T0270984

Alternative Organisations in India

This book provides unheard and emerging accounts of alternative organisations in India. It studies if and why alternative organisations matter to management theory and practice, how it can be applied to the context of alternative organisations, and how, from an alternate organisational perspective, existing debates in management can be enriched. Some other questions examined in this book are: what are the spaces of organising outside corporations? How do these alternative organisational forms challenge our assumptions about a globalised, monolithic capitalist order? How do we understand the organisational lives of the marginalised, silenced and oppressed? How can we imagine an alternative organisational reality?

The book includes cases from India that richly explore the functioning of a Special Investigation Team constituted by the Supreme Court of India, *mritshilpis* (idol-makers), homeless shelters, panchayats, Shahid Hospital, Budhan Theatre, Swaraj University, and of organisations that promote social inclusivity. The overall approach draws upon multiple strands of critical thought to open fresh conversations within the management discipline in India and abroad. The book will be helpful for researchers and students of management, and also for practitioners in non-business and community based organisations.

Devi Vijay teaches at the Indian Institute of Management Calcutta. She is currently a Fulbright-Nehru Postdoctoral Fellow at the Mailman School of Public Health at Columbia University. Her research interests are inequality, institutions, social movements, alternative forms of organising, and qualitative methods.

Rohit Varman teaches at the Indian Institute of Management Calcutta, and is also affiliated with Deakin University, Australia. His research interests are critical theory, subalternity and markets, corporate violence, and interpretive research.

Alternative Organisations in India

Undoing Boundaries

Edited by

Devi Vijay
Rohit Varman

Shaftesbury Road, Cambridge CB2 8EA, United Kingdom

One Liberty Plaza, 20th Floor, New York, NY 10006, USA

477 Williamstown Road, Port Melbourne, VIC 3207, Australia

314–321, 3rd Floor, Plot 3, Splendor Forum, Jasola District Centre, New Delhi – 110025, India

103 Penang Road, #05–06/07, Visioncrest Commercial, Singapore 238467

Cambridge University Press is part of Cambridge University Press & Assessment, a department of the University of Cambridge.

We share the University's mission to contribute to society through the pursuit of education, learning and research at the highest international levels of excellence.

www.cambridge.org
Information on this title: www.cambridge.org/9781108422178

© Cambridge University Press & Assessment 2018

First published 2018

A catalogue record for this publication is available from the British Library

ISBN   978-1-108-42217-8   Hardback

To all those who believe in another world

As Brecht would say:

There was little I could do. But without me
The rulers sat more securely, or so I hoped.

Contents

List of Tables and Figures

Tables

Figures

Acknowledgements

Over the course of the two years that we worked on this book, we got to know very inspiring people. Our contributors have chosen not to take the well-trodden path, choosing instead to enter worlds very different, and often far hostile from their own. Their chapters are truly their own stories. It was our privilege to work with them and we are grateful that they placed their trust in our maiden effort. So many people, including our friends, teachers, students, who may not appear in the pages of this book, have nonetheless inspired us with their passion and commitment, and reinforced, time and again, our conviction in an alternative imaginary.

We are so grateful to our participants whose stories we carry in this book. Many of them are extraordinary individuals who continue to search for alternatives and a better world. Individuals like Dr Saibal Jana have inspired this book. They embody the spirit of our writing.

Our thanks go to Rajesh Dey, Qudsiya Ahmed, Anwesha Rana, Aditya Majumdar and Suvadip Bhattacharjee from the Cambridge University Press team that worked very closely and patiently with us in the development of the book. We are also grateful to the two anonymous reviewers who provided constructive and timely insights.

Deepest thanks to Uma Malhotra who, often at very short notices, carefully read and edited multiple drafts of the chapters with her characteristic diligence and conscientiousness.

This book was conceived and developed over cups of coffee at the Indian Institute of Management Calcutta (IIM Calcutta). We are indebted to the institution for providing spaces for alternative dialogues, conversations and imaginations. By safeguarding academic freedom and by providing a liberal environment, in many ways IIM Calcutta has facilitated our work.

Where would a search for alternatives be without revolutionary poetry? Brecht, Faiz, Hikmet, Pash and Neruda have been our inspiration and have kept us charged while working for long hours on the book.

Introduction
Undoing Boundaries

Devi Vijay and Rohit Varman

Introduction

The water sold itself
and from the desert's
distilleries
I've seen
the last drops
terminate
and the poor world, the people
walking with their thirst
staggering in the sand.
I saw the light
at night
rationed,
the great light in the house
of the rich.
All is dawn in the
new hanging gardens,
all is dark
in the terrible
shadow of the valley.

***

The day is coming
when we will liberate
the light and the water,

earth and men,
and all will be
for all, as you are.
For this, for now,
be careful!

(From 'Ode to the Air' by Pablo Neruda)

In the last twenty five years of neoliberal governance, India has witnessed a dramatic shift to privatisation and corporatisation. The new regime of governance has allowed accumulation of wealth for a few with an accompanying rise in inequity at an unprecedented scale. In this neoliberal era, discourse of management is exalted and allows a significant symbolic capital to accrue to managers. Such a discourse fosters conditions for managementality, or the the mentalities and rationalities of management, to determine subject positions that are economically and culturally privileged. While most people struggle for their survival, neoliberalism creates the condition for a small elite to become entrepreneurial, prudential and active to exploit the opportunities offered by corporatisation in a socially uneven India. As Neruda perceptively observed, the corporate-state nexus commodifies and sells everything to the highest bidder leaving the majority of the Indian population in a state of abject poverty. In such times of abundance for a few and deprivation for the vast majority, the question of alternative organisations becomes particularly relevant in India.

Our ideas of alternative organisations in this book are inspired by critical traditions in social and management theory to imagine a different world in which there are emphases on human emancipation, equity and justice. We believe academic writings create counter-discourses that may lead to conditions of what Neruda describes, 'The day is coming when we will liberate'. Such conditions often hinge on the creation and dissemination of alternative imaginations that are repressed by dominant management discourses under neoliberalism. As Bourdieu (1998, 9) incisively observed:

> now that the great utopias of the nineteenth century have revealed all their perversion, it is urgent to create the conditions of a collective effort to reconstruct a universe of realist ideals, capable of mobilizing people's will without mystifying their consciousness.

Therefore, we see a need to attend to organisational situations and settings that are silenced by mainstream managerial discourses. We believe a search for alternatives has to begin by casting in high-relief, silent spaces that lie within and yet outside the capitalist imagination of the world around us.

✳   ✳   ✳

We take into account the two social vectors of space and time in our engagement with alternatives. We believe that much of our imagination of organisations is still colonised by dominant Western capitalist discourses of progress and modernity. In this book, we would like to attend to alternative realities of organising that are rooted in India. Hence, we are interested in alternative representations of organisational realities that broaden our understanding of management. In doing so, we are interested in recontextualising theories of organisation and management in non-Western institutional contexts. Moreover, discussions of organisations in India are primarily located in capitalist time and are often limited to different corporate forms. As Gupta (1998, 9) puts it, these discussions of organisations are 'fundamentally shaped by colonial modernities', in which ideas and ideals of Western capitalism dominate.

We interrogate management theory in a 'Third World' context to develop alternative perspectives in not only the spatio-cultural sense of a different geography or culture but also to emphasise a different institutional imperative that casts in high relief non-corporate settings in which vast subaltern groups participate. These settings can be outside capitalist time and follow from Chakrabarty's (2000) call to distinguish between two types of historic timelines: History 1 and History 2 that have arisen with the spread of capitalism and the emergence of the modern world. History 1 'is a past posited by capital as part of its precondition' (63); and History 2 that does not belong to the 'life process of capital, which may not be subsumed in the narrative of its progress, yet live in intimate and plural relationships with it, and which allow us to make room for human diversity and the politics of belonging' (66–67). It becomes necessary to understand alternative organisational forms that exist at the margins of the life process of capital. Therefore, we are interested in alternative organisations as organisational forms whose core logics, values, principles and outcomes diverge from dominant businesses (see Parker et al., 2014). These are organisations that present alternative imaginations to contemporary dominant organisational forms, in particular, the corporation. In doing so, we need to draw upon Chatterjee's (1983) call to attend to how different institutional configurations get combined in the so-called backward country to produce unique possibilities of furthering alternative management theories.

We are conscious of the fact that imagining alternatives to the current trajectory of management theories under neoliberalism is not an easy task. In his essay on 'The Spectre of Ideology', Slavoj Zizek notes 'it seems easier to imagine the end of the world than a far more modest change in the mode of production, as if liberal capitalism is the "real" that will somehow survive even under conditions of a global ecological catastrophe' (2012, 1). Elsewhere, in the midst of the 'Occupy Wall Street' protests, Zizek (2014) quintessentially shared the following joke to convey his point:

> In an old joke from the defunct German Democratic Republic, a German worker gets a job in Siberia; aware of how all mail will be read by friends, he tells his friends. 'Let's establish a code: if a letter you will get from me is written in ordinary blue ink, it is true; if it is written in red ink, it is false'. After a month, his friends get a first letter, written in blue ink: 'Everything is wonderful here: stores are full, food is abundant, apartments are large and properly heated, movie theaters show films from the West, there are many beautiful girls ready for an affair – the only thing unavailable is red ink'. And is this not the situation till now? We have all the freedoms one wants - the only thing missing is the red ink. We 'feel free' because we lack the very language to articulate our unfreedom.

Paraphrasing Zizek, all the terms we use today are false terms, mystifying our perception of the situation, instead of allowing us to think it. Our task then in this book is to provide the red ink.

Such a task of finding alternatives is difficult in times of 'erasure of political reflexivity…and a normalization of conservative neoliberalism' (Eckhardt and Bradshaw, 2014, 181). We are living in times when enlightenment has become a new source of darkness. Emancipation and freedom have become harbingers of new forms of enslavement as Horkheimer and Adorno (1976) have brilliantly exposed in their analysis of a negative dialectical relationship in the culture industry. Alternatives have become particularly difficult to imagine because various possible sources of knowledge and political reflexivity are treacherously redirected towards capitalist domination (Marcuse, 1991). Moreover, as Lash and Lury (2007, 4) delineate, we are living in an era when culture has become 'thingified'. Lash and Lury (2007, 8) further observe, 'there is such a thingification of media when, for example, movies become computer games; when brands become brand environments, taking over airport terminal space and restructuring department stores, road billboards and city centres'. In other words, culture does not exist primarily as a superstructure, but thoroughly infiltrates all parts of economy leaving fewer spaces outside it for resistance. Such a shift helps capitalism hide its real motives and as Baudrillard (1981, 71) insightfully suggested, 'to become an end in itself, every system must dispel the question of its real teleology'. Yet, none of this means that we should or we can give up in our attempts to look for alternatives. Invoking Antonio Gramsci, these are notes of pessimism of the intellect, but optimism of the will.

Giddens' (1990) appeal for utopian realism influences this enquiry into alternatives. Accordingly, utopian realist vision requires a combination of emancipatory and life politics. Emancipatory politics refers to, 'radical engagements concerned with the liberation from inequality or servitude', and life politics implies 'radical engagements which seek to further the possibilities of a fulfilling and satisfying life for all, and in respect of which there are no "others"' (Giddens, 1990, 156). Such an orientation hinges on imagining a post-capitalist order that strives to overcome the ravages of class-based society and exploitation of nature. In doing so, we see a need to closely examine alternatives that exist around us and to understand how they can be harbingers of another world. We particularly see the need to comprehend organisations that offer alternatives to the hegemonic corporate order and attend to social movements that often impel such transformations. As Marx (1843) incisively observed:

> We develop new principles for the world out of the world's own principles. We do not say to the world: Cease your struggles, they are foolish; we will give you the true slogan of struggle. We merely show the world what it is really fighting for, and consciousness is something that it *has to* acquire, even if it does not want to.

Moreover, it is imperative that we cast in high-relief alternative arenas of organising that often lapse into the discursive ellipsis of mainstream managerial narratives. These alternative arenas are particularly important because the people exploited or cast aside by the corporate order usually exist in such spaces. We further believe that any idea of alternative is closely related to theoretical understandings that we develop of the world around us.

As an edited volume, this book includes various unheard and emerging accounts of alternative organisational realities. It provides an alternative account of contemporary organisational practices in India, which rejects overdependence on narrowly defined mainstream management theory that draws upon for-profit, large corporations primarily situated in the West. It contests the stereotyped portrayal of management as a control apparatus that is meant to regulate workers, consumers and other environmental factors for greater profits. The overall approach in this book draws upon multiple strands of critical thought.

In the next sections, we elaborate on some key theoretical considerations. We first engage with why there is a need for alternative theorisation of organisations and what are the limitations of mainstream management theories. We identify an increasing body of work that points to a crisis in management – both in terms of the discontents in its practice as well as in the scientific knowledge of management. Subsequently, we elaborate on critical traditions and symbolic power of Western theories in management. Finally, we discuss our chapters that offer alternatives to mainstream organisational and management thought.

Limitations of mainstream management theory

Management is a pervasive institution with unprecedented legitimacy amongst global elite. On one hand, the recent rise of management is closely tied to what Boltanski and Chiapello (2006) label as the 'new spirit of capitalism' that justifies people's commitment to capitalism in a way that renders it attractive. The new spirit of capitalism is marked by the spread of managerialism from the sphere of work to social and private domains. In these fields, it serves the ideological function of making human actors as managers, workers, consumers and entrepreneurs follow the insatiable logic of capitalism to accumulate more and more. On the other hand, management also serves the function of creating extra-ideological violence against vulnerable stakeholders to improve corporate profitability. Extra-ideological violence manifests in scientific management of workers, manipulation of consumers and exploitation of natural resources.

As is the case with capitalism, the managerial approach, that forms the basis of most existing interpretations of how businesses should operate, has arisen in particular historical, economic, political and cultural circumstances (Alvesson and Willmott, 2003). For example, the origins of managerial thought can be traced to when firms largely operated in national markets in the West. Their strategies, therefore, first and foremost, arise within a national context and then are adapted for deployment in other countries. Some argue that contemporary management discourse rarely questions its foundations that stem from a Western/Anglo-Saxon viewpoint and are flawed when applied to other cultural, economic and institutional contexts (Boyacigiller and Adler, 1991; Jack, Westwood, Srinivas and Sardar, 2011). Such a monoculture of management theory is not only problematic from different cultural and institutional standpoints, but is also limiting from the perspective of different regimes of justification or worth that prevail within any social order (Boltanski and Thevenot, 2006).

Indeed, over the last few decades, management theory, as an ideological and extra-ideological apparatus that supports capitalism, has come under increasing scrutiny. Despite its legitimacy, several problems associated with capitalism are also attributed to the idea of management. For example, excessive ecological crises and repeated corporate scandals of growing proportions over the last two decades have brought managerial transgressions to sharp relief. Similarly, critics have pointed to the role of corporate managers in exploitation of workers, consumers and disempowered stakeholders (Banerjee, 2008a; Burawoy, 1979; Jhally, 1991). Rather than dismiss these as the anomalous, dark side of corporate capitalism, some scholars point to such breaches as an 'extreme manifestation of neoliberal corporate normality' when you factor in the complicity of auditors, regulators, government bodies and professional associations (Willmott, 2011, 109). That no lessons were learnt and aggressive capitalist forces continue to strengthen unhindered by the financial crisis of 2008, has hardly been cause for pause, correctives, or alternatives in mainstream management discourse. Thus, we contend that contemporary management thought has been narrow in its perspective and does not adequately reflect problems faced by organisations today.

Managerialist ideology has been steadily transforming not just business, but also professional associations, public sector firms, non-governmental organisations, schools, hospitals and universities (for example, Avis, 1996; Doolin, 2002; Noordegraaf and Stewart, 2000; Terry, 1998). Fournier and Grey (2000, 174) contend, this iconic status of management has found legitimacy on 'ontological grounds (managers as the bearers of the real world), epistemological grounds (management as the embodiment of expert knowledge) and moral grounds (managerialisation being equated with greater justice, public accountability, democracy and quality in public services)'. Indeed, where earlier management gained its legitimacy by associating with government and political functions, today the situation is reversed. Government programmes are transformed around managerial parameters of effectiveness (Anthony, 2005). For example, new public management, which has emerged as a dominant approach to public administration, is underpinned by a managerialist ideology, which redefines citizens as customers and fashions a results-oriented, customer-driven, enterprising and market-oriented model of public administration (Terry, 1998).

A deepening of managerialist ideology is closely related to the structural shift to neoliberalism in the last three decades (Harvey, 2005). As Bourdieu (1998, 95, emphasis in original) insightfully observes:

> In the name of the scientific programme of knowledge, converted into a political programme of action, an immense *political operation* is being pursued (denied, because it is apparently purely negative), aimed at creating the conditions for realizing and operating of the 'theory'; *a programme of methodological destruction of collectives.*

This era is marked by marketisation of various spheres of lives in which market success has become the sole criterion for rewarding achievement (Eckhardt, Dholakia and Varman, 2013; Hartmann and Honneth, 2006). In a scathing criticism of neoliberalism, Conway and Heynen (2006, 17) lament:

> the consummate power of market exchange, privatization and capital accumulation as the defining features of human action and activity has been raised to unprecedented levels, so that neoliberalism disciplines, destroys, dehumanizes and destabilizes, while such outcomes are rationalized as social inevitabilities.

Boltanski and Chiapello (2006) point to two types of criticisms against capitalism. They label the first type as social criticism that draws attention to inequities, exploitation and loss of solidarities under capitalism. Boltanski and Chiapello (2006, 38) call the second one as an 'artistic critique' that highlights the problems of disenchantment, alienation, commodification and inauthenticity. While Boltanski and Chiapello (2006) have observed that capitalism has benefitted from these criticisms by adapting, neutralising these critiques and creating justifications for its spread, they also point to inherent paradoxes in such pursuits under neoliberalism with exacerbation of the very problems that capitalism tries to neutralise (also see Hartmann and Honneth, 2006).

This unreflexive universality of managerial thought becomes problematic particularly when the broader context of advanced capitalism, within which this approach is entrenched, is brought to question. The triumph of capitalism is underpinned by characteristic private appropriation of means of production and a division between capital and labour, the principle of free markets as a coordinating mechanism and a profit motive (Parker *et al.*, 2014). Capitalism has no doubt flourished with significant material achievements and rapid advancements in technology and scientific knowledge (Hobsbawm, 1975). However, many writings on contemporary capitalism point to the violent nature of extraction and accumulation that is inherent to it (Harvey, 2003; Roy, 2012; Sassen, 2014; Varman and Al-Amoudi, 2016). Bourdieu (1998, 98) incisively observes that, 'The ultimate basis of this economic order placed under the banner of individual freedom is indeed the structural violence of unemployment, of insecure employment and the fear provoked by the threat of losing employment'. Banerjee (2008b) borrows from Mbembe (2003) and coins the term necrocapitalism to describe this phase of capitalist accumulation that is based on violence, dispossession and death. Banerjee (2008b, 1544) astutely notes, 'violence, dispossession and death that result from practices of accumulation occur in spaces that seem to be immune from legal, juridical and political intervention, resulting in a suspension of sovereignty'. In necrocapitalism private acts of corporate violence get combined with state violence to produce what Harvey (2003) calls accumulation by dispossession that is commonly visible in battles for control of natural resources in postcolonial societies (Banerjee, 2011). Some examples of necrocapitalistic practices are violent privatisation of commons, expulsion of indigenous people to grab their shared assets and use of modern slavery for private accumulation. Many of these practices across the world, especially in the Global South are justified in the name of progress that has become a key nodal point in discourse of development (Escobar, 1995; Rahnema, 1997).

The 'drama of progress' associated with the gains of capitalism comes with several costs across the Global North–South divide (Hobsbawm, 1975, 4). For instance, Goh, Pfeffer and Zenios (2015), in examining workplace stressors such as long working hours, job insecurity, work-family conflict, job demands and low social support at work, point to how more than 120,000 deaths per year and approximately 5–8 per cent of annual healthcare costs in the US may be attributable to how US firms manage their workforce. This study's conservative estimate of workplace-mortality is comparable with fourth and fifth largest causes of mortality in the US – cerebrovascular disease and accidents, respectively – and exceeds deaths caused by Alzheimer's, diabetes, or influenza. Pfeffer (2016) laments that responses to the study's findings have centred around the economic costs of such dysfunctional workplaces rather than the human aspects.

Further, the focus on achieving efficiency to further the profit motive has impelled rising negative externalities – or the hidden costs borne neither by producer or consumer, but passed on to a third party (Parker *et al.*, 2014). For example, Bavington (2011), in his book titled *Managed Annihilation* exposes advanced capitalism's managerialist impulse that underpinned the extreme exploitation of cod fisheries eventually resulting in a catastrophic collapse in northern codfish stocks and the criminalisation of fishing in the Newfoundland region, Canada. Bavington challenges the use of management practices as a solution to global fisheries crises, given how these practices have not only resulted in irreparable drops in codfish numbers, but also create further social and ecological problems that are further solved by new management techniques. Rather than arriving at radical alternatives, politicians, academic researchers and bureaucrats are complicit in reconstructing cod as an element to be managed in a complex system and in transforming traditional fishermen for whom fishing is a way of life into professional fish harvesters.

Klein (2008) in her incisive analysis of capitalism argues that neoliberal states make use of disasters to implement far-reaching structural changes that rob people of their resources and incomes. Accordingly, such measures are often introduced at times of disasters when people are particularly vulnerable and have a limited ability to resist. Some of these shocks and disasters are deliberately introduced to create conditions for pro-business interventions. Klein (2008) insightfully gives the example of the coup in Chile led by Augusto Pinochet that helped Milton Friedman and other Chicago School economists to pry open the Chilean economy under the banner of market reforms for exploitation by businesses. Her analysis not only helps us see newer trajectories of exploitation within capitalism but also understand the complicity of academics and their theories in such pursuits.

Closer home, even as India is one of the fastest-growing economies poised to shed its colonial past and transition into a 'superpower', predatory growth threatens its ecological sustainability. A dramatic increase in demand for minerals has resulted in thousands of hectares of barren and unproductive land, poisoning of rivers and streams, generation of billions of tonnes of waste that is inadequately disposed and the unapologetic diversion of ecologically sensitive biodiverse regions for mining. Compounding these ecological crises is the disruption of local communities which besides being directly dependent on natural resources are also victims to waterlogging, pollution and displacement. The very deprivations that were to be alleviated by such forms of development have in fact been aggravated under neoliberalism (Shrivastava and Kothari, 2012).

Deem and Brehony (2005) label management theories associated with neoliberalism as new managerialism and suggest that it should be understood as an ideological configuration that helps strengthen the position of upper classes in a society. Accordingly, new configurations of privatisation are glossed as public-private partnerships and there is emphasis on importing ideas from the private world business into the world of public services. In the new logic of managerialism,

Hartmann and Honneth (2006, 49) observe, employees are made into 'entreploys', who are expected, 'not only to dutifully fulfil externally given production quotas, but also to bring communicative and emotive skills and resources to bear in order to meet project goals and…softening the separation of private and professional spheres of actions'. Thus, we find new managerialism generalising the language of business and helping its ideals to permeate not just economic spheres, but also our political, social and private lives (Anthony, 2005; Deem and Brehony, 2005).

The second key crisis of management as we see it, and one that is closely intertwined with the practice of management, is the crisis of production of knowledge on management and organisations. Boyacigiller and Adler (1991) referred to organisation studies as a parochial dinosaur, pointing out that most studies of organisational science are situated in the US context (contextual parochialism), with several countries under-represented in the production of management discourse (quantitative parochialism), leaving organisational theory with a set of core concepts that have diffused globally strongly imbued with US-centric cultural values and orientations (qualitative parochialism). Indeed, Burrell (1996) referred to this body of work as NATO or the North American Theory of Organisation. Over the years, this parochialism has barely receded, evidenced for instance by the North American and Western European domination of editorial boards within fields such as 'International' Human Resource Management (Ozbilgin, 2004). More recently, Aldrich (2009) lamented the absence of attention to temporal and spatial dimensions of context in organisational theory. In his examination of 128 papers published in *Administrative Science Quarterly* between 2000 and 2007, he found, over 90 per cent of the papers covered only a single nation and that 88 per cent of the single nation studies were conducted in the United States. Aldrich warns of decontextualised and ahistorical theories imbrued with misattribution of causal effects and inappropriate cultural arguments.

Further, the production of knowledge on management is crafted around ideals of rationalisation, efficiency and productivity of organisations (Alvesson and Willmott, 2003). In particular, management discourse has been centred around the corporate form reckoned as 'one of the most successful inventions in history' and 'the primary vehicle for the spread of capitalism' (Butler, 1988, 99 in Veldman and Willmott, 2013). In its contemporary form that grants exclusive rights to shareholders and where pursuit of shareholder value is prioritised, the corporate form has created particular problems such as the concentration of power and wealth (Micklethwait and Woolridge, 2005; Veldman and Willmott, 2013). In effect, contemporary management discourse is knowledge for management, and not an examination *of* management (Alvesson and Willmott, 2012), and in its practice and ideology renders invisible, wide swathes of populations including the marginalised and outcastes (Imas and Weston, 2011).

In order to overcome some of these challenges we need to develop critical theory of organisations in India. In particular, we draw attention to the field of Critical Management Studies (CMS) that has evolved in response to some of the points of criticism against capitalist practices and mainstream management theories. It is to this theorisation that we turn to next in our analysis.

Critical theory of organisations in India

In this book, we build on the critical tradition in management theory and particularly on CMS to attend to alternative organisations in India. Critique of management and the dominance of large organisations in the context of capitalist development have long existed, undertaken from various standpoints by seminal theorists such as Karl Marx, Emile Durkheim and Max Weber. In particular, critical theory as a philosophical tradition, which unmasks hidden assumptions and purposes of existing theories and practices, gained momentum in Europe between World War I and World War II, as the exploitation, alienation and repression embedded within modern organisational forms in Western civilisations were called to attention. However, CMS emerged over the last two decades as a discipline and movement that holds the mirror up to management given the powerful status it has achieved (for a review of historical emergence of CMS see Fournier and Grey, 2000; Tadajewski, 2010).

In borrowing from CMS, our intent is then that of scrutinising the assumptions of established management practices in order to interrogate legitimised practices and institutions and to call attention to the unreflexive reproduction of dominant discourses (Alvesson and Willmott, 2012; Parker, Fournier and Reedy, 2007). In doing so, we make this book into fundamentally a political project with the objective of exposing power relations in organisations in the context of a totality, or the wider system within which these organisations function (Grey and Willmott, 2005).

CMS enfolds a wide range of critical traditions including Marxism, Frankfurt school of critical theory, labour process theory, poststructuralism, feminist theory and postcolonial analysis. Within the plurality introduced by these diverse epistemological and political commitments and theoretical traditions, we particularly attend to denaturalisation, non-performativity and reflexivity as shared orientations for critical theory of organisations in India (Fournier and

Grey, 2000). In mainstream management discourse, assumptions like the role of management is to ensure profitability, growth, efficiency and to satisfy interests of shareholders, or that share prices are indicators of managerial effectiveness are natural or 'real'. The critical project *denaturalises* the authority of this scientific knowledge by drawing attention to the socially repressive, alienating, violent and ecologically destructive institutional structures that underpin the knowledge production process (Adler *et al.*, 2007).

CMS is non-performative in its rejection of the assumption of performativity inherent in dominant management discourse, which places emphasis on knowledge imbued with a means-ends rationality, with an expected alignment between knowledge, truth and efficiency (Flemming and Banerjee, 2015; Fournier and Grey, 2000). Austin (1962, 99) describes performativity as a 'performance of an act *in* saying something as opposed to performance of an act *of* saying something'. We thus condemn, in managerial reasoning, assumptions that reify human relations as instrumental means to ensure efficiency and profitability. We object to the scope of managerial reasoning as limited to refining means of accomplishing established ends, instead broadening this reasoning for instance to analysing whether the existing ends generate waste, exploitation and destruction (Adler *et al.*, 2007; Alvesson and Willmott, 2012). We are particularly wary of terms like critical performativity as Spicer *et al.* (2009, 544) have used for 'subversive mobilisation and citations of previous performances'. We believe that such an emphasis on performativity can engender simplistic and flawed engagements with corporate managers. We agree with Flemming and Banerjee (2015, 15) that:

> if CMS is to make an impact, it needs to be highly committed to what ostensibly appears to be a non-performative activity; namely, a prolonged engagement with abstract, often difficult ideas and phenomenon: *study*. Without an informed and critical understanding of power, capitalism, gender, environmental issues, post-colonialism and other area, when called upon to speak (by students, the media, the state, activists, etc.) we will have little 'useful' to say.

Finally, reflexivity – both methodological and philosophical – is crucial to the critical management tradition to scrutinise how organisational and managerial realities are constructed, rather than discovered, in the research process (Alvesson *et al.*, 2008). Reflexivity implies taking stock of the situated nature of knowledge, the author's social positions, language conventions and the political, social and institutional milieu within which research is conducted (Adler *et al.*, 2007; Calas and Smircich, 1999).

In trying to achieve these objectives, our attempt is to present management as a historically and contextually contingent phenomenon that is not inevitable and thus that alternatives are imaginable (Adler *et al.*, 2007; Clegg and Dunkerley, 1980; Fournier and Grey, 2000). Indeed, underpinning the critical tradition is a commitment to radical change. Implicit in the critical project is a transformative intent, a micro-emancipation effort and the generation of alternatives that may be otherwise silenced (Alvesson and Willmott, 1992; Parker, 1995; Parker, Fournier and Reedy, 2007).

In order to create a critical orientation, we further call for a reduction in the excessive dependence on mainstream or uncritical scholarship in the West that continues to wield symbolic power in Indian management schools. We briefly examine the symbolic power enjoyed by mainstream Western theories in Indian management studies.

Symbolic power of the West in Indian management studies

Scientific knowledge and practice of management and organisations have been exapted from the original North America-centric context within which they originated, to different political, social and cultural contexts (see Djelic, 1998; Jack *et al.*, 2011). While the organisational forms may have been translated to local institutional requirements, the content of this American model of management education has more readily travelled (Kipping *et al.*, 2004), riding on arguments of the universality of management (Srinivas, 2012). The ethnocentric assumption of knowledge developed in the West as modern, rational and homogenous versus that of the East as less progressive and irrational has been pivotal to the spread of Western scientific discourse (Frenkel and Shenhav, 2003).

This paved the way for the construction of an ideological system of education that valourised the West and devalourised indigenous knowledge systems. It concurs with Mignolo's (2000) observation that the West works as a ubiquitous referent in the Global South. As a result, much of management scholarship in India has sought legitimacy by borrowing and building on Western theoretical developments (Chakrabarty, 1997). As Bourdieu and Wacquant (1999) insightfully observe, national intellectual fields can have 'passeurs' or carriers who dehistoricise concepts that have been developed in particular societies and contexts, and propagate them.

Indeed, mainstream Western theories wield dominant status in the Indian context. Bourdieu delves into political functions of dominant symbolic systems and questions their taken-for-granted character as worldviews of a society. From this perspective, he develops the idea of symbolic power 'that is not perceived as power but as legitimate demands for recognition, deference, obedience, or the services of others' (Swartz, 1997, 43). In a similar vein, mainstream management theories developed in the West have gained symbolic power and have become the dominant lens through which Indian scholars interpret their context. Such symbolic power creates a status hierarchy in which the West is at the top. Such a hierarchy is based on social domination that often goes misrecognised as a form of power. Therefore, Bourdieu (1990, 141) contends:

> this mis-recognition, unaware that it produces what it recognizes, does not want to know that what makes the most intrinsic charm of its objects, its charisma, is merely the product of the countless crediting operations through which agents attribute to the object the powers to which they submit.

Such a system of power creates symbolic violence in which subordinates accept as legitimate their own condition of domination (Bourdieu, 1977). Therefore, symbolic power often manifests itself in violence that is, 'invisible, unrecognized as such, chosen as much as undergone, that of trust, obligation, personal loyalty... of all virtues honored by the ethic of honor' (Bourdieu, 1990, 127). Accordingly, adherence to a particular logic of symbolic power is situated in habitus or dispositions that are acquired in a certain field. Postcolonial theorists point that colonialism leaves the colonised with a sense of inadequacy and inferiority that results in a postcolonial dispositions characterised by dependence on the West (Fanon, 1952). Bourdieu (1990) observes that when distinctive dispositions are acquired as self-evident from early childhood, they contain their own legitimation. In a situation of structural homology, or correspondence between habitus and practices in a field, actors unwittingly reproduce relationships of domination and subordination (Bourdieu, 1984).

As a result of dependence on the West, knowledge generation in the field of management writings in India seems to have been reposed on many ambiguities and misunderstandings about our social, political, economic and institutional context (Srinivas, 2013; Varman and Saha, 2009). Examples of such misconceptions are abundant: typically and perhaps most crucially, the existing literature has not acknowledged the historical development of markets and organisations as a set of socio-cultural and economic formations (Varman and Sreekumar, 2015). As also highlighted by a large number of scholars (Srinivas, 2013; Varman and Saha, 2009), this literature has been based on ahistorical and decontextualised approaches to studying management and organisations in India. Thus, much of the existing literature on India has overlooked the diversity of socio-cultural, economic and political dynamics that have historically shaped organisational practices, contents, and structures in the country. For instance, Varman and Sreekumar (2015) find that a large part of the analysis of the Indian context is done through mainstream frameworks developed in the West, such as Hofstede's framework, CETSCALE, and SERVQUAL. As a result of such oversight, problematic conclusions have been drawn from flawed assumptions.

Scholars working within the domain of postcolonial theory have questioned dependence on the West (Chakrabarty, 2000; Nandy, 1983). It is evident from the debates in postcolonial theory that there is a need for Indian scholars to be cautious in according canonical status to Western authors. This note of caution not only applies to management theory but to critical theory as well. For example, Michel Foucault failed to account for the European colonial project and did not take into consideration how elements of imperialism and race inscribed disciplinary and bio power in Europe. Thus, Stoler (1995, 5–7) argues:

> the discursive and practical field in which nineteenth century bourgeois sexuality emerged was situated on an imperial landscape where the cultural accoutrements of bourgeois distinction were partially shaped through contrasts forged in the politics and language of race.... In short-circuiting empire, Foucault's history of European sexuality misses key sites in the production of that discourse, discounts the practices that racialized bodies, and thus elides a field of knowledge that provides a contrast for what a 'healthy, vigorous, bourgeois body' was all about.

In a similar vein, Spivak (1988, 289) has suggested that Foucault ignores the 'epistemic violence' of imperialism and the international division of labour. Accordingly, in Foucault's conceptualisation this oversight leads to rendering colonial subjects either invisible or transparent. Such invisibility and transparency are common features of the Western (imperialist) discourse and act to the effect of silencing the subaltern while hindering the possibility of resistance to oppression.

The trajectories and configurations of capitalism in postcolonial settings also deserve a note, for they are distinct from Europe's. Postcolonial theorists have indeed observed that India continues to see a coexistence of capitalist and pre-capitalist modalities after its political independence in 1947 (Chatterjee, 2008; Sanyal, 2007). Moreover, a large part of the capitalist enterprise in the country makes gains through primitive forms of accumulation (Sanyal, 2007). This form of accumulation often leads to a compromise between the capitalist class and old feudal lords, and results in unique modes of domination and power. For example, Kaviraj (1988) has argued that the postcolonial India in the 1950s witnessed a passive revolution in which the bourgeoisie and the feudal classes came together to consolidate their positions (see also Gramsci, 1971). The passive revolution in India led to the state becoming relatively independent of the capitalist class and an instrument of negotiation of conflicts among capitalists, feudal lords, and other sections of the population (Chatterjee, 2008). And Sanyal (2007, 33) insightfully observes:

> In the post-colonial situation, the nation is reified in the body of the state, and the bourgeoisie is able to establish its dominance only by coming to terms with the other constituents of the nation to construct a hegemonic order that is necessarily complex.

As a result of these conflicts, the postcolonial Indian state devised welfare measures and other policies such as labour laws to check exploitation of the disempowered and to ameliorate the ill-effects of capitalist developments.

The project of Westernisation of knowledge has also led to questions around the relevance of imported management knowledge and its appropriateness for specific locations (Srinivas, 2012). As a result, a critically-oriented sub-stream of research on India has begun to emerge (Arora and Romijn, 2012; Jagannathan and Rai, 2015, Mirchandani, 2015, Srinivas, 2012, 2013; Varman and Belk 2012). This scholarship in management adopts a situated approach and investigates the complex and multifaceted intersections between social, cultural, political, economic and institutional dimensions. In this book, we hope to take this pursuit further and to delve into alternative contexts within India that need to be understood to broaden our imagination about management theories.

Narratives of alternative organisations in India

The diverse narratives curated in this volume span organised spaces of contestation among social movements, state and capital. They also include construction of alternative organisational spaces constituted within and as extensions of the state apparatus and community-based organising in a marginalised and stigmatised community. Thus, we provide accounts of alternative organisational spaces, forms of organising and organisational lives.

The collection of studies present in this book may be seen as an eclectic collection that includes a wide range of theories (e.g., on violence, ideology, power and institutions) and organisational domains (e.g., theatre groups, artisan guilds, social movement, shelter homes, social enterprises, local self-governing institutions). The commonalities can be seen as following two threads divided as Part I and Part II in this book. Part I focuses on alternative representations of organisational realities that provide different perspectives to contemporary understanding of management and organisational knowledge. For example, in Chapter 2, Jaggannathan and Rai examine the alternative organisational mechanism of the Special Investigation Team (SIT) that was created by the Supreme Court of India to facilitate the delivery of justice following the riots in Gujarat in 2002. This was following widespread sentiment that the criminal justice system was failing to deliver justice to riots victims. The SIT, comprising retired and serving police officers, was articulated as an independent agency, which would deliver justice to the riots victims. Through an examination of the formal and informal technologies that describe the enactment of the SIT, Jaggannathan and Rai argue that the SIT embodied processes through which narrative claims of injustice could be isolated and disciplined.

In Chapter 3, Vijay draws on an empirical study of the work practices of a neighbourhood of *mritshilpis*, or clay image makers, to examine the institutional contexts for practice reproduction. The study unpacks *mritshilpis'* everyday work practices and the institutional orders within which these practices are produced and reproduced. Further, Vijay identifies three scripts – embodying *gharana*, mobilising place and enacting community – that mediate practices and their institutional contexts. She unpacks the relational, historical and spatial elements that underpin the durability of practices and institutional maintenance. In doing so, she sheds light on non-instrumental, value-based, context-specific rationalities that drive work and organisation and offers an account of the organisational realities of those otherwise silenced.

In Chapter 4, Vikas studies the marginalised lives of the homeless, who exist in a state of invisibility. He enquires into invisibility of the homeless as an outcome of the disposition of the State. He examines how the State structures the invisibility of its own vulnerable citizens and how the homeless respond to it. Vikas conducts ethnography to understand the design and operational deficiencies of homeless shelters. By examining these questions, Vikas attempts to lay the groundwork through which more effective alternatives may be created for the homeless that reduce their vulnerability.

In Chapter 5, Guha and Chakrabarti explore how panchayats, India's rural local government institutions, manage conflicting organisational requirements. Although panchayats play a pivotal role in providing citizen centric services and in implementing developmental programmes, accounts of organising in panchayats are rare. Guha and Chakrabarti undertake a three-district study of implementation of the rural employment guarantee scheme in the state of West Bengal. Their study reveals that functioning of panchayats involves balancing conflicting requirements that often involves deviation from prescribed procedures. However, as a part of a hierarchical organisation in which relationships among different tiers of administration are guided by partisan politics, it becomes necessary to camouflage such deviations. This is done by stakeholders' formulation of informal rules and their enforcement.

Part II engages with alternative organisational forms – organisations that contest the status quo and experiment with imaginations of organisational forms built on alternative principles. These accounts contest taken-for-granted assumptions about a globalised, monolithic capitalist order. For instance, in Chapter 6, Khare and Varman examine how the role of ideology, which underpinned a worker's movement helped create an alternative to capitalist institutions. Drawing on the context of Shaheed Hospital at Dalli Rajhara in the state of Chattisgarh, the authors point to how counter-ideology is used to challenge prevailing market-based norms and to denaturalise existing social relations. While the health facility materialised the counter-ideology of Marxism-Leninism, it also fuelled a broader participation that was necessary for the workers' movement in its early years.

In Chapter 7, Kandathil, Shah and Kapoor apply Clegg's (1989) circuits of power framework to analyse the power asymmetries that plague a Denotified Nomadic Tribe (DNT) living in Ahmedabad, Gujarat. The label of 'born criminals' and the lack of economic and political opportunities contribute to the powerlessness of the Chharas, rendering any resistance along the episodic circuit ultimately futile. Kandathil and colleagues analyse the attempts of the Budhan Theatre, a collective of actors and activists from the Chharas, which creates an alternative organisational space for more effective resistance.

In Chapter 8, Kothiyal undertakes a critical commentary on the dominant ways of understanding and organising learning in mainstream organisations

where there is increasing commodification of higher education She examines the
alternative organisational form embodied by Shikshanter, 'The Peoples' Institute
for Rethinking Education and Development', based in Udaipur, Rajasthan.
Shikshanter works towards creating alternate spaces and ways for learning that
radically depart from the prevalent commercialised and commodified models
of education. As an organisation, it is ideologically committed to preserving
and building local knowledge system(s), advocating against ever-increasing
commodification of education leading to the 'degree/certification' culture, and to
inculcate learning in the true Gandhian spirit. An offshoot of this thinking is the
'Swaraj University', which provides a sharp contrast to the contemporary milieu
of 'accreditation driven' education system in India.

Finally, in Chapter 9, Sarin and Sriram contend that organisations seeking to
promote social change often have to engage with markets, even while resisting
the ideology on which they are based. This is particularly true of organisations
trying to promote and preserve livelihoods in spaces increasingly dominated by
market-based values. This chapter explores the tension that such organisations
face and how they negotiate them. Using brief case studies of organisations such
as Decentralised Cotton Yarn Trust, Dastakar Andhra, Selco and Pratham Books,
the authors describe non-market motivations that explain the origin of these
organisations and the manner in which these are expressed. They also probe
into why engaging with markets becomes a necessity, tensions the engagement
creates, and different ways in which organisations have tried to address them. In
analysing their contrasting trajectories vis-à-vis their stated missions, the authors
argue that such organisations have no alternative but to continuously contest and
negotiate conflicting ideologies.

Taken together, these chapters represent contexts that seldom find space in
mainstream management writing today. The common thread through all these
pieces is that they represent alternative ways of thinking about organising and
bear evidence to various alternatives to dominant neoliberal discourse. In doing
so, we hope to advance emerging critical perspectives, offer a critique of long-
standing conceptual and methodological imperfections and provide new insights
that will influence the generation and application of management knowledge in
the Indian context.

References

Adler, Paul S., Linda C. Forbes and Hugh Willmott. 2007. 'Critical Management Studies.' *The
    Academy of Management Annals* 1(1): 119–79.

Aldrich, Howard E. 2009. 'Lost in Space, Out of Time: Why and How We Should Study Organizations Comparatively.' *Research in the Sociology of Organizations* 26: 21–44.

Alvesson, Mats and Hugh Willmott. 1992. 'Critical Theory and Management Studies: An Introduction'. In *Critical Management Studies*, edited by Mats Alvesson and Hugh Wilmott, 1–20. London: Sage Publications.

———— (eds). 2003. *Studying Management Critically*. London: Sage Publications.

————. 2012. *Making Sense of Management: A Critical Introduction*. Second edition. London: Sage Publications.

Alvesson, Mats, Cynthia Hardy and Bill Harley. 2008. 'Reflecting on Reflexivity: Reflexive Textual Practices in Organization and Management Theory.' *Journal of Management Studies* 45(3): 480–501.

Anthony, Peter D. 2005. 'Management Ideology'. In *Critical Management Studies: A Reader*, edited by Christopher Grey and Hugh Willmott, 21–28. New York: Oxford University Press.

Arora, Saurabh and Henny Romijn. 2012. 'The Empty Rhetoric of Poverty Reduction at the Base of the Pyramid.' *Organization* 19(4): 481–505.

Austin, J. L. 1962. *How to Do Things with Words*. Oxford: Clarendon Press.

Avis, James. 1996. 'The Enemy Within: Quality and Managerialism in Education'. In *Knowledge and Nationhood: Education, Politics, and Work*, edited by James Avis, Martin Bloomer, Geoff Esland, Denis Gleeson and Phil Hodkinson, 105–20. London: Cassell.

Banerjee Bobby S. 2008a. 'Corporate Social Responsibility: The Good, the Bad and the Ugly.' *Critical Sociology* 34(1): 51–79.

————. 2008b. 'Necrocapitalism.' *Organization Studies* 29(12): 1541–63.

————. 2011. 'Voices of the Governed: Towards a Theory of the Translocal.' *Organization* 18(3): 323–44.

Baudrillard, Jean. 1981. *For a Critique of the Political Economy of Sign*. Candor: Telos

Bavington, Dean. 2011. *Managed Annihilation: An Unnatural History of the New found land Cod Collapse*. Vancouver: UBC Press.

Bhabha, Homi. 1994. *The Location of Culture*. New York: Routledge.

Boltanski, Luc and Laurent Thevenot. 2006. *On Justification: Economies of Worth*. Princeton, NJ: Princeton University Press.

Boltanski, Luc and Eve Chiapello. 2006. *The New Spirit of Capitalism*. New York: Verso.

Bourdieu, Pierre and Loic Wacquant. 1999. 'On the Cunning of Imperialist Reason.' *Theory, Culture and Society* 16(1): 41–58.

Bourdieu, Pierre. 1977. *Outline of a Theory of Practice*. New York: Cambridge University Press.

————. 1984. *Distinction: A Social Critique of the Judgement of Taste*. Translated by Richard Nice. Cambridge, MA: Harvard University Press.

————. 1990. *The Logic of Practice*. Translated by Richard Nice. Stanford, CA: Stanford University Press.

————. 1998. *Acts of Resistance: Against the New Myths of Our Time*. Cambridge: Polity Press.

Boyacigiller, Nakiye Avdan and Nancy J. Adler. 1991. 'The Parochial Dinosaur: Organizational Science in a Global Context.' *Academy of Management Review* 16(2): 262–90.

Burawoy, Michael. 1979. *Manufacturing Consent: Changes in the Labor Process under Monopoly Capitalism.* Chicago: University of Chicago Press.

Burrell, Gibson. 1996. 'Normal Science, Paradigms, Metaphors, Discourses, and Genealogies of Analysis.' In *Handbook of Organization Studies,* edited by Stewart R. Clegg, Cynthia Hardy and Walter R. Nord, 642–58. London: Sage Publications Ltd.

Butler, Henry N. 1989. 'Contractual Theory of the Corporation.' *George Mason University. Law Review* 11(4): 99–123.

Calas, Marta B. and Linda Smircich. 1999. 'Past Postmodernism? Reflections and Tentative Directions.' *Academy of Management Review* 24(4): 649–72.

Chakrabarty, Dipesh. 1997. 'The Time of History and the Times of Gods.' In *The Politics of Culture in the Shadow of Capital,* edited by Lisa Lowe and David Lloyd, 35–60. Durham: Duke University Press.

_____. 2000. *Provincializing Europe: Postcolonial Thought and Historical Difference.* New Jersey: Princeton University Press.

Chatterjee Partha.1983. 'More on Modes of Power and the Peasantry'. In *Subaltern Studies II: Writings of South Asian Histories and Society,* edited by Ranajit Guha, 311–49. New Delhi: Oxford University Press.

_____. 2008. 'Democracy and Economic Transformation in India.' *Economic and Political Weekly* 43(16): 53–62.

Clegg, Stewart and David Dunkerley. 1980. *Organization, Class and Control.* London: Routledge & Kegan Paul.

Clegg, Stewart R. 1989. *Frameworks of Power.* London: Sage.

Conway, Dennis and Nik Heynen. 2006. 'The Ascendancy of Neoliberalism and Emergence of Contemporary Globalization'. In *Globalization's Contradictions: Geographies of Discipline, Destruction and Transformation,* edited by Dennis Conway and Nik Heynen, 17–33. New York: Routledge.

Deem, Rosemary and Kevin J. Brehony. 2005. 'Management as Ideology: The Case of New Managerialism in Higher Education.' *Oxford Review of Education* 31(2): 217–35.

Djelic, Marie-Laure. 1998. *Exporting the American model: The Post-war Transformation of European Business.* Oxford: Oxford University Press.

Doolin, Bill. 2002. 'Enterprise Discourse, Professional Identity and the Organizational Control of Hospital Clinicians.' *Organization Studies* 23(3): 369–90.

Eckhardt, Giana M. and Alan Bradshaw. 2014. 'The Erasure of Antagonisms between Popular Music and Advertising.' *Marketing Theory* 14(2):167–83.

Eckhardt, Giana, Nikhilesh Dholakia and Rohit Varman. 2013. 'Ideology for the 10 Billion: Introduction to Globalization of Marketing Ideology.' *Journal of Macromarketing* 33 (1): 7–12.

Escobar, Arturo. 1995. *Encountering Development: The Making and Unmaking of the Third World.* Princeton: Princeton University Press.

Fanon, Frantz. 1952. *Black Skin, White Masks.* New York: Grove Press.

Flemming, Peter and Subhabrata Bobby Banerjee. 2016. 'When Performativity Fails: Implications for Critical Management Studies.' *Human Relations* 69(2): 257–76.

Fournier, Valerie and Chris Grey. 2000. 'At the Critical Moment: Conditions and Prospects for Critical Management Studies.' *Human Relations* 53(1): 171–93.

Freire, Paulo. 1990. *The Pedagogy of the Oppressed*. New York: Continuum.

Frenkel, Michal and Yehouda Shenhav. 2003. 'From Americanization to Colonization: The Diffusion of Productivity Models Revisited.' *Organization Studies* 24(9): 1537–61.

Giddens, Anthony. 1990. *The Consequences of Modernity*. Cornwell: Polity.

Goh, Joel, Jeffrey Pfeffer and Stefanos A. Zenios. 2015. 'The Relationship Between Workplace Stressors and Mortality and Health Costs in the United States.' *Management Science* 62(2): 608–28..

Gramsci, Antonio. 1971. *Selections from the Prison Notebooks*. Edited and translated by Quintin Hoare and Geoffrey Nowell Smith. New York: International.

Grey, Christopher and Hugh Willmott. 2005. *Critical Management Studies: A Reader*. Oxford: Oxford University Press.

Gupta, Akhil. 1998. *Postcolonial Developments: Agriculture in the Making of the Modern India*. Durham: Duke University Press.

Hartmann, Martin and Axel Honneth. 2006. 'Paradoxes of Capitalism.' *Constellations* 13(1): 41–58.

Harvey D. 2003. *The New Imperialism*. Oxford: Oxford University Press.

Harvey, David. 2005. *A Brief History of Neoliberalism*. Oxford, UK: Oxford University Press.

Hobsbawm, Eric J. 1975. *The Age of Capital: 1845–1878*. New York: Scribner and Sons.

Horkheimer, Max and Theodor Adorno. 1976. *Dialectic of Enlightenment*. New York: Continuum.

Imas, J. Miguel and Alia Weston. 2011. 'From Harare to Rio de Janeiro: Kukiya-Favela Organization of the Excluded.' *Organization* 19(2): 205–27.

Jack, Gavin, Robert Westwood, Nidhi Srinivas and Ziauddin Sardar. 2011. 'Deepening, Broadening and Re-asserting a Postcolonial Interrogative Space in Organization Studies.' *Organization* 18(3): 275–302.

Jagannathan, Srinath and Rajnish K. Rai. 2015. 'Organizing Sovereign Power: Police and the Performance of Bare Bodies.' *Organization* 22(6): 810–31.

Jhally, Sut. 1991. *The Codes of Advertising: Role of Fetishism and the Political Economy of Meaning in Consumer Society*. London: Routledge

Kaviraj, Sudipto. 1988. 'A Critique of the Passive Revolution.' *Economic and Political Weekly* 23(45/47): 2429–44.

Kipping, Matthias, Behlul Usdiken and Núria Puig. 2004. 'Imitation, Tension, and Hybridization: Multiple "Americanizations" of Management Education in Mediterranean Europe.' *Journal of Management Inquiry* 13(2): 98.

Klein, Naomi. 2008. *The Shock Doctrine: The Rise of Disaster Capitalism*. London: Penguin.

Lash, Scott and Celia Lury. 2007. *Global Culture Industry*. Cambridge: Polity.

Marcuse, Herbert. 1991. *One-Dimensional Man*. Boston: Beacon

Marx, Karl. 1843. *Letter from the Deutsch-Französische Jahrbücher to Ruge*. Accessed on 15 December 2016. Available at https://www.marxists.org/archive/marx/works/1843/letters/43_09.htm#p144.

Mbembe, Achille. 2003. 'Necropolitics.' *Public Culture* 15(1) :11–40.

Micklethwait, John and Adrian Wooldridge. 2005. *The Company: A Short History of a Revolutionary Idea*. Volume 12. New York: Random House LLC.

Mignolo, Walter. 2000. 'The Many Faces of Cosmo-polis: Border Thinking and Critical Cosmopolitanism.' *Public Culture* 12(3): 721–48.

Mirchandani, Kiran. 2014. 'Flesh in Voice: The No-touch Embodiment of Transnational Customer Service Workers.' *Organization* 22(6): 909–23.

Nandy, Ashis. 1983. *The Intimate Enemy: Loss and Recovery of Self under Colonialism*. Delhi: Oxford University Press.

Noordegraaf, Mirko and Rosemary Stewart. 2000. 'Managerial Behaviour Research in Private and Public Sectors: Distinctiveness, Disputes and Directions.' *Journal of Management Studies* 37(3): 427–43.

Ozbilgin, Mustafa. 2004. '"International" Human Resource Management: Academic Parochialism in Editorial Boards of the "Top" 22 Journals on International Human Resource Management.' *Personnel Review* 33(2): 205–21.

Parker, Martin. 1995. 'Critique in the Name of What? Postmodernism and Critical Approaches to Organization.' *Organization Studies* 16(4): 553–64.

Parker, Martin, Valérie Fournier and Patrick Reedy. 2007. *The Dictionary of Alternatives: Utopianism and Organization*. London: Zed Books.

Parker, Martin, George Cheney, Valérie Fournier and Chris Land. 2014. *The Routledge Companion to Alternative Organization*. London: Routledge.

Pfeffer, Jeffrey. 2016. 'Why the Assholes are Always Winning: Money Trumps All, in JMS Says'. Accessed on 26 January 2016. Available at http://www.socadms.org.uk/why-the-assholes-are-winning.

Rahnema Majid. 1997. 'Introduction'. In *The Post-Development Reader*, edited by Majid Rahnema and Victoria Bawtree, ix–xix. London: Zed Books

Roy, Arundhati. 2012. 'Capitalism: A Ghost Story.' *Outlook*. Accessed on 6 February 2016. Available at http://www.outlookindia.com/article.aspx?280234.

Sanyal, Kalyan. 2007. *Rethinking Capitalist Development: Primitive Accumulation, Governmentality and Post-colonial Capitalism*. London: Routledge.

Sassen, Saskia. 2014. *Expulsions: Brutality and Complexity in the Global Economy*. Cambridge: Harvard University Press.

Shrivastava, Aseem and Ashish Kothari. 2012. *Churning the Earth: The Making of Global India*. New Delhi: Penguin India

Spicer, André, Mats Alvesson and Dan Kärreman. 2009. 'Critical Performativity: The Unfinished Business of Critical Management Studies.' *Human Relations* 62(4): 537–60.

Spivak Gayatri C. 1988. 'Can the Subaltern Speak?'. In *Marxism and the Interpretation of Culture*, edited by Cary Nelson C and Lawrence Grossberg, 271–313. Urbana: University of Illinois Press.

Srinivas, Nidhi. 2012. 'Epistemic and Performative Quests for Authentic Management in India.' *Organization* 19(2): 145–58.

Srinivas, Nidhi. 2013. 'Could a Subaltern Manage? Identity Work and Habitus in a Colonial Workplace.' *Organization Studies* 34(11): 1655–74.

Srivastava, Mukesh. 1994. 'A Critique of the History of Higher Education in India.' Indian Institute of Management Ahmedabad Working Paper 1220. Ahmedabad: Indian Institute of Management Ahmedabad.

Stoler, Ann Laura. 1995. *Race and the Education of Desire: Foucault's History of Sexuality and the Colonial Order of Things.* Durham: Duke University Press.

Swartz, David. 1997. *Power and Culture: The Sociology of Pierre Bourdieu.* Chicago: Chicago University Press.

Tadajewski, M. 2010. 'Towards a History of Critical Marketing Studies.' *Journal of Marketing Management* 26(9/10): 773–824.

Terry, Larry D. 1998. 'Administrative Leadership, Neo-managerialism, and the Public Management Movement.' *Public Administration Review* 58(3): 194–200.

Varman, Rohit and Biswatosh Saha. 2009. 'Disciplining the Discipline: Understanding Postcolonial Epistemic Ideology in Marketing.' *Journal of Marketing Management* 25 (7–8): 811–24.

Varman, Rohit and Hari Sreekumar. 2015. 'Locating the Past in its Silence: History and Marketing Theory in India'. *Journal of Historical Research in Marketing* 7(2): 272–79.

Varman, Rohit and Russell W. Belk. 2012. 'Consuming Postcolonial Shopping Malls.' *Journal of Marketing Management* 28(1–2): 62–84.

Varman, Rohit and Ismael Al-Amoudi. 2016. 'Accumulation through Derealisation: How Corporate Violence Remains Unchecked.' *Human Relations* 69(10): 1909–35.

Veldman, Jeroen and Hugh Willmott. 2013. 'What is the Corporation and Why does it Matter?.' *M@ n@ gement* 16(5): 605–20.

Weber, Max. 1968. *Economy and Society.* New York: Bedminster.

Willmott, Hugh. 2011. 'Enron Narrative'. In *Business Ethics and Continental Philosophy*, edited by Painter-Morland, Mollie and René ten Bos. Cambridge, UK: Cambridge University Press.

Zizek, Slavoj. 2012 (ed). *Mapping Ideology.* London: Verso.

―――――. 2014. *Žižek's Jokes.* Cambridge MA, USA: MIT Press.

2

Formal and Informal Technologies of Alternative Organisational Spaces within the State

An Analysis of Violence, Wrongdoing and Policing

Srinath Jagannathan and Rajnish Rai

When violence occurs, and nothing happens to those responsible for the violence, what is the nature of society that we create and live in? When the sanctity of human life is cast aside, questions are raised about the credibility and legitimacy of democratic institutions. Life is mobilised by the ruling elites of the state as a political and communicative play to reproduce their power over society. The state is characterised by the site of a durbar where the politics of subservient courtiers structures administrative action. The durbar becomes the centripetal locus of action and other claims of justice are cast aside. The possibility of dissent against the durbar becomes difficult in the wake of organisational dynamics, which marginalise ethical acts of dissent.

We examine these questions of life, death, state, police, riots, violence, investigations and justice in the context of Gujarat. In February 2002, as a part of right wing mobilisation for building a temple in Ayodhya at a site where a mosque had been demolished by rioting mobs in 1992, a few activists were returning from Ayodhya to Gujarat (Jaffrelot, 2012). A train compartment in which they were travelling was burnt leading to the loss of fifty nine lives (Dhattiwala and Biggs, 2012). Following this incident, there were large-scale violent riots in Gujarat directed against Muslims leading to the loss of nearly 2,000 lives (Jaffrelot, 2012). There was widespread sentiment that not only had the state of Gujarat not done enough to prevent the riots but might even have been complicit in the violence directed against Muslims (Noorani, 2004). Dhattiwala and Biggs (2012) argue that the state of Gujarat administratively retaliated against those police officers who tried to uphold law and order by not allowing riots or mass violence to occur, while facilitating the advancement of careers of those police officers who turned a blind eye towards the riots.

Amidst claims of inducement, coercion and intimidation of witnesses in the investigations of riots cases, the Supreme Court of India intervened to constitute a SIT to investigate the riots cases (Mitta, 2014). In this chapter, we explore the politics of the SIT, which was articulated as an alternative organisational space within the state. We explore the informal technologies deployed by the state to assess whether the SIT had the organisational and ethical capacity to provide justice to riots victims (Chatterjee, 2014). By tracing multiple narratives of the SIT, we engage with the genealogical project (Burrell, 1988) through which the state sought to re-acquire legitimacy for itself. According to Rasche and Chia (2009), engaging with genealogical projects involves at least two important forms of analysis. First, they involve analysing the multiple root tributaries of emerging practices in terms of understanding various historical elements that created the conditions for the present practices to be possible. Second, they also involve an analysis of background tacit knowledge and the identity formation of actors, which enables current practices to be seen as legitimate.

In this context, alternative organisational spaces such as the SIT constructed by the state are attempts at branding, in creating impressions of the state acting with velocity and urgency to resolve people's issues (Yakhlef, 2004, 242). Also, such a scheme of velocity may also be associated with the state playing an active role in vectorising the space of society, involving the replacement of pluralist social memories with dominant, majoritarian anchors of social meaning. Specifically, the political ideology of Hindutva, which seeks to re-interpret the Indian nation from the standpoint of a narrow, majoritarian imagination, is an example of the vectorisation of space. The Hindutva project works towards forgetting India's syncretic and plural past, and instead builds discourses of the Indian nation being centred around a narrow sense of Hindu pride with only a subordinate role being envisaged for religious and cultural minorities (Das, 2008). We explore whether the alternative space of the SIT embodies a similar vectorisation of space. Re-cast within the social relations of a durbar, the SIT could imply an organisational process, where complex socio-political memories associated with the riots are forgotten, and instead the administrative practice of the state is firmly anchored in narrow technical imaginations, where a few convictions (and many clean chits and acquittals) absolve the state of larger political complicity in the violence directed against minorities.

Violence, state and the technology of alternative organisational spaces

Right-wing captures of the state often involve control of the police and prosecution agencies (Chatterjee, 2014; Jaffrelot, 2012) to ensure that right-wing violence directed against cultural minorities does not face legal barriers. At the same time, right-wing projects also articulate themselves as projects engendering strong institutions, thus activating vectors of 'social fantasy, instigated by citizen's unconscious expectations in the process of the continuous recreation of social reality' (Fotaki, 2010, 705). Stories are circulated articulating the state as being strongly in pursuit of equity and justice, producing narratives of the moral righteousness of the state. However, when a state fails and people see through its violent character, it may need to take recourse to creating an alternative organisational space. This is a further push into informality, processes of territorialisation through which the state cements its vectored association with majoritarian moorings.

Territorialisation involves vectoring of organisational spaces in ways where their ability to reflect a tension between multiple identities is erased. Vectored organisational spaces are characterised 'not so much by multiple identities but by an absence of identity, constituting a context with no context, whose difference is indifference' (Yakhlef, 2004, 242). Right-wing projects have often attempted to violently erase cosmopolitan urban identities by demonising and labelling them as places of 'excessive individualism, artificiality, and a den of immorality fostering the loss of traditions' (Vari, 2012, 715). Territorialisation thus involves categorising spaces as being guilty of hybrid and impure possibilities and sanitising these spaces to produce politically pure identities.

Riots are often deployed by right-wing forces as a form of savagery and disrespect towards cultural minorities (Kumar, 2007). Territorialisation involves making the cultural 'Other' unsafe and rendering cultural 'Otherness' as a suspect, inadequate and illegitimate form of citizenship (Vari, 2012). However, projects of resistance can often advance claims of justice and disturb the stability of projects of territorialisation engendered by the state. Since resistance projects can threaten the stability of right-wing state driven territorialisation agendas (Desai, 2014), the state may constitute alternative organisational spaces to reclaim its legitimacy (Rajeshwari, 2013). Alternative organisational spaces may be particularly required when the mainstream organisational agencies associated with the state lack credibility and are tainted as lacking independence and autonomy (Rajeshwari,

2013). Further, alternative organisational spaces within the realm of the police, prosecution or judiciary shift the public discourse of resistance to a new vectored, technical space (Rajeshwari, 2013).

An alternative organisational space is only likely to add to exceptional decisionism, a strategy of reproducing the legitimacy of the state by resorting to exceptions (Jagannathan and Rai, 2014). As passive consumers of alternative organisational spaces, we may be rendered as spectators or 'patients absorbing stimuli rather than agents exercising active discrimination and intelligent reflection' (Beiner, 1983, 162). The important question in thinking about alternative organisational spaces is whether acts of the state or other influential political actors 'positions the audience more inside politics than outside' (Manolescu, 1998, 62). When the state constitutes alternative spaces because of lack of credibility of the regular organisational spaces, it needs to be seen whether the spectacle of the alternative space closes the possibility of political debate or enables it.

Alternative organisational spaces constituted by the state may embody a communicative play of progressive engagement with critique. Right-wing propaganda often relies on simplistic and charismatic tropes, which encourage 'counter-subversion panics using populist rhetoric and producerist narratives to enlist a mass base to defend their unfair power, privilege and wealth' (Berlet, 2012, 565). Right-wing rhetoric obfuscates issues of equity and justice to target projects of resistance. Through the orchestration of right wing propaganda, 'the blame for economic, political and social tensions is transferred away from free market capitalism to mythical conspiracies' (Berlet, 2012, 565) staged by those resisting hegemonic discourses. When states are held to be complicit in regimes of violence (Jaffrelot, 2012) and there is a coalition of activists engaged in resistance (Setalvad, 2013), then states may simulate the rhetoric of right-wing propaganda to obfuscate issues of justice and shift the discourse to a plane of nationalist righteousness. Through this rhetoric, the institutional configuration of an alternative organisational space is positioned as if the alternative space is a world of its own in 'which the rules of everyday' micropolitics of the state 'are suspended' (Sorensen and Spoelstra, 2011, 85). Alternative organisational spaces are meant to convey the fantasy that the failure of the state will be corrected and the desires of justice advanced by citizens will be fulfilled.

Right-wing narratives often justify the violence inflicted, sanctioned or permitted by the state. Such violence is justified by situating it as 'productive: of truth, knowledge and the prevention of prospective violence and terror' (Pugliese, 2013, 1). Similarly right-wing forces have justified the riots which occurred in

Gujarat in 2002. The right-wing thesis about the Gujarat riots suggests that for many years the media and the state have ignored the violence inflicted on Hindus by the religious minorities (Deshpande, 2014). Right-wing propaganda contends that during the Gujarat riots, minorities were taught an effective lesson (*Hindu*, 28 February 2007). Consequently, the minorities continued to live in fear and thus would never again dare to inflict violence against Hindus, bringing an atmosphere of peace in Gujarat (*Hindu*, 28 February 2007). Thus, right-wing forces have argued that the violence inflicted during the 2002 riots was productive and prevented future occurrence of violence. However, the culture of fear nurtured by right-wing politics was soon resisted by a variety of civil society actors standing up for justice (Setalvad, 2013). This forced the state to resort to institutional means to exonerate itself from the charge of being complicit in the 2002 riots. Since the agencies of the state were accused of impeding fair investigations (Jaffrelot, 2012), an alternative organisational space such as the SIT could have had greater credibility in exonerating the state. The findings of the SIT were triumphantly marshalled by right-wing forces to indicate the innocence and righteousness of the state (Deshpande, 2014). Through the findings of the SIT, the state had reacquired legitimacy, and the 'institutional logics promoted and endorsed by organisational leaders' had triumphed in opposition to claims which emerged from 'bottom-up practices accorded through individual agency' (Drori and Honig, 2013, 347).

In the context of allegations of wrongdoing, the state attempts to re-establish its legitimacy by rhetorically relying on the symbolic autonomy of alternative organisational spaces. The state rhetorically distances itself from investigations into its wrongdoing and claims that an independent agency has vindicated its innocence. Resistance has often been staged even in the context of severe social constraints and local enactments of resistance have often attempted to subvert centralised state power (Scott, 1990). In the context of resistance directed against the violence enacted with the complicit sanction of the state power, alternative organisational spaces are another attempt at counter-subversion. The state attempts to label resistance figures as having made false allegations and suggests that these figures are resisting the development and evolution of the state for malicious purposes. Alternative organisational spaces authorised by the state are attempts to enhance the credibility of official narratives while contesting the legitimacy of locally staged resistance.

Methods

We wanted to trace how a society and a state engage with issues of mass violence that leave behind deep scars and thus engage with the constitution of fields through which regimes of symbolic violence were enacted (Everett, 2002). We wanted to understand how grievances and angsts of injustice find institutional expression. As authors of this chapter, we shared a sense of anxiety about the possibilities of violence and the state not doing enough to prevent violence. One of us is an officer of the Indian Police Service (IPS) in India and the other has taught in a social science university in India. We met while completing our doctors of philosophy (PhDs) around five years ago and as our relationship of friendship evolved, we collaborated on a number of themes pertaining to business, ethics, justice, society, state and administration around which we had a shared sense of anxiety.

Our situatedness influenced the partisan knowledges that we accessed and articulate here in the endeavour 'to make linkages between history, structure and individual lives in the service of an intellectual and political transformation' (Mir and Mir, 2002, 105). The role of the author who works in the police is well recognised for standing up for justice against numerous odds during several points in his career. This mediated our access within a broad sense of solidarity with journalists, lawyers, police and administrative officers and riot victims who have been following the investigation of cases pertaining to the riots in Gujarat in 2002. We interviewed four journalists, five lawyers, seven police officers and two administrative officers for the purposes of this study. We assured all our participants of confidentiality and discussed a range of issues pertaining to the investigations of the riots cases through the mechanism of the SIT.

Our conversations revolved around the constitution of the SIT, actions taken by different members of the SIT, interventions of the Supreme Court, the interface between politics, ethics, SIT and investigation, other issues of organisational dynamics that influenced the functioning of the SIT and the quest for justice of riots victims. The conversations were often held in an informal setting, in terms of actors catching up with each other over a period of time to discuss developments as they were emerging, thus exploring a range of human vulnerabilities (May, 2003) and their intersection with rich narratives of survival, resilience and resistance. In our conversations, we uncovered accounts which questioned the official narratives of the state and the SIT. We wanted to explore the gaps between the SIT's formal commitment to processes of justice and its numerous actions. We did not record any of our conversations, as they followed several informal contours. We maintained detailed field notes of our conversations pertaining to the issues that were of interest to us.

Our identities influenced the actors to who we spoke. While we contacted actors such as a former Director General of Police and a former Home Minister of the state of Gujarat for their views on the subject, in order to access narratives from actors who had been a part of the innermost circles of the state, they declined to speak to us. We also relied on a careful engagement with texts such as newspaper reports, court orders and judgments, investigation notes, depositions of witnesses, statements before investigators and affidavits to engage with the institutional unfolding of the SIT. Following Jagannathan and Rai (2014), we adopted the approach of combining journalistic texts, interview data, archival data of court and investigation proceedings and our own personal insights to engage with the complexity of narratives. We do not offer any legal arguments or coherent truths here. We believe that the magnitude of violence was spread across an extremely large canvas and there are multiple local narratives, which make the project of discovering linear truths epistemically unviable and unproductive.

Instead, we problematise several narratives that exist about the SIT and the institutional unfolding of events. We wrote extensive memos about the data in order to analyse the contradictions and tensions that often informed the tension between institutional rhetoric and concrete action. In these memos, we engaged with official narratives of the SIT and problematised the administrative actions that informed the enactment of the SIT. We examined how informal positions in the background were shaping the institutional structuring of SIT. Our analysis was less historical and more genealogical (Burrell, 1988), as we attempted to understand, how the enactment of the SIT was embodied in the state's quest for legitimacy.

Narratives of the SIT

We articulate the enactment of the SIT in the form of three broad themes. In each of these themes, we combine interview data, journalistic accounts and texts pertaining to court and investigation proceedings. Our attempt here is not to offer an authentic truth about the processes surrounding the SIT's investigations of the Gujarat riots, but to problematise the SIT as an alternative organisational space within the state. We wish to raise questions about the efficacy of alternative organisational spaces within the state and argue that these alternative spaces do not further the quest for justice.

State, special actions and vectorisation of space

The Gujarat riots of 2002 embodied the sociology of damage. Damage was not only with respect to the loss of human life and the magnitude of violence, but also about the balance of power that rested at the intersection of the state and the mob. The right-wing project of constructing majoritarian narratives of society, and pushing other dissenting narratives seeking justice to the margins was at play immediately after the riots (Jaffrelot, 2012). Consequently, the National Human Rights Commission (NHRC) (11 July 2003) approached the Supreme Court urging that the human rights of riot victims were being violated:

> Deeply concerned about the damage to the credibility of the criminal justice delivery system and negation of human rights of victims, the National Human Rights Commission, on consideration of the report of its team which was sent to Vadodara, has today filed a Special Leave Petition under Article 136 of the Constitution of India in the Supreme Court with a prayer to set aside the impugned judgement of the Trial Court in the Best Bakery case and sought directions for further investigation by an independent agency and retrial of the case in a competent court located outside the state of Gujarat.

The Supreme Court of India transferred the trial of the Best Bakery Case to Mumbai after the court in Vadodara had acquitted the accused. The Best Bakery Case is seen as an important test case for the possibility of justice in the aftermath of the Gujarat riots (Bunsha, 2006). Rioters killed fourteen people who had taken shelter in the Best Bakery in Vadodara by burning it on 1 March 2002. However, 68 witnesses turned hostile during the trial in a session's court in Vadodara leading to allegations that they had been coerced and intimidated. As mandated by the Supreme Court, when the retrial took place in Mumbai, only seven of the 74 original witnesses turned hostile, leading to the conviction of nine of the seventeen accused in 2006. After hearing the petition filed by the NHRC with respect to other sensitive cases, the Supreme Court constituted a SIT to reopen the investigations in these cases (Supreme Court of India, 26 March 2008). Interestingly, the state of Gujarat did not oppose the constitution of the SIT. It submitted to the Supreme Court (26 March 2008, Paragraph 3) that it was not:

> interested in shielding any culprit or a guilty person, but on the other hand, would like all those who are guilty, to be punished.

A lawyer representing the cases of riot victims in Gujarat questioned the efficacy of constituting a SIT for investigating the riots cases:

> The SIT was a five member body. The head of the SIT was Dr R. K.

Raghavan, a former director of the Central Bureau of Investigation (CBI), and the SIT comprised one more independent member. This independent member was also a former Special Director of the CBI who had worked with Dr Raghavan. Many people were asking legitimate questions. By what rules of conduct were Dr Raghavan and the independent member governed? They were private citizens. What would happen to them if they did not discharge their responsibilities in an accountable manner? Further, the SIT comprised three police officers representing the state of Gujarat itself – Ms Geetha Johri, Shri Shivanand Jha and Shri Ashish Bhatia. Thus, the state of Gujarat controlled the majority in the SIT. NHRC had demanded probe by an independent body. In what way was a body still controlled by the state of Gujarat an independent agency?

The apparatus of the SIT was a formal technology of instituting an alternative organisational space within the state. It is interesting to note that the NHRC called for an independent investigation and the solution that was mediated by the judiciary resulted in a 'special' investigation. It was clear that the SIT was a temporary body and would be dissolved after it had completed its role. Given the ephemerality of its existence, its accountability to long-term democratic concerns was questionable.

'Special' also has a connotation of eliteness associated with it, indicating a mediation between elite echelons of the state from which the commons are excluded. Within the metaphorical cosmos of the 'special', justice is reduced to an ephemeral quest, a temporary apology through which the state crafts a body that is firmly within its control and yet has the pretence of a 'special' outsideness. When the state articulates special actions, it mobilises the tropes of an outsider in order to reclaim legitimacy, and yet fills the outsider body with entrenched insiders.

The 'special' is formally outside the reach of the normal state, but it is through informal conversations of the everyday that the politics of control is exercised over insiders. The 'special' is an embodiment of a formal technology, which will be principally enacted through the gravitational pull of informal cultures. The state urgently needed to reclaim legitimacy as even the Supreme Court of India (26 March 2008, Paragraph 1) acknowledged the scale of horror:

> If in the name of religion, people are killed, that is essentially a slur and blot on the society governed by rule of law... Religious fanatics really do not belong to any religion. They are no better than terrorists who kill innocent people...

Yet, while the SIT was a rhetorical move towards claiming legitimacy, there were several questions. A police officer familiar with the investigations said:

> The credibility of police officers on the SIT was questionable. The state of Gujarat suggested names of three officers as members of SIT with whom they felt comfortable. Later, the Supreme Court of India removed two officers – Shri Shivanand Jha and Ms Geetha Johri – as members of the SIT.

Ms Geetha Johri was charge-sheeted by the CBI on charges of conspiracy of killing a witness and destroying evidence, thus obstructing investigation in another case of police killing (*Hindustan Times*, 4 September 2012). Though she was later discharged by a court of law, the discharge was purely on technical grounds for want of sanction for prosecution required under the Criminal Procedure Court from the state government of Gujarat rather than on factual merits of the case (*Hindu*, 2 March 2015). While passing strictures against Ms Geetha Johri, the Supreme Court of India (12 January 2010, Paragraph 42) transferred the investigation of the police killing case from the Gujarat Police to the CBI,

> From the above factual discrepancies…we, therefore, feel that the police authorities of the state of Gujarat had failed to carry out a fair and impartial investigation…It cannot be questioned that the offences the high police officials have committed was of grave nature which needs to be strictly dealt with…Ms Johri had not been carrying out the investigation in the right manner…Therefore we are of the view that her mentioning…the discussion among the accused officers…was meant to obfuscate the enquiry.

The SIT thus embodies a vectorisation of space and eliminating the possibility of organisational politics leading to unpredictable outcomes. Within the police, state and other social spaces, actors cannot be controlled in a universal and comprehensive manner. The disagreements of actors with each other can lead to actions, which question the ethical content of state decisions.

However, the SIT is a carefully chosen body. It is free from the inconvenience of dissent and unpredictable micropolitics. The SIT reflects the need of the state to reorder the unpredictability of space and replace it with the intersection of predictable vectors in order to reclaim its legitimacy. The imperative of vectorisation and comfort thus led the state to questionable appointments such as that of Ms Geetha Johri.

The news magazine *Tehelka* alleged that Ms Geetha Johri had been pressurised into diluting a police killing case as a quid pro quo for diluting a departmental enquiry against her husband Shri Anil Johri, an Indian Forest Service officer of Gujarat cadre (Ayyub, 2010). Ms. Geetha Johri was also nominated by the Gujarat government for the President's Police Medal despite her name not featuring in the list prepared by the Director General of Police (DGP) of the state of Gujarat (Ayyub, 2010). Ms Johri was also rewarded through her posting as the Commissioner of Rajkot Police (Ayyub, 2010). In the light of questionable appointments of SIT members, an official of the state of Gujarat said:

> It is extremely important to appreciate the circumstances in which the state government agreed for reinvestigation and proposed the names of three senior officers to be part of the SIT. The order of constitution of SIT by the Honourable Supreme Court was the result of the petitions filed by the NHRC, the Citizens for Justice and Peace (CJP) and other non-governmental organisations (NGOs) in 2002 and 2003 seeking re-investigation of some of the cases by CBI and transfer of the cases outside Gujarat, to enable a free and fair trial after several witnesses turned hostile amid allegations of threat, coercion and inducement. All these years the state government had consistently opposed these pleas on the ground that entrusting the investigation of these cases to CBI or transferring the trial of these cases outside the state would imply that the courts and law-enforcement machinery of Gujarat are not trustworthy and would sabotage delivery of justice.

Thus, the stand taken by the state of Gujarat before the Supreme Court agreeing to the constitution of SIT was a reversal of its previous positions. An official of the state of Gujarat who has been following these developments remarked:

> It is intriguing that the state government's arguments on March 25, 2008 were in total contrast to the stand taken by the state since 2003 and it agreed for investigation by a SIT provided that the officers constituting the team are not from outside the state. The Supreme Court appreciated the stance of Gujarat government in not objecting to the setting up of a SIT. While the government in Gujarat was led by the Bharatiya Janata Party, the central government was led by the rival political formation of the United Progressive Alliance

(UPA) led by the Congress Party. The UPA had soft peddled its interventions in the riots cases till then because it was afraid of alienating the vote bank of the majority Hindu community.

Amidst these suggestions of party politics and partisan interests, an official of the state of Gujarat said:

> Did the stand of the Gujarat government change because the UPA was changing its stand? After losing the elections in the recently conducted Gujarat polls in December 2007, the UPA suddenly expressed its willingness before the Supreme Court in February 2008 to get the cases investigated by CBI. Therefore, was the state government engaging in a pre-emptive move to prevent the transfer of cases to CBI, by agreeing for constitution of SIT for re-investigation of the cases, and man the SIT with pliable officers who would toe its line?

A journalist questioned the role of the judiciary as well:

> The NHRC had approached the Supreme Court in 2003. The Supreme Court gave its ruling in 2008. What took the Supreme Court five years to decide that an independent investigation is needed in these cases to meet the ends of justice? Why did the Supreme Court agree to the state of Gujarat suggestion of nominating Gujarat Cadre officers as members of the SIT? Even if the best officers with the most impeccable credentials were to be chosen, they should have been from outside Gujarat. It was unreasonable to expect Gujarat cadre officers to act with functional autonomy. A large portion of the blame for the SIT failing to deliver justice must lie with the Supreme Court as well.

Thus, the politics of alternative organisational spaces within the state is the vector of compliance and pliability, sanctified by judicial interventions. The special actions of the state such as the SIT are a site of communicative hyperbole. They are strategies through which issues of wrongdoing are prevented from being problematised in diverse local spaces.

Statist alternatives and the rationality of enchantment

When the state advances arguments for an alternative organisational space, it is attempting to enchant the public with the imagination of action. An alternative organisation is the entrepreneurship of the new, an act of creation itself. Thus, it is argued that an alternative organisation is immersed in the purity of authentic innovation that will enable the state to uphold the tenets of justice. That the alternative organisation is a careless mythology is evident from the almost ahistorical imaginary through which the alternative is articulated as being independent and separate from the state. With respect to the formation of the SIT, a police officer said:

> The state government was apprehensive that investigations will slip out of its hand. It had already burnt its fingers earlier. Police officers who were involved in false police encounters along with ministers had tried to fix investigations. However, some officers had stood up and gone beyond all pressures to effect arrests of such officers in cases of police killings. The state government therefore wanted to control the investigations of these cases and had suggested the names of its trusted officers for nomination as members of the SIT.

A human rights activist remarked about the micropolitics of the SIT,

> Within normal policing processes, people can still stand up and do the right thing. Because of the earlier experience in investigation of an encounter case known as Sohrabuddin murder case, the state government was apprehensive and was not sure whether some police officers could again stand up and pursue the path of justice seriously, which would hurt its interests. However, the SIT removed these uncertainties and the handpicked officers of the government went about protecting their bosses.

An official of the state of Gujarat, disturbed by the constitution of the SIT said,

> It appears most likely that the state of Gujarat wanted to pre-empt the transfer of cases to CBI. The learned Senior Counsel Shri Rohatgi, representing the state of Gujarat was prepared with the list of three senior IPS officers of the Gujarat Cadre who would be part of the SIT. How did he come prepared with the list? How could he know beforehand that the Supreme Court would propose constitution of an SIT during the hearing on that day? It is especially intriguing because the Supreme Court had for the first time proposed constitution of SIT on 25 March 2008, and on the same day the lawyer representing the state of Gujarat proposed the

name of the officers who could be part of the SIT. What informal
negotiations took place in the background and what was the role of
the Supreme Court in these negotiations? Was the Supreme Court
so naive that it did not understand that the dangerous consequences
of the state government proposing the names of those officers who
would investigate the top political functionaries who were alleged
to be involved in the post-Godhra carnage? This was like the
state government proposing who from the state government will
investigate the role of the state government itself.

Another official of the state of Gujarat said:

> The Government of Gujarat had always rewarded those who stood
> by it. It had also punished those who were not compliant. The senior
> counsel, Shri Rohtagi, who represented the state of Gujarat in the
> Supreme Court is today the Attorney General of India, when the BJP
> formed the Central Government in 2014. Looking at the patterns
> of rewards and punishments, I wonder whether a Government was
> being run or was it a King's durbar.

Entrusting the investigation to a SIT and staffing it with pliable officers limited
the region of surveillance for the state. The SIT became a process of vectorising
subjectivities. The SIT was articulated as an extraordinary effort made by the state
and the Supreme Court. The SIT was articulated as an agency that would have
the last word on truth claims about the riots. It was almost as if the SIT was the
arbiter of theological imaginations of ultimate justice. These arguments conceal
the informal negotiations that the state of Gujarat had entered with the amicus
curiae and probably with the judiciary as well to decide who would be a part of the
SIT. A curious incident that took place during the hearing in the Supreme Court
resulting in the constitution of the SIT raises serious questions on the role of the
amicus curiae, Shri Harish Salve who was supposed to give an independent opinion
to the Supreme Court. A lawyer familiar with the investigations of riots cases said:

> In court, Shri Salve supported the state of Gujarat. He did not endorse
> the views of NHRC, CJP or the Union of India. Thus, Shri Salve must
> be held complicit for the appointment of individuals like Ms Geetha
> Johri, whose ability to conduct a free and impartial investigation
> was in doubt, as allegations of obstruction of investigation and
> destruction of evidence had been levelled against her.

Newspaper reports support the above allegations that Shri Salve was involved in finalising the names of Gujarat cadre IPS officers who were included in the SIT (Khetan, 12 March 2011). Although the Supreme Court had permitted the petitioners to suggest the names of officers who could be included in the SIT, these names were eventually not accepted by the Supreme Court. Interestingly, the Supreme Court staffed the SIT with the officers who were suggested by the state, against whom the investigations were to be carried out.

CJP, an NGO pleading on behalf of riot victims was of the view that Shri Salve had not taken complaints about the shoddy investigations of the SIT seriously. He had not taken a firm stand on them, thus bringing into question the credibility of the amicus curiae (Khetan, 12 March 2011). For instance, the role of the SIT was questioned in one of the riot's cases known as the Gulberg Society Massacre Case, where sixty nine people, largely Muslims, were killed by rioters in a residential building (NDTV, 11 March 2010).

In the Gulberg Society Massacre Case, the SIT held a police inspector responsible for the breakdown of the law and order machinery while failing to initiate legal action against police officers of the rank of Joint Commissioner and Deputy Commissioner (Khetan, 12 March 2011). There were at least two allegations of conflict of interest against Shri Salve (Khetan, 12 March 2011). A lawyer familiar with the allegations said:

> Shri Harish Salve had written to the Government of Gujarat through the Additional Advocate General, Tushar Mehta (now Additional Solicitor General in the Supreme Court) forwarding the proposal of a UK based company Eros Energy requiring government land to set up a solar energy project. He was also representing the state of Gujarat in the Supreme Court in another case, famously known as the Ishrat Jahan encounter case, where he was defending the police officers accused of carrying out a false police encounter of four persons, including Ishrat Jahan. These informal friendships and networks cannot be ignored while examining the role of actors who created the SIT.

A police officer questioned the credibility of Shri Shivanand Jha, another member of the SIT:

> Shri Shivanand Jha was an establishment man. As a reward for his services, he had been appointed as the Home Secretary in the state of Gujarat. Moreover, Shri Jha was a person who had been accused

for his role in the Gujarat riots by Ms Zakia Jaffrey in her complaint dated 8 June 2006. Ms Jaffrey was a riot victim whose husband had been killed during the Gulberg society massacre. Her husband was a former Member of Parliament and had called several bureaucrats, politicians and police officers for help. But none of them responded and he was finally killed in the violence. Can you imagine? Nearly seventy people were killed by a mob of rioters. The scale of the massacre is a blot on modern Indian society. How can we allow the people responsible for this to go unpunished? The inclusion of Shri Jha in the SIT called into question the principles of natural justice as he would be expected to investigate his own role in the riots.

A lawyer who has represented several riots victims, said:

When something as horrible as the riots occurred, we need to question whether election victories are enough to absolve you of the crime. You may have won the ballot box. But the riot victims continue to languish in the refugee camps and are screaming for justice. You cannot ignore their legitimate demands for justice. Instead of rendering justice to victims, the state adopted dilatory tactics to tire the victims so that they give up their fight.

The state re-enchants the public away from the narratives of injustice by authoring an institutional entrapment of these narratives. While the SIT could not repress the public memory of riots and injustice, it could still frame the state as a site of institutional action. It could move the state away from tropes of apathy, neglect or explicit intimidation to a space of slow institutional censorship through which narratives of injustice could be slowly deflated, one by one, until their capacity to advance a truth claim could be significantly diminished. These narrative claims of injustice could then be articulated as the clichéd rant of a stubborn past that refuses to die in a present that is becoming golden by the day.

The role of Shri Ashish Bhatia, another member of the SIT was also questioned by the Special Public Prosecutor in the Gulberg Society Massacre Case, Shri R. K. Shah, who resigned from his job (*Times of India*, 3 March 2010). In his letter of resignation, Shri Shah pointed out how two contradictory sets of statements of witnesses, putatively recorded at different instances of time, with the second set of statements containing very weak evidence, were submitted by the SIT before the trial court in the Gulberg Society Massacre Case,

Worse was to follow. The SIT has placed on record two sets of statements of key eyewitnesses (one set recorded in May–June 2008 and the second ostensibly in September 2008). Witnesses denied ever recording statements for a second time. The second set of statements completely weakened the case made by the eyewitnesses in their first statements before the SIT.

A lawyer who has followed the developments in the Gulberg Society Massacre Case, said:

Shri Bhatia insisted that the second set of statements should be considered. Relying on the second set of statements suited the government. The SIT took several such decisions which prevented the hands of law from reaching those who were at the very top of the government.

Finally, after hearing the complaints of victims who had suffered during the communal riots, the Supreme Court directed Ms Geetha Johri and Shri Shivanand Jha to be removed from the SIT (*Outlook*, 6 April 2010). While these officers were replaced by two IPS officers Shri Y. C. Modi and Shri K. Venkateshan from outside the state of Gujarat (*Outlook*, 26 October 2010), the nature of the investigations whose directions had already been set, did not undergo a dramatic change. Moreover, the new members of the SIT were included on the recommendations of Dr R. K. Raghavan, the Chairman of the SIT, whose role itself was under cloud. By the time the new officers had joined the SIT, much of the investigations had been completed including examination of key functionaries of the state such as the Chief Minister. A police officer familiar with the investigations argued:

The role of the then Commissioner of Police, Shri P. C. Pande was also in doubt. Later he went on to become the Director General of Police (DGP) of the state. There are several allegations that Shri P. C. Pande neglected his duty in preventing riots in Ahmedabad after the 27 February 2002 Godhra incident.

When power is exercised repeatedly, then the violence of power reproduces its own legitimacy. Authority is the consolidation of the possibility of violence over a period of time. Thus, when officers such as P. C. Pande are promoted without their role in the riots being investigated thoroughly, the very action of their hierarchical ascent creates the impression that nothing was wrong with the police during the riots (Dhattiwala and Biggs, 2012).

The articulation of the state appears to be that even if something was wrong, it needs to be forgotten and people should carry on with the amnesia of the police ever having done any wrong (Setalvad, 2013). When the SIT carries forward the project of such amnesia then the state is enchanting the public through a play of memory. By re-inventing the careers of those who were accused of wrongdoing, the state appears to suggest that these officers have survived the test of institutional and judicial time.

The argument of the state appears to be that if these officers had done anything wrong, then by now institutional and judicial processes would have caught up with them. However, since nothing has happened to them, and instead they have been promoted, there exists no evidence against them or the state about any wrongdoing. Thus, the politics of administrative survival is posed as the temporality of legitimacy and the sense of permanence of actors accused of wrong doing is used to enchant the publics by suggesting that it was only the allegations against these actors which were ephemeral.

Wages of consenting to an alternative state

The anger with respect to the Gujarat riots in 2002 emerges from the allegations that the state did not do enough to prevent the riots (Desai, 2014). The state had a democratic responsibility to uphold the rule of law and prevent the rioters from engaging in violence (Jaffrelot, 2012). Yet, perhaps there was also an alternative state within the state that decided to ignore its duties in preventing violence (Setalvad, 2013).

The alternative state had an atmosphere of informal decision making, with the wages of participating in such cultures of informality being the conversion of administration into a court of the loyals (Dhattiwala and Biggs, 2012). Those who consent to the alternative state are metaphorically transformed into courtiers who will receive wages for their labour. The text of the state then becomes a curious play of legal processes annotated through informal interventions emanating from a sociology of the durbar.

A journalist spoke about the informal culture of the durbar:

> There has been a lot of controversy about a meeting which took place on 27 February 2002 which was chaired by the Chief Minister of Gujarat. The government of Gujarat has consistently denied that the Chief Minister said anything about going soft on rioters in the meeting. A police officer, Sanjiv Bhatt later claimed that he was present in the meeting and heard the Chief Minister said so.

The entire state machinery was pressed into service to deny that Sanjiv Bhatt was ever present during the meeting. This controversy is unfortunate. Rather than debating on whether Sanjiv Bhatt was present during the meeting or not, look at the record of the state. All the officers who acted against rioters have been punished. All the officers who gave the rioters a free hand have been rewarded. What is the Chief Minister likely to have said then?

There were serious allegations against Shri P. C. Pande, who was the then Commissioner of Police, did not faithfully discharge his duties of controlling the riots in Ahmedabad. The most serious allegations against Shri P. C. Pande were regarding the Gulberg Society Massacre; it was alleged that Shri P. C. Pande did not respond and help the residents of the society even after several calls of help from the ex-Congress Member of Parliament, Shri Ehsan Jafri (Soni, 10 May 2012). However, despite these allegations, the state government later appointed him as the DGP in 2006 and his tenure continued till February 2009 (*Indian Express*, 22 February 2009). In 2007, before the Gujarat assembly elections, the Election Commission ordered Shri P. C. Pande's removal as DGP apprehending that he would not play an impartial role in the elections (*Times of India*, 16 October 2007). On expected lines, once Shri Narendra Modi became the Chief Minister once again after the elections, Shri Pande was once again made the DGP. However, the Election Commission once again requested for Shri Pande's transfer as DGP before the parliamentary elections in 2009 (*Indian Express*, 24 February 2009).

In August 2004, during the cross-examination before the Nanavati Commission, which was a judicial commission set up by the Gujarat government to investigate the riots, Shri Pande claimed amnesia and refused to answer any questions about whether he had received any phone calls from Shri Jafri. He said (Soni, 10 May 2012):

> At present I cannot say whether I received direct distress calls from Gulbarg Society between 12.25 and 12.55 hours that day because there is no noting of it and I do not remember anything about it.

Yet six years later while answering questions before the SIT, Shri Pande was able to cast aside his narrative of amnesia and now he had a clear recollection of the fact that he had not received any telephone calls. He said (Soni, 10 May 2012):

> Late Ahesan Jafri, ex-MP, did not contact me either on my landline phone or mobile phone on 28 February 2002, seeking help. No one

from Gulberg society contacted me either on my landline or mobile phone seeking help.

It is important to note that while the Nanavati Commission was a quasi-public hearing with lawyers representing riot victims being present and having rights of cross-examining witnesses, the SIT was an enclosed space. Whereas Shri Pande claimed amnesia before the Nanavati commission, he was more forthcoming before the SIT. This again indicates the degree of comfort that actors, whose role during the riots was questionable, enjoyed with the SIT. Perhaps the SIT was a safe space for the courtiers of the durbar. The wages of giving consent to the alternative state of the durbar was the privilege of patronage. While the SIT was supposed to uncover the apparatus of the durbar and its intersection with the riots, its institutional capacity to pursue justice was limited.

The SIT was an alternative, ephemeral organisation with the pretence of independence. In order to reach the durbar, it would require an entrenched ethnography, a determined pursuit of leads and trails. But the SIT was justice in project mode, a project that had been sanctioned by the formal state. Within the social relations of the durbar, the SIT was a reservoir for disciplining unruly narratives. The SIT as an alternative organisation mediated between the durbar and the state. While the investigations of the SIT would uncover some truths, larger conspiracies would remain concealed.

Some prosecutions would be successful. This was akin to deciding which elements of the durbar could be sacrificed in order to retain the control of the durbar over the state. The SIT served the purpose of spatial distancing so that the sovereign of the durbar could dishonour the wages of some courtiers and punish them in order to retain the legitimacy of the formal state and the durbar's stranglehold over it.

A police officer familiar with the functioning of the SIT asked:

> Till February 2009, Shri Pande was the DGP and had a role in writing the Annual Confidential Reports of Ms Johri, Shri Jha and Shri Bhatia. Would it have been possible for them to investigate Shri Pande's role in a free and impartial manner? When Shri Pande was examined by the SIT on 24 March 2010, Ms Johri and Shri Jha had not yet been restrained by the Supreme Court from being associated with the SIT. How can this be deemed to be a credible investigation exercise?

Another official of the state of Gujarat said:

From the beginning, I had no faith in the SIT. The credentials of the head of the SIT, Shri R. K. Raghavan were questionable. He was the security in charge when a former Prime Minister, Shri Rajiv Gandhi had been assassinated by terrorists. There were several allegations of lapses. How could such a person be expected to lead important investigations by the SIT? His conduct as the head of the SIT raises several ethical questions. Why was the state of Gujarat financing Shri Raghavan's visits to London by air? Wasn't this conflict of interest and inducement? Certainly, no investigations were taking place in London. Why was the state of Gujarat reluctant to reveal this information when details had been sought under the Right to Information Act, 2005? What were the state of Gujarat and Shri Raghavan afraid of? What were they hiding? What was the quid pro quo? More importantly and curiously, why did the Supreme Court not take cognizance of this fact when it was apprised about it?

Another police officer felt that the SIT had not paid serious attention to the issues at hand:

There were six major questions that the SIT had to address. Who overruled the District Magistrate of Godhra in ensuring that the post mortem of the dead bodies of the Godhra train carnage was not carried out in Godhra itself, but in Ahmedabad and did the Chief Minister have a role in this action? Why were dead bodies carried through urban areas in a procession, thus inflaming communal passions? Why were no minutes maintained of the February 27, 2002 meeting of the Chief Minister Shri Narendra Modi with senior civil servants and police officials? Why was immediate action not taken by the Chief Minister and the Home Department against police officials who had not taken action as per law in the riots that followed, leading to a huge loss of life and property in the state? What was the role of ruling party ministers and activists who were allowed to gain access to sensitive points such as the Police Control Room to monitor the riots? Why were several officers who had played an effective role in curbing the riots transferred within very short periods of time – Shri Rahul Sharma (SP) Bhavnagar, 38 days), Shri Himanshu Bhatt (SP Banaskantha, three months)? These six questions contained the key to unearthing a larger criminal conspiracy that might have sustained the Gujarat riots. Yet, the SIT failed to uncover the answers to these questions in a serious way.

While investigating these issues, when the SIT got an opportunity to interrogate the Chief Minister of Gujarat, it did not probe the inconsistencies in his statements adequately and also refused to indict other administrators for their conscious intent in allowing the riots to occur (Mitta, 2014). The institutional processes of justice did not rigorously pursue investigations about allegations that the very top echelons of the state of Gujarat had allowed the riots to occur in 2002 for political benefits (Dhattiwala and Biggs, 2012). Several decisions of the SIT were questionable. It soon began to appear that the SIT was an instrument for the state to re-claim its legitimacy, particularly since calls for the Chief Minister's prosecution for being complicit in the riots had been made by a variety of actors (Noorani, 2004). With the pretence of an alternative and independent organisation, perhaps the SIT was supposed to discipline and deflate allegations of injustice directed against state actors and conclude that there was no prosecutable evidence against these state actors (Chatterjee, 2014).

Thus, once the SIT had interrogated the Chief Minister and given him a clean chit, the case was closed (Jaffrelot, 2012). While the SIT concluded that there existed no prosecutable evidence against the Chief Minister or other important actors of the state, the amicus curiae Raju Ramchandran, 'in his report dated 25 July 2011 told the Supreme Court that there was a clear case for the prosecution of' the Chief Minister and 'three others, at the least' (Setalvad, 2013, 12). Thus, the democratic public could once again be re-enchanted that the top echelons of the state had been innocent with respect to the riots, and it could be forgotten that the-then Chief Minister's:

> destination may have been very different if the Indian criminal justice system had met the standards of more robust democratic legal systems that make strict adherence to due process and timely delivery of justice an article of faith and everyday practice (Nair, 2014, 13).

There were several other issues with the ways in which the SIT functioned.

A human rights activist described developments pertaining to the Godhra Riots Case:

> The investigations were kept by the SIT with officers in whom the victims had little faith. For instance, the investigation of the

Godhra case continued to rest with Deputy Superintendent of Police, Shri Noel Parmar even after the setting up of the SIT. The victims continued to feel intimidated by this decision. There was a sense of carelessness in the entire manner in which the SIT went about the investigations.

Through questionable decisions such as those in the investigation of the Godhra riots, the performance of the SIT was reduced to the fatigue of institutional inertia. The durbar had built complex institutional coalitions on the ground. Actors such as Shri Noel Parmar were a product of this complex. The complex had also tried to erase dissenters like Shri Rahul Sharma and Shri Himanshu Bhatt from the ground. Many of the SIT's contradictions are intertwined with the complex linkages between formal and informal practices which defined the state's actions. The social relations of the durbar were the central anchor of these complex linkages between actors of the state on the ground.

The SIT had no formal authority to cut through these complex linkages. The careers of SIT officers were still being determined by state actors such as Shri P. C. Pande whose role during the riots was questionable. The SIT was the outcome of consenting to the culture of the durbar that permeated the formal state. In fact, in several instances, the functioning of the SIT itself was anchored around complex informal linkages. Shri Sanjiv Bhatt, an IPS officer of the Gujarat cadre, who was later dismissed on disciplinary grounds, alleged in a petition before the Supreme Court that a legal officer representing the state of Gujarat were passing SIT documents and other affidavits to totally unrelated people and thus subverting the integrity and confidentiality of SIT investigations.

The Supreme Court of India (13 October 2015) however ruled that the allegations made by Shri Sanjiv Bhatt did not warrant investigation. The Supreme Court advanced three arguments while arriving at this conclusion. First, the petitioner lacked credibility as he was in connivance with representatives of rival political parties and activists. Second, informal consultations with people not connected to the matter did not subvert justice as investigation officers and lawyers representing the state were entitled to consult people in whom they had confidence. Third, the SIT reports submitted to the Supreme Court materially did not contain confidential information and therefore sharing these reports with private persons did not erode the legitimacy of investigation processes.

A journalist critiques the conclusions of the Supreme Court:

I do not want to go into questions of Shri Sanjiv Bhatt's credibility, but only want to point out my disappointment with the Supreme Court's substantial position. The Supreme Court says that anybody, including those with well-known affiliations to right wing political formations can be consulted before you file affidavits. Similarly, you can also share SIT reports with these people? Should not common sense tell you that these people are actually connected to those who are accused of wrong doing? The SIT reports were also submitted in sealed cover to the Supreme Court. The riots victims and their lawyers could never see the contents of these reports. Then how could these reports be informally passed on to private persons with well-known sympathies for those against whom serious allegations were pending?

Thus, we find the Supreme Court legitimising the informal consultations of the SIT and legal officers of the state of Gujarat with a variety of actors having known right wing sympathies. In many ways, it is these complex interlinkages between informal and formal practices that constituted the social relations of the durbar. The institutional wage of the durbar was the intersection of the fantasy of power with the reality of injustice. Thus, the everyday institution of life was saturated with the mechanics of power. The durbar operates sometimes through explicit instructions, but more often through intrigue. The wage of the durbar was the unpredictability of its violence. It was the wait for the retaliation.

Standing up for the truth had become an unpleasant exercise and compliance with the durbar was easier. Police officers who stood up for riot victims were transferred, denied promotions, and harassed by bringing disciplinary charge-sheets on a variety of trivial issues against them (Dhattiwala and Biggs, 2012; DNA 28 January 2015; Langa, 22 February 2012; *Times of India* 4 March 2014). On the other hand, police officers who stood by the narratives of the state were rewarded through promotions, important postings and post-retirement jobs (Dhattiwala and Biggs, 2012).

However, the consequences were damaging for riot victims. It was only after strong protests from civil rights organisations that the SIT agreed to remove officers like Shri Noel Parmar from handling investigations. A relative of a person arrested under Prevention of Terrorism Act (POTA), 2002 spoke to the *Indian Express* (29 April 2008),

> We did not want to meet the SIT when they came to Godhra because of Parmar. Now, we might even send our testimonies to the

team. Those arrested are innocent and now have a better chance of getting justice.

The sociologist, Shiv Visvanathan (2010) critiqued the functioning of the SIT:

> Can an organisation whose entrails are local transcend its biases? Can one really expect a local officer to investigate a DGP like P. C. Pandey whose role during the events is under a cloud? Pandey, after all, is the reality principle who writes their ACRs. How does one guarantee the secrecy and integrity of an investigation allowing the SIT to be a lens and not a local net leaking information?

The SIT as an alternative organisation thus raised several questions about the pursuit of justice. The contours of injustice had already been outlined by the Supreme Court of India (12 and 24 April 2004) when it transferred the trial of the Best Bakery Case outside Gujarat to Maharashtra:

> Those who are responsible for protecting life and properties and ensuring that investigation is fair and proper seem to have shown no real anxiety. Large number of people had lost their lives. Whether the accused persons were really assailants or not could have been established by a fair and impartial investigation. The modern day 'Neros' were looking elsewhere when Best Bakery and innocent children and helpless women were burning, and were probably deliberating how the perpetrators of the crime can be saved or protected. Law and justice become flies in the hands of these 'wanton boys'. When fences start to swallow the crops, no scope will be left for survival of law and order or truth and justice. Public order as well as public interest become martyrs and monuments.

A lawyer outlined how public interest continued to remain a martyr with respect to the investigations carried out by the SIT:

> The permission to allow ruling party politicians in the police control room and its implications for the riots needed to be investigated. However, this was never pursued seriously. One of the members of the SIT, Shri Jha had been the Home Secretary of the Government of Gujarat for three years, and he had toed the line of the Government that the riot's cases should not be transferred outside Gujarat. Given these circumstances, not only was his ability to investigate others in

doubt, but justice was reduced to an absolute farce in the expectation that he would be able to investigate his own role in the riots. More than the agency, it was important that investigations be carried out by officers who were not afraid of authority or consequences for their careers, officers who could be trusted to unearth the truth without fear. Unfortunately, this did not happen.

The SIT functioned more as a by-product of the durbar than as an entity that could cut through the complex webs of governmentality that the durbar had manufactured. The SIT could not overcome the administrative psychosis of fear that the durbar had created and independent officers were not a part of the SIT. Thus, there were several informal negotiations of fear, compliance and rewards that formed a part of the everyday sociology of the SIT.

If the durbar persuaded actors of the state to allow the riots to occur, the SIT did not have the democratic, ethical, or organisational capacity to raise questions about the functioning of the durbar. At best, it could bring a few actors to justice without uncovering the criminal conspiracy and dereliction of duty by the highest echelons of the state which allowed the riots to occur. The SIT was akin to a Shakespearean fool in the sovereign's durbar (Kavanagh, 2009).

The SIT had the independence of a fool in an emperor's durbar. Just like the fool in an emperor's court stands as an alternative to the other courtiers (Kavanagh, 2009), the SIT stood as an alternative to other institutional processes of the state. However, the independence that is available to the fool is only that of mock audacity and censored courage.

The fool is not yet a part of the apparatus of moral outrage, democratic critique and uncensored dissent that can transform society. The wages of the fool are the enchantment of the status quo and the pretence of tolerance. The wages of the SIT were a pretence of independent investigation and the relegitimisation of the durbar as an entrenched informal mechanics of the formal state.

Discussion

When the NHRC approached the Supreme Court for transferring the trial of riot related cases outside Gujarat, the state was drawn into a vector of special action in order to reclaim its legitimacy. While the SIT was technically answerable to the Supreme Court, the formal norms of accountability of retired senior police officers were questionable. Further, since the careers of a majority of the officers of the SIT were configured by the state of Gujarat, it was unlikely that the SIT could overcome the vectoring staged by 'the symbolic environment of the elite' (Yakhlef,

2004, 243). Since the state of Gujarat had selectively managed the careers of police officers in a partisan manner during the riots and its aftermath (Dhattiwala and Biggs, 2012), the memories of rewards and retaliation vectored the spatiality of the SIT. Since 'the claim of objectivity masks subjective motivations, high sounding stories hide the lowest of motives' (Burrell, 1988, 224), in a genealogical sense, the objective processes of investigation and prosecution advanced by the state concealed the subjective-political processes of marginalisation and inequity in which the state is embedded.

While stringent provisions of POTA and the accompanying standards of evidence, which made the possibility of conviction easier, were mobilised against the accused in the burning of a coach of the Sabarmati Express Case in Godhra, POTA was not used against those accused of post-Godhra rioting. While ruling party politicians were allowed to be present in the police control room when riots were occurring in Gujarat, the Chief Minister refused to appear before the Nanavati Commission where human rights lawyers could cross-examine him, and only appeared before a SIT, which was staffed by police officers with whom the state had comfortable equations. In a genealogical sense of locating traces of the present in the past (Burrell, 1988), we find that present outcomes of no prosecutable evidence being available against high functionaries of the state can be traced in the efforts of the state in the past to control the production of narratives pertaining to the riots. Thus, the transfer of police officials who stand up for justice is a testimony of the disciplinary devices of the state at play in creating narrow regimes of accountability.

The rational credibility of the state was important to justify the actions of the state as being 'somehow necessary to the protection of what was putatively at risk and that will now be surely safeguarded... security, liberty and sovereignty' (Pugliese, 2013, 2). By concentrating the investigations in the hands of a few officers with whom the state was comfortable, others in the police could be prevented from resorting to unpredictable actions, which could inconvenience the ruling elites of the state. The organisational tactic of the SIT also needs to be seen in the broader context of right wing politics. Right-wing political propaganda has claimed that the riots were a response to provocation, which could not be tolerated (Deshpande, 2014). According to the right-wing, the riots took place because the media had historically ignored the angst of Hindus, who had suffered injustice and violence (Deshpande, 2014). Such propaganda built the discursive foundation that legitimised the inaction of the state of Gujarat in adequately intervening to prevent the riots during 2002 (Jaffrelot, 2012).

Since the ethical principles behind the functioning of the SIT were questionable and a variety of informal instrumentalities such as the conflict of interest of the amicus curiae, Shri Harish Salve existed, lawyers representing victims and activists had to keep the pressure alive on investigative and judicial institutions. It was the perseverance, skill and resourceful display of solidarity, struggle and commitment of lawyers such as Mukul Sinha and the resilience shown by riot victims which led to the conviction of former ministers in the Gujarat government for their role in the 2002 riots (Desai, 2014). What civil society activists, lawyers and even officials of the state willing to stand up for the right were engaging in was a project of resistance, 'a trial of courage' (Folkers, 2016, 6) to ensure that justice was done. On the other hand, actors of the state who abided by the social relations of the durbar continued to change their positions as per convenience as embodied in the inconsistent statements given by former Gujarat DGP Shri P. C. Pande about riot victims calling him for help.

It is necessary to pay attention to the allegations of informal deals being struck between Ms Geetha Johri and the government, which eventually led to the Supreme Court directing Ms Johri to be excused from the SIT. Further, there were suggestions that the head of the SIT, Shri Raghavan was not paying adequate attention to details and was allowing matters to drift with the majority view articulated by officers of the state of Gujarat (Visvanathan, 2010).

In view of these allegations, it is the farce of the durbar, which is played out when the SIT examines Shri P. C. Pande. Similarly, the SIT enacts a farce when it states that there is no prosecutable evidence against actors, who occupied the highest echelons of the state for enabling the riots of 2002 (Chatterjee, 2014).

The SIT comprises three officers, whose annual confidential reports are written by Shri Pande. The SIT's investigation of Shri Pande embodies how spaces are 'encountered in a habitus-like manner, to a large extent unconsciously and preconsciously, rather than in a reflective mode' (Yakhlef, 2004, 243). The habitus of the police is that of junior officers unconsciously obeying their senior officers. Thus, Shri Pande makes contradictory statements during the SIT investigations and the junior officers obediently allow these contradictions to persist. It is important to note that the role of one of the officers who is a part of the SIT itself is suspect with respect to the riots. The formal technology of the SIT itself thus appears to be a mock medieval courtroom drama of slapping the emperor on his wrist.

The performance of the SIT appears to be that of a consenting fool rather than a critical fool (Kavanagh, 2009). As a journalist points out, the SIT as an alternative was acceptable to the state of Gujarat because it prevented the cases from being transferred to CBI. The CBI worked under the Union of India, and the Union of India itself had not intervened in a serious sense and had been soft-peddling the issue of riots in order to conform to the norms of cultural majoritarianism as a part of vote bank politics. Thus, the SIT was embedded in a politics of conformity rather than a critical inquisition of the state's role in the riots of 2002. The head of the SIT, Shri R. K. Raghavan often appeared on television channels and gave interviews to the press defending the findings of the SIT. While television channels chronicled the rhetorical positions of the SIT, they clearly lacked the capacity to intimately engage with the ordinary, everyday resistance (Scott, 1990) of riot victims who continued to stay in refugee camps years after the riots were over (*Hindu*, 28 February 2007).

The SIT's was the craft of 'a rhetor in a potentially adversarial relationship with the audience, a relationship where the rhetor seeks to control and/or impose her will upon the audience' (Manolescu, 1998, 64). We argue that the state attempted to control the emergent claims of justice through various formal and informal organisational technologies, which were embodied in the SIT which was presented as an alternative organisational space within the state. Once the SIT provided a clean chit to several influential actors of the state, those engaged in resisting the state began to be targeted as engaging in conspiracies to defame the state which was carrying forward projects of development and progress with sincerity and commitment (Deshpande, 2014). Thus, the SIT as an alternative organisational space helped in promoting 'a counter-subversion panic targeting scapegoats accused of subversive conspiracies' (Berlet, 2012, 566).

Conclusion

We hope to have performed an exercise of public lamentation regarding the enactment of the alternative organisational space of the SIT. The SIT was an imagination of the alternative. The state argued that if its normal institutions had failed then it had the organisational capacity to create an alternative institution, which would deliver justice. The executive and the judiciary were as much complicit in producing this fantasy as the political class, which urgently needed to renew its sense of legitimacy. The political class had discovered that when a wrong occurs, it is not enough to win elections to wipe out the sense of wrong. A wrong does not become right just because a majority derives its sense of agency from the wrong.

Further, democracy is not as much about majorities as it is about dissent, debate, dialogue, and public discourse. We argue that alternative organisational spaces within the state further diminish the space for democratic public debate. Alternative organisational spaces such as the SIT appear to be the product of communicative mediation between different wings of the elite echelons of the state. They create a fantasy of hope but soon reveal their genealogical imperative of controlling the narratives of violence, and repressing local possibilities of resistance. We hope to have shown that alternative organisational spaces are part of a narrative complex for producing state-sanctioned knowledges of violence.

However, resistance does not come to an end with such attempts at institutional configuration of memory. Instead, the realisation dawns that the quest for justice can be fulfilled only by democratising the institutional apparatus of the state. The quest for establishing a politics based on the social relations of democracy becomes more urgent in such a circumstance. The realisation dawns that the institutional tensions between the executive, judiciary, and the legislature are not enough to deliver democracy. The factional micropolitics within the state is also not enough to deliver justice. An alternative organisational space only banishes local narratives, memories and claims for justice rather than advancing them. Thus, the realisation becomes concrete that democracy and justice can only be advanced by enabling collective performances of dissent, critique, and opening up public spaces for debate and dialogue. We hope to have contributed to one such public performance of dissent here.

References

Ayyub, Rana. 2010. 'Geeta Johri was Known to be a Fearless Officer. So, What Accounts for her Flip-Flops?' *Tehelka*, 11 September. Accessed on 20 January 2015. Available at http://www.tehelka.com/geeta-johri-was-known-to-be-a-fearless-officer-so-what-accounts-for-her-flip-flops/.

Beiner, Ronald. 1983. *Political Judgment*. Chicago: University of Chicago Press.

Berlet, Chip. 2012. 'Collectivists, Communists, Labor Bosses, and Treason: The Tea Parties as Right-Wing Populist Counter-Subversion Panic.' *Critical Sociology* 38(4): 565–87.

Burrell, Gibson. 1988. 'Modernism Post Modernism and Organizational Analysis: The Contribution of Michel Foucault.' *Organization Studies* 9(2): 221–35.

Bunsha, D. 2006. 'Verdict in Best Bakery Case.' *Frontline*. Accessed on 7 October 2016. Available at http://www.frontline.in/static/html/fl2304/stories/20060310005611700.htm.

Chatterjee, Moyukh. 2014. 'After the Law: Notes on Gujarat 2002.' *Economic and Political Weekly* 49(16): 12–15.

Das, Runa. 2008. 'Nation, Gender and Representations of (In)Securities in Indian Politics:

Secular Modernity and Hindutva Ideology.' *European Journal of Women's Studies* 15(3): 203–21.

Desai, Mihir. 2014. 'A Combative Hero: Mukul Sinha.' *Economic and Political Weekly* 49(23): 29–30.

Deshpande, M. D. 2014. *Gujarat Riots: The True Story: The Truth of the 2002 Riots*. New Delhi: Partridge India.

Dhattiwala, Raheel and Michael Biggs. 2012. 'The Political Logic of Ethnic Violence: The Anti-Muslim Pogrom in Gujarat, 2002.' *Politics and Society* 40(4): 483–516.

DNA. 2015. 'Gujarat: IPS Officer Who Assisted CBI in Ishrat Case Chargesheeted.' 28 January. Accessed on 21 May 2015. Available at http://www.dnaindia.com/india/report-gujarat-ips-officer-who-assisted-cbi-in-ishrat-case-chargesheeted-2056409.

Drori, Israel and Benson Honig. 2013. 'A Process Model for Internal and External Legitimacy.' *Organization Studies* 34(3): 345–76.

Everett, Jeffrey. 2002. 'Organizational Research and the Praxeology of Pierre Bourdieu.' *Organizational Research Methods* 5(1): 56–80.

Fletcher, Denise and Tony Watson. 2007. 'Voice, Silence and the Business of Construction: Loud and Quiet Voices in the Construction of Personal, Organizational and Social Realities.' *Organization* 14(2): 155–74.

Folkers, Andreas. 2016. 'Daring the Truth: Foucault, Parrhesia and the Genealogy of Critique.' *Theory Culture and Society* 33(1): 3–28.

Fotaki, Marianna. 2010. 'Why Do Public Policies Fail So Often? Exploring Health-Policy Making as an Imaginary and Symbolic Construction.' *Organization* 17(6): 703–20.

Hindu. 2007. 'Five Years after Godhra and the Pogrom.' 28 February. Accessed on 21 May 2015. Available at http://www.thehindu.com/todays-paper/tp-opinion/five-years-after-godhra-and-the-pogrom/article1803452.ece.

_____. 2015. 'Sohrabuddin Fake Encounter Case: Charges Against Geeta Johri Dropped.' 2 March. Accessed on 19 May 2015. Available at http://www.thehindu.com/news/national/charges-against-geeta-johri-dropped-in-fake-encounter-cases/article6951527.ece.

Hindustan Times. 2012. 'CBI Charges Amit Shah, Geeta Johri with Murder.' 4 September. Accessed on 20 January 2015. Available at http://www.hindustantimes.com/india-news/cbi-charges-amit-shah-geeta-johri-with-murder/article1-924568.aspx.

Indian Express. 2008. 'Godhra Celebrates Exclusion of Noel Parmar from Team Assisting SIT.' 29 April. Accessed on 21 January 2015. Available at http://archive.indianexpress.com/news/families-of-godhra-accused-celebrate-as-police-officer-dropped-from-sit/302915/.

_____. 2009. 'Five Top Cops were Shifted on EC Orders, admits Shah.' 24 February. Accessed on 7 October 2016. Available at http://indianexpress.com/article/cities/ahmedabad/five-top-cops-were-shifted-on-ec-orders-admits-shah/.

_____. 2009. 'Khandwawala is New state DGP, Pande to Swap Post with Him.' 22 February. Accessed on 21 January 2015. Available at http://archive.indianexpress.com/news/khandwawala-is-new-state--dgp-pande-to-swap-post-with-him/426687/.

Jaffrelot, Christophe. 2012. 'Gujarat 2002: What Justice for the Victims? The Supreme Court, the SIT, the Police and the state Judiciary.' *Economic and Political Weekly* 47(8): 77–89.

Jagannathan, Srinath and Rajnish. K Rai. 2014. 'Organizing Sovereign Power: Police and the Performance of Bare Bodies.' *Organization*. DOI: 10.1177/1350508413518265.

Kavanagh, Donncha. 2009. 'Institutional Heterogeneity and Change: The University as Fool.' *Organization* 16(4): 575–95.

Khetan, Ashish. 2011. 'Whose Amicus is Harish Salve?' *Tehelka*, 12 March. Accessed on 20 January 2015. Available at http://archive.tehelka.com/story_main49.asp?filename=N e120311WhoseAmicus.asp.

Kumar, Manasi. 2007. 'A Journey into the Bleeding City: Following the Footprints of the Rubble of Riot and Violence of Earthquake in Gujarat, India.' *Psychology and Developing Societies* 19(1): 1–36.

Langa, Mahesh. 2012. 'Role of IPS Sreekumar in Exposing Gujarat CM.' *Hindustan Times*, 22 February. Accessed on 21 May 2015. Available at http://www.hindustantimes.com/india-news/role-of-ips-sreekumar-in-exposing-gujarat-cm/article1-814940.aspx.

Manolescu, Beth. I. 1998. 'Style and Spectator Judgment in Fisher Ames's Jay Treaty Speech.' *Quarterly Journal of Speech* 84(1): 62–79.

May, Reuben. B. 2003. '"Flirting with Boundaries": A Professor's Narrative Tale Contemplating Research of the Wild Side.' *Qualitative Inquiry* 9(3): 442–65.

Mir, Raza and Ali Mir. 2002. 'The Organizational Imagination: From Paradigm Wars to Praxis.' *Organizational Research Methods* 5(1): 105–25.

Mitta, Manoj. 2014. *Sins of Gujarat 2002 and their Long Shadows*. Noida: Harper Collins.

Müller, Ulrich, Emanuela Yeung and Sarah Michelle Hutchison. 2013. 'The Role of Distancing in Werner and Kaplan's Account of Symbol Formation and Beyond.' *Culture and Psychology* 19(4): 463–83.

Nair, Ravi. 2014. 'The Ehsan Jafri Case: Modi's Banquo Ghost.' *Economic and Political Weekly* 49(24): 13–15.

National Human Rights Commission. 2003. 'Orders Passed by the Commission on Gujarat.' 11 July. Accessed on 20 January 2015. Available at http://www.nhrc.nic.in/GujratOrders.htm.

NDTV. 2010. 'The Gulberg Society Massacre: What Happened'. 11 March. Accessed on 20 January 2015. Available at http://www.ndtv.com/article/india/the-gulbarg-society-massacre-what-happened-17556.

Noorani, Abdul. G. 2004. 'Gujarat Riots: Bringing the Guilty to Court.' *Economic and Political Weekly* 39(27): 29–50.

Outlook. 2010. 'SC Asks SIT to Drop Johri, Jha from Gujarat Riots Probe.' 6 April. Accessed on 21 January 2015. Available at http://www.outlookindia.com/news/article/SC-Asks-SIT-to-Drop-Johri-Jha-from-Guj-Riots-Probe/678745.

———. 2010. '2002 Gujarat Riots: SC Paves Way for Judgement.' 26 October. Accessed on 19 May 2015. Available at http://www.outlookindia.com/news/printitem.aspx?698768.

Pugliese, Joseph. 2013. *State Violence and the Execution of Law: Biopolitical Caesurae of Torture, Black Sites, Drones*. New York: Routledge.

Rasche, Andreas and Robert Chia. 2009. 'Researching Strategy Practices: A Genealogical Social Theory Perspective.' *Organization Studies* 30(7): 713–34.

Rajeshwari. 2013. 'Judicial Inquiries into Communal Violence.' *Economic and Political Weekly* 48(40): 13–15.

Scott, James. C. 1990. *Domination and the Arts of Resistance: Hidden Transcripts*. New Haven, CT: Yale University Press.

Setalvad, Teesta. 2013. 'The Importance of Zakia Jafri's Protest Petition.' *Economic and Political Weekly* 48(21): 10–13.

Soni, N. 2012. 'Former Gujarat DGP's SIT Statement Belies his Amnesia Claim.' DNA, 10 May. Accessed on 21 January 2015. Available at http://www.dnaindia.com/ahmedabad/column-former-guj-dgps-sit-statement-belies-his-amnesia-claim-1686933.

Sorensen, Bent. M. and Sverre Spoelstra. 2011. 'Play at Work: Continuation, Intervention and Usurpation.' *Organization* 19(1): 81–97.

Supreme Court of India. 2004. 'Appeal (CRL) 446-449 of 2004'. *Zahira Habibulla H Sheikh and Another versus State of Gujarat and Others*. 12 April.

_____. 2008. 'Write Petition (CRL) No. 6 2007'. *National Human Rights Commission versus State of Gujarat and Others*. 26 March.

_____. 2010. 'Writ Petition (CRL) No. 6 2007'. *Rubabbuddin Sheikh versus State of Gujarat and Others*. 12 January.

_____. 2015. 'Writ Petition (CRL) No. 135 2011'. *Sanjiv Rajendra Bhatt versus Union of India and Others*. 13 October.

Times of India. 2007. 'EC Transfers Gujarat DGP, Five Other Police Officers.' 16 October. Accessed on 21 January 2015. Available at http://timesofindia.indiatimes.com/india/EC-transfers-Guj-DGP-five-other-police-officers/articleshow/2461697.cms.

_____. 2010. 'Upset with the SIT Attitude, Gulbarg Prosecutors Quit.' 3 March. Accessed on 21 May 2015. Available at http://timesofindia.indiatimes.com/india/Upset-with-SIT-attitude-Gulbarg-prosecutors-quit/articleshow/5635393.cms.

_____. 2014. 'Gujarat Harassing Me Over Riot Cases: IPS Officer.' 4 March. Accessed on 21 May 2015. Available at http://timesofindia.indiatimes.com/india/Gujarat-harassing-me-over-riot-cases-IPS-officer/articleshow/31364914.cms.

Vari, Alexander. 2012. 'Re-territorializing the "Guilty City": Nationalist and Right-Wing Attempts to Nationalize Budapest during the Interwar Period.' *Journal of Contemporary History* 47(4): 709–33.

Visvanathan, Shiv. 2010. 'The Unmaking of an Investigator'. *Seminar*. Accessed on 21 January 2015. Available at http://www.india-seminar.com/2010/605/605_shiv_visvanathan.htm.

Yakhlef, A. 2004. 'Global Brands as Embodied "Generic Spaces": The Example of Branded Chain Hotels.' *Space and Culture* 7(2): 237–48.

3

Scripting Alternative Images

Institutions, Practices and Scripts of the *Mritshilpis* of Kumortuli

Devi Vijay[1]

The onset of Durga Puja, a popular religious festival among the Bengalis celebrated during four days in the lunar month of *Ashwin* (September-October), transforms the city of Kolkata, West Bengal into a grand, if ephemeral, spectacle. The festival weaves around twin narratives of Goddess Durga, consort of Shiva: the popular narrative of the dutiful daughter and benevolent mother visiting her maternal home with her four children (Ganesh, Kartik, Saraswati and Lakshmi) and the mythical story of Durga's fierce form as the ten-armed, victorious demon-slayer. Distinctive to Kolkata, *protimas* (or images of deities) of Durga and her family are worshipped with much ceremony in the thousands of *pandals* (make-shift structures usually made of bamboo and coloured cloth) that occupy public spaces across the city. The festival constitutes a cornerstone of Bengali socio-cultural life: an annual event that is welcomed in anticipation and excitement. At the end of the festival, reflecting the ethos of the cyclicality of life, these *protimas* are immersed in the river Hooghly that flows through Kolkata.

In this chapter, I look behind the scenes of this large-scale dramaturgy to catch a glimpse of the lives of the *mritshilpis*, or the clay sculptors, who sculpt the *protimas* that occupy centre-stage for popular consumption during these annual religious festivals. Despite the centrality of these images in arguably the most significant popular culture event of Bengali life, and proliferation of accounts on Durga Puja (for example, Ghosh, 2000; Guha-Thakurta, 2014; McDermott, 2010; Nicholas, 2013), there is a dearth of research on the social world of the *mritshilpis*. An examination of the 'ordinary accounts of ordinary adventures' stands to better explain the social world in which we live (Bourdieu *et al.*,1999, 624). As I will elaborate in the following sections, *mritshilpis*' practices constitute an institutional context with its own particularities and cultural specificities characterised by seasonal work around religious festivals and high uncertainty in terms of orders, flow of labour and raw materials. During peak season, more than half the workforce in an artisanal studio would be constituted of temporary and casual workers. Nevertheless, this occupational practice constitutes one of the oldest, proliferating trades in West Bengal distinguished by an unbroken hereditary tradition (Guha-Thakurta, 2015). Organisational research stands to benefit from such 'unconventional contexts' (Bamberger and Pratt, 2010). The focus of this chapter is then to examine the social organisation of the *mritshilpis*' craft, their occupational practices and the processes by which these actors produce and reproduce their social world.

Through a fifteen month qualitative fieldstudy of the *mritshilpis* of Kumortuli, a renowned potters' neighbourhood in Kolkata, I unpack the practices that are reproduced in this institutional setting that is simultaneously a site of commerce, residence, apprenticeship and craftwork. I contend that beneath the apparent ephemerality and transience, scripts of *gharana*, community and place constitute organising principles that underpin the reproduction of this institutional context over time. In doing so, this chapter seeks to develop an alternative account that breaches established images of organisations and responds to calls to 'get closer to work/organisational practices happening' (Samra-Fredericks and Bargiela-Chiappini, 2008, 654), to bring 'work back in' (Barley and Kunda, 2001) and to understand occupations as situated and negotiated orders (Bechky, 2011).

Theoretical orientation

Dominant organisational accounts of economic forms are anchored around concepts of firms, markets, hierarchies and networks, ignoring a swathe of economic forms arising in settings such as informal economies and trust networks (Zelizer, 2010). Borrowing Weber's switchman metaphor:

> the 'world images' that have been created by ideas have, like switchmen, determined the tracks along which action has been pushed by the dynamic of interest. 'From what' and 'for what' one wished to be redeemed, and let us not forget 'could be' redeemed depended on one's image of the world (Weber, 1946, 280; cited in Swidler, 1995, 25–26)

Such 'world images' of economic structures have set us along established tracks that have resulted in lacunae in our understanding of the multiple ways in which people organise their economic lives.

In addressing these exclusions, scholars have undertaken economic analyses of contexts that economists typically overlook, or have examined the various social contexts in which economic action is embedded. However, considerable attention to macro-perspectives of organisational activities has resulted in a dearth of conceptual grounding of individual and interpersonal workplace action and relations (Barley and Kunda, 2001). Such situated accounts of work beyond established occupations such as medicine, accounting, law and engineering are particularly sparse (Bechky, 2011). To be sure, studies have explored craft industries, distinguishing craft-based 'quasi-firms' (Eccles, 1981) from 'formal organisations' on the grounds of bonds of allegiance, dense associational ties, personal relations (Eccles, 1981; Coser *et al.*, 1982), project-based work, relatively unique products, non-routine search procedures as well as experimental and intuitive bases for work processes (e.g., Perrow, 1967). Craft sectors are understood to have sub-contracting and freelance labour, highly porous and ill-defined boundaries, with cultural industries in the craft sector mired with high variance, great unpredictability, complexity and dynamism (Faulkner and Anderson, 1987; Powell, 1990). Artisans in particular lead increasingly vulnerable lives with intensified competition, the vagaries of a global market and a range of exploitative conditions like low wages and health hazards (Scrase, 2003). But there is scant empirical evidence on the nature of work and how coordination is accomplished in such settings (Anteby and Bechky, 2016; Bechky, 2011; Hallett and Ventresca, 2006). In particular, the importance of different types of coordination practices can vary across different settings and depend on the structural contexts of such practices (Bechky, 2006). Given the greater prevalence of such contingent, temporary and project-based work across various occupations today (Kunda *et al.*, 2002), gaps in our understanding of such forms of work should be cast in sharp relief.

One key mechanism by which we can further a situated understanding of work and occupations, is by examining work practices and the institutions they enact (Bechky, 2011). Examining practices, or 'shared routines of behaviour' (Whittington, 2006, 619) mitigates the particular challenges of more individualist approaches that involve conjectures of attributes such as shared beliefs, theories, norms and understandings internalised within individuals. Focusing on practices enables an examination of the more visible and manifest shared routines of behaviour. While practices are not reducible to individuals, they are more closely tied to individuals than macro social systems, in effect serving as a useful conceptual linkage between broader structures and belief systems and individual action (Barnes, 2001). Practices are shaped by institutional spaces. In the following section, I examine institutional contexts, embedded social practices and scripts that mediate the institutional and action realm.

Institutions, practices and scripts

Institutions can be defined as 'shared rules and typifications that identify categories of social actors and their appropriate activities or relationships' (Barley and Tolbert, 1997, 3). Institutions manifest as more or less enduring elements of social life (Hughes, 1936) that constrain, enable and provide blueprints for orienting action. While institutions structure culture by patterning channels for social action, institutions are also an emergent property of social action (Swidler, 1995). Elaborating on this duality of social structures, Giddens (1984, 25) contends that 'the structural properties of social systems are both medium and the outcome of the practices they recursively organise...the moment of the production of action is also one of reproduction in the contexts of the day-to-day enactment of social life'.

Through the interplay between the institutional realm and the realm of action, institutional practices shape actions which, in turn, reconstitute or modify institutional structure. The institutional realm thus encodes idealised patterns derived from past social practices (Barley, 1986). This structuring of institutional structures unfolds as actors draw upon different structural dimensions of signification (such as symbolic orders), domination (such as normative sanctions) and legitimation, to construct social positions of actors and the position-practice relations (Giddens, 1984).

An institutional realm comprises a set of scripts that characterise a social setting's activity with scripts linking the institutional realm to the realm of action (Goffman, 1967; Barley, 1986). Scripts can be understood to be 'observable, recurrent activities and patterns of interaction characteristic of a particular setting' (Barley and Tolbert, 1997, 7). Scripts play a role in the structuring process by constituting the 'behavioural grammars that inform a setting's everyday action' (Barley, 1986, 83). Scripts do not imply that actors are cultural dopes. Rather actors actively seek strategic advantage by using culturally scripted skills (Swidler, 1995). Actors can invoke scripts that work best for them, given that institutions vary in their visibility, degree of institutionalisation and acceptance (Tolbert and Zucker, 1996). I contend that, conceptually, scripts are useful in examining social processes at different levels, and enable us to develop a theoretical middle range (Davis and Marquis, 2005). Building on this body of work, I am guided by the research question: What are the scripts that actors invoke in the maintenance and reproduction of institutional contexts?

Methods

This study is part of a larger project that commenced in October 2013 with the intent to examine the work organisation of the *mritshilpis*. This qualitative field study followed an emergent research design that is amenable to understanding phenomena that are poorly understood (Lincoln and Guba, 1985; Strauss and Corbin, 1990). Data were collected with the help of a research assistant who accompanied me on field visits. The research assistant helped with asking questions, recording and transcribing interviews.

I began with an initial visit to neighbourhood artisan workshops where I gained insights about the seasonal nature of workflow, the informal economies of the workforce, and about Kumortuli, the artisan neighbourhood and marketplace where many artisans across the city visited for raw materials and for recruitment of *karigars* or apprentices. Following a visit to Kumortuli in October 2013, I adopted Kumortuli as the research site.

Research setting

Kumortuli presents an important site for the study of *mritshilpis* on account of its uniqueness as one of the oldest, and perhaps largest, surviving neighbourhood of *mritshilpis* in Kolkata. Kumortuli is placed in Ward No. 9 of the North Kolkata Municipal Corporation, located between Chitpore Road (now Rabindra Sarani) and the Hooghly River. It is at once a place of residence, production and commerce. As of 2006–07, there were about 527 artisan families that were residing there. Most artisans bear the surname of Pal, common within this *Kumhar* caste, and workshops are known by their owners. Within the Pal caste, there are two lineages – the natives of West Bengal, colloquially referred to as *ghotis* or as *epar Bangals* and those from what is now Bangladesh, also referred to as the *opar Bangals*. These two lineages are broadly organised into two different unions: the older Kumortuli Mritshilpi Sanskriti Samity (predominantly constituted of the *ghotis*) and the Kumortuli Mritshilpi Samity (predominantly of the *opar Bangals*). The *karigars*, or the skilled apprentices who work in these workshops, are organised under the Kumortuli Mritshilpa Karigar Samity. *Mritshilpis* are traditionally, and even today, predominantly male. However over the last two decades, women have entered the craft and have carved a niche, winning several state awards and a dedicated clientele.

Kumortuli is characterised by rows of open-front workshops with asbestos roofs and tarpaulins to keep away the rains. Figure 3.1 shows *karigars* in their road-side workshops working on *protimas* during peak season.

Figure 3.1: *Karigars* working on *protimas* during peak-season

There are about 500 such workshops within a total area of 6.6 acres (Guha-Thakurta, 2015). Every nook of a workshop has images at various stages of completion that often spill over into the narrow alleys outside the workshop. Grey mud, straw, and bamboo are strewn across the alleys and the workshop floor. The bigger workshops are usually two-storeyed – with the second-floor visible from the street much like an open doll-house. Workshops are colloquially referred to as studios with some dating back to over 100 years. The studio-owner usually sits in the second-floor or in an ante-room when he is not engaged in clay modelling with the *karigars* on the ground floor. Alongside studios stacked with clay *protimas* in different stages of production are shops with colourful accessories such as the clothes and jewellery used to adorn the deities. The workers in these shops are also locally referred to as craftsmen. While some of these artisans were interviewed, their identities and practices are distinct, and are therefore not included among the category of artisans who are referred to as *mritshilpis*. For the purpose of this study, henceforth I use the term artisan and *mritshilpi* interchangeably, at all times referring to those engaged in clay sculpting of the deities.

Work in Kumortuli is seasonal with peak season running from August to November (see Appendix Table 3A). The peak season, artisans start work often as early as 6 am and work through the night. The air is rent with the collective work-cry of men moving idols from studios to their destinations, or chants of enthused customers who come in groups to transport the *protima* ceremonially. *Karigars* apply finishing touches to *protimas*, moving finished ones out in the sun to dry, while the studio owner shouts orders to a novice to fix the tarpaulin atop the studio, lest the rains come and soak the clay sculptures kept out to dry. Labourers haul handcarts atop which are the prepared Durga deities – towering images resplendent in shimmering *sarees* (see Figure 3.2 and Figure 3.3). Jostling through the narrow roads, often not more than six feet wide, and in certain alleys, tapering down to 3–4 feet, children run around on errands for their parents, bringing stocks of paint, or pieces of jewellery from a relative or the store next door. Photography enthusiasts crowd the alleys seeking to acquire, retain and transport images to a realm removed from this space that blends survival and the sacred. The narrow lanes are crowded with customers, tourists and photographers consumed by their interest in this chaotic, iconic dramaturgy.

Figure 3.2: A resplendent Durga *protima* en route to its *pandal* from Kumortuli

Figure 3.3: Labourers hauling the prepared *protima* by handcart

Data collection

I first began my fieldwork in Kumortuli in October 2013, with data collection distributed across fifteen months, given the seasonal nature of work. The first interview at Kumortuli was with the secretary of one of the three unions in Kumortuli. He then referred us to a few studio owners including one of the first women to enter the craft. For the subsequent visits, interviews were fixed through the union, until I became more familiar with the locality. While the union secretary continued to be a key liaison, from July 2014, interviews were conducted independent of the *mritshilpi* unions' contacts. I followed a purposive sampling approach. I interviewed artisans from both *ghoti* and *opar Bangal* lineages, male and female artisans and owners of large, mid-sized as well as small studios. Given a specific interest in organisational practices, I focused on the studio-owners, as they, and not the *karigars*, interface with customers, are involved with procurement of raw materials and finances. Thirty interviews were conducted: twenty four with studio owners and six with *karigars*.

Interviews were conducted in Bengali and later transcribed and translated to English. Initial interviews were unstructured, focusing on artisan family histories, workflows, recruitment of *karigars* and other aspects of the trade such as activities during peak and off-peak seasons. As the study evolved, interviews were revised to a semi-structured format. Questions were focused on understanding aspects of artisanal aesthetics, seasonality and engagement with customers. On an average interview response time lasted for 45 minutes.

In addition to the interviews, I spent several days across months observing artisans' work, their interactions with others in the neighbourhood and with customers. Given the seasonal nature of work, I was particular about visiting Kumortuli prior to key festivals to observe production. Thus, there are fieldnotes from both lean and peak seasons.

Although empirical studies on *mritshilpis* of Kumortuli have been limited (Bhattacharya, 2008; Goldblatt, 1979, 1981, 1983; Guha-Thakurta, 2015 are exceptions), the place is frequented by students on college projects as well as photographers and documentary film-makers. Some respondents had voiced concerns about these perennial intrusions. I was therefore cautious not to interrupt workdays, especially during the peak season when artisans work from six in the morning till well past midnight to meet customer deadlines. Instead, I, with my research assistant, spent time outside the workshops, clarifying parts of the workflow while the artists worked if necessary, or when they took a break.

I supplemented my contextual knowledge with scholarship on Durga Puja (Bhattacharya, 2007; Ghosh, 2000; Guha-Thakurta, 2015), few empirical studies of Kumortuli (Goldblatt, 1979, 1981, 1983), publications on religious festivals in West Bengal (Nicholas, 2013), arts and aesthetics in West Bengal (Guha-Thakurta, 1992). In addition, I drew upon available media accounts, videos, documentaries, and journalistic accounts that specifically referenced the *mritshilpis* or Kumortuli.

Given an emergent research design, data analysis was simultaneous with data collection. Fieldnotes were maintained meticulously during and after each field visit. The research assistant and I had debriefings together after every field visit on the basis of which further questions and respondents were identified. Data were analysed in three stages.

First, iterating between data collection and analysis and informed by both primary and secondary data sources, I developed a thick description of the institutional context of Kumortuli. By developing a dialogue between theory and data (Langley, 1999), I sharpened emergent themes. For example, literature on different types of institutional orders (for example, Friedland and Alford, 1991; Thornton *et al.*, 2012), enabled us to group themes as constituting the artisanal professional, the market and the religious orders.

Second, to map the realm of action (Barley and Tolbert, 1997), I generated a description of the routine activities of modelling *protimas*. In this stage, I distilled two constellations of practices. First, the practice of 'modeling *protimas*' was constituted of four occupational micropractices – i.e., mixing the clay, preparing the *kathamo*, preparing the *ekmete* and *domete* and painting the eyes of the *protima*. These practices have remained relatively unchanged over time. Each of these practices may be constituted of further micropractices. There may also be a larger arrangement of practices that could be clustered. However, these four were isolated given their relevance and ubiquity to all *mritshilpis'* occupational practices. Second, I identified 'work organisation' that included aspects of division of labour, managing customers and suppliers and workflows. Finally, I went back to the data and relied on focused coding, identifying recurring words, phrases, or themes to isolate the scripts characteristic of this social setting. I distilled three scripts – i.e., embodying *gharana*, mobilising place and enacting community – by which the institutional contexts were interpreted and instantiated. To give voice to our respondents, I include within the text, excerpts from their interview responses.

In the following sections, I describe the diverse institutional orders and elaborate step-by-step the activities that constitute the *mritshilpis'* occupational practices in order to show how and with what resources these practices endure. I then present three scripts that mediate practices and institutional contexts and which provide insights into practice durability and institutional maintenance.

Institutional context and practices at Kumortuli

As per folklore, the first celebration of *puja* (ritual worship) with Durga's clay image is attributed to Raja Krishna Chandra Ray (1710–82) of Nabadwip who commissioned a potter to sculpt the clay form. Prior to this, artists represented deities symbolically by a clay mound, a pot or a painted picture (Dutta, 2003). Raja Krishna Chandra Ray's extravagant form of celebration of a festival was appropriated and propagated by the nouveaux riche upper caste Hindu elites of Kolkata, who had acquired wealth through their transactions with the British. Religious celebrations presented a legitimate way to convert their new wealth into status. Increasing demand for images of deities brought migrant workers of the *Kumhar* caste from rural Bengal to the city of Kolkata for the three to four months of the festivals. Towards the second part of the eighteenth century, in order to accommodate the growing demand for clay idols, Kumortuli was carved out in the 'black town' region (the area inhabited by Indians) of Kolkata, itself a city born as a colonial outpost to serve British interests (Dutta, 2003; Goldblatt, 1981). By the turn of the nineteenth century, migrants had begun to settle and there were about fifty image-making workshops in Kumortuli. By the early twentieth century, the *Kumhars* of Kumortuli had given up the practice of pottery altogether (Goldblatt, 1981).

Kumhar – from which Kumortuli is derived – is a vernacular term associated with the potters' caste. Within older guild systems, *Kumhars* specialised in making earthen vessels such as water jars and cooking pots (Coomaraswamy, 1909). Kumortuli as an organised space was thus traditionally dominated by the occupational caste of the *Kumhars*, although this caste monopoly eroded over the years (Goldblatt, 1981). These artisans today identify themselves as *mritshilpis* (clay idol-makers) or *protima shilpis* (*protima* translates to image of a deity or idol). Although similar occupational communities formed around the same time, such as weavers of Jogipara and oil-pressers of Telipara, declined and disappeared due to competition from industry and changes in consumer preferences, the demand for Kumortuli's products has steadily increased over the years (Goldblatt, 1981). By the 1830s, as the grand lavish *pujas* receded and *pujas* conducted within households began to increase, poorer residents who were prior beneficiaries of the generosities during festivals were cut off from festivities. In response, people collected money to form associations and celebrate the festival (Goldblatt, 1979). Today, the majority of images sold in Kumortuli cater to associations in different neighbourhoods of Kolkata and to associations of the global Bengali diaspora.

The *mritshilpis*' practices are embedded within an institutional context that is constituted of three dominant institutional orders – artisanal professional, market and religion. I elaborate on these three below and illustrate how these institutional orders manifest in everyday practices of 'modelling the *protimas*' and 'work organisation'.

Artisanal professional order

The boundaries between art and craft are often blurred and frequently transgressed (Becker, 1978). For analytic specificity, I consider the *mritshilpis*' organisation of work and aesthetic as being informed by practical utilitarianism that characteristically underpins the artisanal crafts. Thus, while there may be *mritshilpis* who produce a few pieces of art-for-arts'-sake (e.g., for exhibitions, museum pieces, and so on), production of *protimas* is predominantly for livelihood. Aesthetics, or the systems through which attributions and judgements of value of particular items are based, are integral to the operation of the artisanal order (Bielby *et al.*, 2005). The aesthetic order specifies and authorises certain kinds of practices, techniques and skills, norms of excellence, style and taste.

Modelling *protimas*

Mritshilpis draw upon a body of knowledge and skills on the aesthetics of modelling *protimas* that are passed on from master to apprentice. Idol-making is distinct from other kinds of pottery by virtue of the fact that the potters' wheel is not used; rather this craft is distinctive in its use of the unfired clay technique that artisans model with their hands, resulting in a reference to the craft as modelling. Clay is the primary material in the making of the idol. At Kumortuli mounds of clay outside workshops is ubiquitous and the smell of freshly mixed clay hangs thick in the air and permeates. Novices learn that the clay used for idol-making is primarily of two types: the *entel* or *chit mati*, which is blackish sticky alluvial soil, and the *bele mati*, which is white and comes off one's hands more easily. While the former is procured from Diamond Harbour or Budge Budge, the *bele mati* is procured from the Ganga along the *ghats* and is more expensive (Agnihotri, 2001). Over centuries, potters' settlements and their prices have been determined by their access to clay. The soft alluvial soil of the Hooghly River in Kolkata is particularly amenable to later stages in idol-making to achieve a smooth finish. Artisans mix different varieties of clay, sprinkle the mixture with water and knead to achieve the right composition. Straw, jute and paddy husk are the main ingredients used to alter the consistency of the clay being used.

Underpinning these practices of processing the clay are certain normative beliefs about the aesthetics of how the idol must look. For instance, the efficacy of the image rests depends on how it evokes *bhakti*, or devotion, among the viewers. There are certain aesthetics of depicting devotion, as explained by Bhabesh Pal:

> In *protima* making many things are not accurate. An accurate figure may not evoke bhakti (devotion) among the worshippers. The way we make Durga *murti*, it is able to evoke bhakti when the shape is healthier. Human figure cannot match this; it has less of facial curves. For theme *pujas*, the Durga *murti* is not the conventional type, it does not evoke *bhakti* among people. Say the *murti* in Bagbazar, it arouses devotion in you… (Bhabesh Pal, interview, November 2014).

The *protima* is modelled by *karigars* over a wooden base structure built in proportion to the idol. Bamboo structures are erected over the wooden base constituting the *kathamo*. This primary model of the *protima* is created using hay and thick ropes over the bamboo frame. The next stage is termed the *ekmete*, or the single-coated stage, where coats of clay composed primarily of the sticky *entel mati* are applied by *karigars* onto the hay and bamboo frames. Once dried, the model is evened out with *bele mati* for a smooth finish and is dried in the sun for about four to five days. This stage of applying the second coating of clay is termed the *domete* (Bhattacharya, 2008). Fragments of cloth are placed over the wet clay to hold the clay together and prevent it from cracking. White paint is used initially to coat the *protima*, followed by coloured coats usually using water-based colours. While there have been changes in the materials used over the years, *mritshilpis* retain the basic clay form as the basic structure on top of which other materials are experimented with.

The head is later attached to the body of the *protima*, resulting often in rows of headless deities that line the streets of Kumortuli, especially around the festive season. The idol's head is crafted by the most skilled craftsperson in the studio using a mix of *bele mati* (sandy clay) with *entel mati* (humus clay). Using a knife-like tool, the *mritshilpi* gives details to the face such as sharpening the nose, giving shape to the eyes and so on. This head is left to dry for three to four days after which it is fixed on the prepared body. Workshops often use their moulds made of cement, clay or plaster-of-Paris. These moulds are prized possessions re-used year after year and are fiercely protected as a trademark of a workshop's distinctive aesthetics especially among renowned *mritshilpis* (Guha-Thakurta, 2015).

Work organisation

Emblematic of craft organisations where occupational training and mentoring constitute the means of control (Stinchcombe, 1959), clay idol-making is a competence learnt through apprenticeship. *Karigars* come from across the state of West Bengal to apprentice, often working up to two decades with the same studio.

In the everyday division of labour, the studio owner is at the top of the hierarchy, after which comes the more experienced *karigars* and the novices. The novices are usually tasked with elementary, lower-skilled tasks such as mixing clay to the right consistency, transferring crafted *protimas* out into the sun to dry, and so on. In large studios, the *karigars* undertake most tasks in the modelling process described above, while the studio-owner is directly involved in the smaller studios. Typically, the master artist works on the face while the *karigars* prepare the rest of the model.

Novices or part-time labourers looking for casual work usually engage in mixing clay. Although novices take up this stage, it is crucial to the finish of the final product. If the composition does not have adequate water, the mud dries up resulting in shrinkage of the *protimas*. To prevent this, the mud is soaked three to four times a day and is kept in an airtight polythene bag. Artisans start off with mixing the clay, but as some *mritshilpis* say, learning the craft also depends on 'aptitude'. If an individual does not have the aptitude, he may remain a *karigar* who mixes clay. While the wooden base and bamboo frame of the *kathamo* are erected by semi-skilled *karigars*, the hay and bamboo frame is prepared by skilled *karigars* or by the studio owner, depending on the size of the studio. This stage is pivotal in the modelling process, on account of the need to manage the hay and in ascertaining the appropriate proportions to shape a human-like body. Any artisan who cannot make this structure is not considered a good *mritshilpi*. Apprentices became 'all-rounders' after three to four years of apprenticeship and only then are involved in all aspects of production.

Figure 3.4: A master-artist on Mahalaya painting the eyes that give life to the *protima*

Figure 3.5: Durga with her children Kartik, Ganesh, Saraswati and Lakshmi at the Milan Chakra Pandal on Hazra Road, Kolkata

Reserved for the most skilled and senior artisan in the community is the task of drawing the eyes, a ritual called *Chakshu-daan* (literally translated as *offering eyes*). The true potency of an idol rests in its eyes – how expressive and life-like they appear. Hence, this is the highest skill performed by the most skilled artisan. Often, an artisan renowned for his skill with painting the deities' eyes offers his services to several studios. Figure 3.4 captures an artist painting the eyes on a Durga *protima*. Figure 3.5 shows the final decorated tableau of Durga and her four children in a *pandal*.

Market order

The exchange between *mritshilpis* and their customers is mediated by market institutions. *Protimas* are produced not just for local, but also for global consumption driven by the demands of deadlines, quality and customisation. Larger workshops have better access to capital and labour and are therefore able to cater better to larger orders and tide over the risk associated with the seasonality and perishability of the product. For instance, a *protima* that remains unsold has no value the day after the festival, and is then destroyed to salvage the raw material. Thus, artisans are vulnerable to the demands and bargains of the customers. Collapse or near absence of formal market institutions such as access to credit and better infrastructure for living and working compound everyday challenges. Thus, customer's requirements, access to labour, financial capital and raw materials and the risk involved in the occupation constitute a market order, which influences craft practices.

Modelling the *protima*

Protimas are bought by customers, who may be classified into three categories: (a) individual households; (b) *rajbaris* or traditional aristocratic households; and (c) the *baroary* or *sarbajanin pujas* or community *pujas* organised by local clubs and neighbourhood associations. The size of a *protima* typically increases across these three categories: i.e., householders typically buy miniature *protimas* while *protimas* for community *pujas* are large. *Protimas* may be made-to-stock or made-to-order and are of two primary kinds: the individual *protimas,* and the *ekchalas.* The *ekchalas* are images on a single frame. The individual *protimas* are of different sizes, with standard sizes being 4 feet, 5 feet and 7 feet, and customised *protimas* going up to 25 feet.

Work organisation

Studio size varies in terms of physical space, number of *karigars* and number of images produced. Larger studios often stock the ready images in warehouses outside Kumortuli and the number of *karigars* varies across months. Number of images is a more reliable estimate given that it is more observable (Goldblatt, 1979). Larger studios make around – twenty five to thrity *protimas* during Durga Puja, the most significant festival, while smaller studios make around fifteen. Larger studios, because of the larger physical space available, usually make large-sized deities (5 feet to 7 feet tall), while the smaller ones typically specialise in miniatures and the *ekchalas*.

Production for peak season begins from May, and gains momentum around August giving about nine to ten months of working season. Saraswati Puja falls in the month of January, which sees another spike in activity, following which Kumortuli slips into a lean period, or the off-season from January to early April. During lean months, production is scant and temporary migrant workers return to their native regions to take up agricultural labour or some form of casual work. Owners of larger studios keep production going with fewer workers by procuring orders for exhibitions, images of celebrities, or more recently, decorative sculptures for wedding venues.

The division of labour varies between large studios and smaller ones. Although most workshops today hire some form of wage labour because of the demand for deities, large studios can afford to have two to four permanent workers throughout the year, while smaller ones primarily rely on temporary wage labour. Given that they are unable to sustain demand across the year, coupled with the absence of physical space to store *protimas* prepared earlier, owners of small studios cluster their production around peak season. This is a particular disadvantage because wages spike from INR 400 in off-season to about 2,000 during peak season. In contrast, larger studios can begin production as early as April for the peak season. Number of workers increase to about seventeen to twenty in some of the large established studios during peak season, when many migrant workers return. Indeed, availability of physical space and distribution of labour across months aids the accumulation of capital for these larger firms, while smaller ones remain subsistence-based (Goldblatt, 1981). Wages for hired *karigars* are paid daily and doubled during the peak-season. Getting access to *karigars* is increasingly challenging as they demand higher wages, with alternative available opportunities. While these alternative occupations, such as working on agricultural land or running small shops may not involve the same skill and may in fact involve less skill, these provide higher income.

Religious order

Amidst these social logics of artisanal aesthetics and commercial interests, *mritshilpi* practices are also enmeshed in the traditions of religious festivals and associated rituals. Scholars have ascribed a secular status to Hinduism in Bengal, in particular, highlighting the cross-religious nature of Durga Puja celebrations (e.g., Bhattacharya, 2007; Guha-Thakurta, 2014). However, the association with deities, aspects of worship, religious symbolism, rituals and organisation of work around the Hindu *panjika* or almanac, resonate with prevalent conceptualisations of a religious order (cf. Thornton *et al.*, 2012).

Modelling *protimas*

The processing of clay in idol-making is infused with various normative beliefs and representations that typify the religious institutional order. Worship of clay idols is specific to Bengali Hindu rituals and these images are customarily immersed at the end of the ritual worship as the same clay idol must not be used twice. The clay that is used for idol-making is collected from the Ganga, one of the most sacred rivers in Hindu mythology. Thus, besides the properties of this clay that makes it amenable to idol-making, clay from the Ganges also attains religious and sacred connotations.

Further, the first clay for crafting the *protimas* for the season is ritualistically taken from outside a sex worker's house in the neighbouring Sonagachi district where there is a large concentration of sex-workers. Traditionally, the *mritshilpi* has to beg the prostitute for the clay, and it has to be gifted to him by her. A priest is involved in chanting the pertinent Vedic verses when this clay is taken. This ritual is associated with the belief that a man enters a prostitute's house leaving his virtues at her doorstep therefore the land outside the doorstep is most holy with this collection of virtues. While this practice is not a core invariant feature of all studios today, i.e., as a ritual this has dissipated given the mass production of *protimas* that occur, *mritshilpis* do adhere to this ritual if the customer so specifies. Further, the clay along with other items for ritual worship may be used by the priest for '*pranprotishtha*' or breathing life into the clay figure. Finally, a ritual purity is attributed to this technique of unfired clay modelling by virtue of the fact that clay in its earth and water mixture is seen as purest for crafting gods (Guha-Thakurta, 2015).

Work organisation

Here work organisation includes organising work according to the cyclicality of business across the Hindu *panjika* (Hindu almanac) and the division of labour in a studio. *Mritshilpis'* workflows are anchored around the festivals that are determined by the Hindu calendar (solar and lunar). Although each month of the year involves a festival (See Appendix), Vishwakarma Puja, Durga Puja, Lakshmi Puja, Kali Puja and Jagadhatri Puja (*Ashwin* to *Aghran*: usually September to November) are the significant festivals for the *mritshilpis'* trade. China Pal, one of the first women *mritshilpis* in Kumortuli, explains:

> We begin the work by making the '*kathamo*' (structure) with bamboo poles, wooden planks and hays. Ritualistically, the '*kathamo puja*' (a sacred ritual for artisans to begin work) takes place on the Rathayatra day in the monsoon period, but I begin work for the season on the Akshay Tritiya day to find some more time to cope with the demands (China Pal, *Hindustan Times*, 14 September 2014).

The *kathamo puja* that China Pal mentions is a ritual prayer to the gods to bless their work on the Durga idols and the start of festivities. However, with increase in demand, some of these ritualistic components are accommodated within prevailing normative frameworks, like another auspicious date that falls on a festival or as per the Hindu almanac. *Kathamo puja* is still observed in *rajbaris* and some local clubs organising *sarbajanin pujas*.

The eyes of Goddess Durga are ceremonially drawn on Mahalaya, the day when the Goddess descends from her abode in the mountains and comes home. Mahalaya marks the end of *Pitri Paksh* (a period dedicated to homage to forefathers and ancestors) and the beginning of *Devi Paksh* (period of the Goddess) according to Bengali Hindu rituals. Mahalaya is celebrated seven days ahead of Durga Puja and heralds the advent of Durga. Bengalis remember their deceased ancestors and pray for their souls to rest in peace. Bengalis flock to *Babughat* by the Ganges to take a holy dip in the river and perform rituals of paying obeisance to departed ancestors. In their homes, families wake up at 4 am to listen to the All India Radio's rendition of *Mahishasuramardini*. Closely interwoven with these rituals of Mahalaya, well-known to Bengalis residing in Kolkata in particular, is the painting of the eyes of the Goddesses by the *mritshilpis* of Kumortuli. Underlying this ritual is the belief that it is by painting the eyes, that the craftsmen give life to the *protima*.

Intersection of religious, market and commercial orders

Artisans invoked the artisanal, religious and commercial institutional orders in diverse, often competing ways in their everyday occupational practices. For instance, while a good piece of art was usually one for which a customer paid well, there was simultaneously an artisanal reputation, and prestige to maintain when it came to slashing selling prices. Given the dependence on the craft for their livelihood, artisans often found themselves at the receiving end with customers. Invoking their artisanal pride in the challenge of creating something new artisans lamented the shoddy treatment meted out to them by customers. Some even attributed the increasing disenchantment with the occupation among their next generation to this exploitative behaviour by customers. Formal market institutions – such as access to banks, insurance against risk, infrastructural support from state were all but absent in the context of a craft that is pivotal to popular cultural production and consumption. Few *mritshilpis* availed of the facility of loans from nationalised banks, while most preferred to go to moneylenders despite extortionist interest rates, because of their dependability and presence around the community. Similarly, reflecting the intertwining of religious and aesthetic orders, customer orders are sometimes placed based on a *manoshik* – a religious vow the customer has made, or a conceptualisation of the idol in a particular form which they then convey to the *mritshilpis*. However, since the customer does not often have the necessary skills to draw the desired image, the final product is a co-creation of the customer's vision, and the *mritshilpi's* interpretation. Thus, the final product's aesthetic quality is not necessarily a reflection of the artisan's creativity alone; rather an adherence to the norms and authorised practices of the religious context may make the final *protima* more valued (cf. Asad, 1993). The seasonal nature of the rituals also implied that there were extremely lean spells between the sales of *protimas*. Artisans have to deliver despite vagaries of weather conditions or life events like disease or death of a family member.

In sum, the above descriptions seek to elucidate how the religious, market and artisanal order are realised in *mritshilpis'* occupational practices. We elaborate on specific scripts that *mritshilpis'* invoke to mediate these multiple institutional orders in their everyday practices.

Scripts mediating institutional contexts and practices

Embodying *gharana*

Mritshilpis referred to their own individual distinctive aesthetics or school of art as *gharana*. On the one hand, *gharana* was attributed to one's lineage. As discussed earlier, within the Pal community of Kumortuli, there are two predominant lineages – the *ghotis* or *epar Bangals* and the *opar Bangals*. Within the craft, there are material differences in the practices of the *ghotis* and the *opar Bangals*. For example, the *ghotis* are considered proficient in the *adi roop* or *bangal mukh* of Durga with eyes like bamboo leaves, while the *opar Bangals* are proficient in the human-like eyes of Durga. Further, almost in jest, a *mritshilpi* from the *epar Bangal* lineage pointed out to us that the *opar Bangals* have a penchant for crafting voluptuous figurines with pot bellies. While he professed that he did not discriminate between workers from either lineage, it was easy to spot one trained in the *opar Bangal* form, when the worker would start modelling a pot belly on the figurine. To our *opar Bangal* confidante, how could a 'natural' depiction of a youthful, slim-waisted Durga bear a pot-belly?

On the other hand, *gharana* was also a product of years of mastery, developed and honed through years of practice, discipline, and evolving tastes and preferences. While the skills of *shilpi sastras* are acquired often from childhood through observing elders work, *mritshilpi* was also someone who 'creates something new', someone who could 'crystallise his thought to complete a shape,'[2] who had '*manoshik ekagrota*' (mental integrity and focus), one who withdrew from the world to emerge and portray an expression. Artistic inspiration often struck after hours of meditation and focus on the divine form as Bhabesh Pal explains:

> It depends on the persons' *dhyaan* (meditation, attention). God entirely rests upon one's *dhyaan*. With eyes closed you get a picture. It comes to the mind of a *shilpi* by thinking; say the eyes can be done in this way or that way.

Tarun Pal describes how this visualisation of the form was distinctive of the artisans, 'The way we perceive Ma Durga is different from the common man. It comes from within. Last year I made the eyes relatively bigger and shape of face was a little long. It was beautiful.'

The concept of *embodiment* is important, as it seeks to capture how the body comes to matter within practice of the craft. Art 'runs through your blood', 'comes from your heart', 'depends on your mood', 'cannot be forced', evokes emotions, and must arouse devotion. A *mritshilpi* has *shilpi sattwa*, an artistic instinct, which then gives shape to his ideas. Nimai Pal, a septuagenarian with a long lineage in clay modelling, ties together how lineage and body practices come together:

> I have done a few good projects. I made a Lakshmi and a Saraswati protima with all my heart. I worked on the Lakshmi *thakur* for two to three days with all my heart until I was completely satisfied with

my artwork. This was not for money. I did this well. I pour my heart into two to three projects and use the skills and artwork that I had picked up from my father. We have continued practicing our father's style of work. However, we have to figure out and create our own styles sometime. Our teacher could not have taught us everything. We have to learn certain things on our own.

Embodying *gharana* is one mechanism by which that the normative specificities and particularities of the institutional context are interpreted and instantiated in *mritshilpis*' practices. *Gharana* provides access to specific stylisations and aesthetic beliefs that are produced and reproduced. These aesthetic beliefs are not experienced as just conventional; they are perceived to be 'natural', 'proper', 'moral' (Becker, 1978).

Embodying a *gharana* becomes a way of acquiring and retaining customers, often for generations. Discerning customers ask for certain styles such as the *Bangal mukh*, as discussed earlier. Bhabesh Pal informs:

> Everyone has a particular *gharana*. Like my *protimas* are different from that of my neighbours. This difference attracts my customers. Rakhal Chandra Pal, Nepal Pal have another *gharana*, everyone has specific characteristics. Customers are also (accordingly) different.

By specialising in traditional clay modelling and rejecting the theme *puja* versions, traditional artisans build and retain a clientele by differentiating themselves. Consider how China Pal traces the tradition in her craft and rejects the contemporary demand for Durga *protimas* made of fibreglass:

> I attended stitching classes from Nivedita school. But I wanted to remain in this profession of idol-making. My tradition is *ekchala protima*. My father and grand-father were also makers of *ekchala protimas*. I am not into the theme idol-making sector. Theme *pujas* are in demand; it offers more money when you model with fibres – these fields do not excite me. I want to satisfy my customers with my style of work. I want this tradition to come back.

The traditional approach to crafting the *protima* is pitched against changing aesthetics and preferences to justify the artist's stance. It is through this embodiment of *gharana* that artists engage with questions of 'oughtness' when confronted with change, such as when an artisan whose modelling I was observing shared, 'In the theme *puja* the shape of *protima* is not proportionate. For example, here hands are small. Can Ma (or 'Mother', here referring to Goddess Durga) have small hands'?

In this everyday practice reproduction, the *gharana* of the *mritshilpi* is not one that is handed down from generation to generation as is, but one that is continuously evolving, responding to changing aesthetics, adapting to consumer preferences, tastes and materials. For instance, Narayan Rudro Pal narrates how he navigates customer demands that may not be normatively appropriate:

> Customer tells us what they want. However, we do not make anything that is *Bikritoshilpa* (an image whose form has been spoilt). Since we create *thakur* (god), we ensure that people get the feeling of *bhakti* (devotion) when worshipping the *thakur*. For example, someone asked us to put the face of Hema Malini (a Bollywood actress) on the *thakur*. We will put a face of Hema Malini which people will feel like worshipping. But that does not mean that I am going to put the '*hunterwali*' Hema Malini face (a provocative character). We would never do this. We would use the beautiful, soft, sober Hema Malini playing *veena* (a stringed instrument) [parentheses added].

A specific type of know-how is acquired and continuously augmented by everyday doing. This same know-how and 'logic of appropriateness' of how a *protima* must look is also deployed by others to cater to changing customer preferences.

Mobilising place

The cluster of artisan workshops in Kumortuli present material advantages to the studio-owners in terms of access to a continuous flow of labour seeking employment, access to jewellery and ornamentation shops in the neighbourhood that specialise in accessories for the clay idols, proximity to the riverbed where boats arrive with clay and straw, supply of bulk raw materials such as bamboo, as well as sharing of the skilled Pal *moshai* (elder) who does the *chakshu-daan* for the *protimas* of numerous studio-owners.

However, in addition to these commercial advantages, artisans also accrue symbolic capital by virtue of place. Kumortuli is synonymous with expertise in idol-making within the city of Kolkata and beyond. Artisans articulated that their work was distinct and of superior craftsmanship as compared to artisans outside Kumortuli, attributing perfection, detailing and more natural qualities in their craft over that of outsiders. Artisans also explained how they could improve their craft by watching others at work and observing their styles. Bhabesh Pal describes how residing in Kumortuli enabled vicarious learning from others' craftsmanship:

> Kumortuli is a vast area. Many *shilpis* work over here, so there is an interaction between them. I observe others' work, taking cues from them, then I come up with more enriched work. Another person may learn something from me, there is an on-going process of learning. In other places (outside Kumortuli), the opportunity of learning is limited. They usually repeat things. We simultaneously observe and learn.

Consider for example, how Debabrata Pal elaborates on the learned stylistic differences manifested between Kumortuli artisans and outsiders:

> *Mohishashur* is natural. The way the form of the *asur* has evolved here – like that of a human – they (artisans outside Kumortuli) can't make it. The detailing we have in making of an owl, a mouse or a swan, you won't get it in others' work. There is a skill difference. The artists who are working in Kumortuli they are more skilled. *Shilpis* outside Kumortuli learned the skill from us. They observed our work. They are now doing their business outside.

It is important to note here that there is a certain representation of what is 'natural'. Mohishasur is a demon who is slayed by Goddess Durga in the popular narrative that celebrates her valour. Thus, what constitutes Mohishasur's form is again imbued by certain commonly shared understandings of how he 'ought' to look, which in this case is further specific to Kumortuli artisans' style.

Even those who have expanded their workshops, prospered and taken up larger residences outside Kumortuli, continue to retain their workshops in Kumortuli, indicating the signifying function that a Kumortuli address plays in a competitive market. This comes to sharp relief in the context of the threat of displacement that many artisans were confronted with under a well-intentioned and badly executed (and now abandoned) project by the previous government under the Jawaharlal Nehru National Urban Renewal Mission. Many artisans chose to continue to stay rooted in Kumortuli and face the uncertainty instead of starting a studio elsewhere in the city. Consider how Biswajit Pal situates place amidst a changing environment:

You will see a lot of variety of artwork in Kumortuli now. Kumortuli does not mean just *thakur* anymore. Earlier, Kumortuli used to work for six months and sit idle for the rest six months in a year. Now Kumortuli makes a variety of products.

Thus, Kumortuli is more than just a physical location; it provides material and symbolic resources that shape the *mritshilpis'* practices. Mobilising place is thus another script, which mediates the institutional normative context and work practices. Place here provides a spatial base for organised action.

Enacting community

Artisans who shape clay idols maintain a distinctive occupational identity preferring to call themselves *mritshilpis* or *protima shilpis*, and not *Kumhars* – the parent occupational group to which their ancestors belong. Most *mritshilpis* belong to the Pal caste that engages in pottery – one that is in itself distinct from other Pal communities such as the Teli Pals and the Kundu Pals. Several of the *epar Bangals* trace their lineage to Krishnanagar and Shantipur in West Bengal. This community of *mritshilpis* in Kumortuli enact relational community norms in their everyday practices. Folklores around the practices of the *mritshilpis* were imbued with religious myths. The Rudro Pals were believed to be born from the *rudraksha* (prayer beads) of the Hindu deity Shiva. Certain festivals such as Gopal Dol and Vishwakarma Puja are distinctively important festivals for the community, and are celebrated together. Multiple kinship networks also run across this community through intermarriage. Besides many families, saliently those of Rakhal Pal and Mohan Banshi Rudra Pal, have branched off across generations with multiple studios within Kumortuli.

Residents also mourned together, as I learnt one day in November 2014 when I visited Kumortuli. Most shops had lowered their shutters and the area, typically abuzz with activity, was oddly deserted. Surprised because it was still season, and production for Saraswati Puja should have been in sway, I was apprised by Mala Pal and her brother that a renowned and senior *mritshilpi* had passed away and that shutters were pulled down out of respect and would continue to be so for three days. However, they added, if this was peak season, they could shut down work for only a few hours. This collective mourning is salient given that studios are independent units competing for customer orders and labour. After all, a customer could not care who had passed away, she wanted her ready order.

As a community of practice (Brown and Duguid, 1991), this cluster of *mritshilpis* recognise that their occupation is inherently a collective enterprise.

While *mritshilpis* had essentially autonomous independent studios, they were often interdependent for the supply of raw materials and labour and co-operated in their work practices. The learning in this community-of-practice is inseparable from the practicing. Indeed, the respondents shared that they could distinguish a resident artisan's style from the final product, if they had observed his craft before. Consider how Biswajit Pal explains how he would collaborate with a fellow artisan in Kumortuli:

> For example, an artist comes to me and asks for help. He has tried his best to make a *protima*, but his customer is still not satisfied. Then I ask him to look at the *protima* as if it were a doll and add personality and expression to it. This is how we are different. This is our quality of work – this is our specialty.

Gopal Pal, popularly known as Kalu da, showed us around his workshop where he mechanises the movement of *protimas*, a process for which only a few artisans have the necessary skills and equipment. If a *mritshilpi* receives an order that requires mechanisation, he would come to *Kalu da* for help at this stage. Reflecting on this collaborative endeavour in the production of their craft, Mala Pal described:

> We decorate the *thakur* and Bhanu da enhances that decoration. We have to work together to get a prize. A single contribution does not get you a prize. For example, we have Kalu da, he gives a bit of direction. I do my work in the middle.

Mritshilpis leveraged relational, community norms for access to labour, financial capital, as well as with customers, to manage the risks associated with the profession, vagaries in access to raw materials and labour in a seasonal occupation, and changing customer preferences. Access to *karigars* usually came through personal networks – a father, uncle, or acquaintance from a village would bring their next of kin to Kumortuli to get apprenticed. As Tarun Pal informs:

> They [*karigars*] acquired the skill from their fathers and now working here and their fathers have retired from work. The same in the way that I am running my father's studio now after his demise, maintaining the tradition.

However, the metaphor of community does not take away from tensions and struggles that may arise within. Artisans may get divided along unions; or even get divided between *karigars* and studio-owners. During the eighteenth and nineteenth century, image making was a subsidiary occupation around the – three/four festival months, with the rest of the time spent working as potters or in agriculture (Goldblatt, 1981). Work production was primarily achieved through family labour. For the last 150 years at least, Kumortuli *mritshilpis* have hired wage labour to tackle the increasing demand. On one hand, *mritshilpis* maintained there was no difference in the skill of an experienced *karigar* and the *mritshilpis*, except that the former did not have financial capital. Like the studio owners, the *karigar* had the same *shilpi sattwa*, or artistic instinct, within them to give shape to his ideas, and he complemented the studio owners. Yet, the hierarchy between the two categories is palpable on many fronts. For instance, the workforce is called '*karigars*' – implying craftsman, while studio owners identified themselves as *mritshilpis, protima shilpis* or 'artist' (in English, and not the vernacular). The labourers called the studio owners, '*malik*', implying chief, or owner. During field visits, it was common to find that labourers were reluctant to speak with us unless the *malik* was around and only if he was fine our interaction. All interviews with *karigars* were conducted after 6 pm, and occurred at the Karigar Union premises, in contrast to studio-owners' interviews which were usually during the working day and within their workshop. Indeed, Goldblatt (1983) provides a vivid description about the formation of union for the wage labourers of Kumortuli and their first strike in 1974 which resulted in securing, albeit a compromise, fixed working hours and leave for the workforce. The incident highlighted that social differentiation between the studio-owners and *karigars* exists, and their interests are increasingly polarised. As reported in the *Times of India* on 10 August 2013, the Karigar Union went on a strike because of non-payment of wages and rude treatment at the hands of the studio owners indicating that, perhaps, not much had changed.

It is important to note here that the concept of community employed here cannot be reduced to geographic place or caste-based community alone; while place and lineage are intertwined with the community context, embeddedness within this community also bestows identity, kinship and work-specific cooperation. Thus, enacting community serves as a script by which aspects of the religious, market and artisanal orders are instantiated in practice as well as a script that mediates how these institutional orders are reproduced through everyday practice.

Discussion and conclusion

This study contributes to two key strands of scholarship. First, I contribute to research on work and occupations, not just by engaging with an unconventional context that stands in sharp contrast to dominant accounts of occupations, but also by casting in sharp relief the underlying structures and structuring scripts that underpin what appears to be an ephemeral and transient form of organising. Second, I contribute to scholarship on institutional maintenance in a domain of popular cultural production

Bringing work back in

I make two contributions to scholarship on work and occupations. First, I contribute to furthering our understanding of an alternative context where economic action occurs that is mired with its own specificities and cultural nuances. Dominant accounts of economic action are conceptualised around established frameworks of firms, networks and hierarchies (Zelizer, 2010) and organisational theories focus on highly standardised forms of organising that are assumed to prevail across a wide variety of countries and sectors (Boyacigiller and Adler, 1991). Such ideas fail to capture the complex realities of exchange. Barley and Kunda (2001, 90) lament that the paucity of detailed studies of work that specify practices has resulted in 'anachronistic theories and out-dated images of work and how it is organised', a sentiment that has resonated with other scholars over the years (for example, Barley, 2008; Bechky, 2011). To complement prevailing accounts of hierarchy, authority, reciprocity and collaboration that serve as governance and coordination mechanisms in different forms of organising, I develop an alternative account of organising, where scripts such as *gharana*, place and community hold together a configuration of people, objects, social relations and practices.

Through this situated description of work and organising, I not only seek to provide rich and nuanced images but I also attempt to 'make more embodied the lives of those working or wanting to work, thereby grounding work relations in the material and concrete world'(Anteby and Bechky, 2016, 502). For instance, this account of *mritshilpi* practices and the scripts they invoke reveal the bodily experiences of the job and their corporal relation to work (e.g., the physical labour involved in sculpting the *protima*, requiring touch and hence co-presence with material objects like clay, bamboo and hay, meditating to arrive at a point of artistic inspiration, crafting the expressions of a deity to arouse devotion, and so on).

Second, the nature or work in such a context is seasonal, seemingly fluid and ephemeral with porous boundaries of raw materials and labour. Past studies that have looked at temporary forms of work, focus on the flexibility they afford (Christopherson and Storper, 1989), the absence of formal structures that facilitate coordination and control (Christopherson and Stroper 1989; Meyerson *et al.*, 1996) and the associated mobile and boundary-less careers (Jones and DeFilippi, 1996). However, this study shows that underlying these visible features of uncertainty, fluidity and permeable boundaries are deep processes of structuring that create a complex institutional order that is enacted, maintained and challenged in everyday practices through scripts such as *gharana*, place and community.

My study provides insights into a specific kind of seasonal work that must be done in a particular time and place and opens up questions for future research. For instance, my findings point to the need to conceptualise seasonal work as distinct from temporary work, given the cyclicality, associations with place and migration. What resources and role structures are leveraged to coordinate seasonal work and organise year after year?

Institutional maintenance

The issue of how institutions are maintained has received lesser attention than how institutions are created or how institutions diffuse (Lawrence *et al.*, 2009; Scott, 2001). Considerable institutional work goes into maintaining even highly institutionalised phenomena such as democratic elections in countries with deeply entrenched democratic practices (Lawrence *et al.*, 2009). While regulatory actions, policing and monitoring may be more explicit mechanisms that maintain institutions (for example, Leblebici *et al.*, 1991), my study reveals mechanisms of institutional reproduction that are less visible. Embodying *gharana*, mobilising place and enacting community relations shape how norms of various institutional orders are embedded and routinised in everyday practices. In identifying these scripts, I distil the historical, spatial, and relational constituents of practice that are inadvertently, intuitively, or consciously produced and reproduced every day. The chapter does not claim that these are the only scripts that mediate institutional contexts and practices; rather in this specific institutional context, these scripts are important to understand the interplay between institutional norms and practices.

Further, institutional maintenance does not imply an absence of change. Rather, as this study describes, there is ongoing change in terms of consumer preferences, aesthetics, materials used, and attitudinal shifts across generations towards the occupation. The question of institutional maintenance is then to understand how actors maintain institutions amidst change. By focusing on institutional contexts, I do not conclude that *mritshilpis* within the social space of Kumortuli are passive recipients or cultural dopes enacting institutions.

Rather, I see how actors reflexively engage with these institutional orders. The findings suggest that these scripts affect how artisans learn, navigate changing consumer preferences and aesthetics, changing diasporas, expanding markets, and exogenous threats. These three scripts also help us understand how such changes do not cascade into a story of stagnation at Kumortuli. Rather there is, and has been for decades, adaptation and re-orientation (see Guha-Thakurta, 2015 for a narrative of historical evolution of Durga Pujas and commensurate *mritshilpi* practices). Artisan workshops that for decades have specialised in *protima*-making, are today gradually expanding to fibreglass works both during and off-season, especially taking on orders for weddings and public events. Some families, for example, that of Sunil Pal, have shifted completely to the manufacture of fibreglass products. Here as well, they retain their workshops in Kumortuli, state that they are informed by their *gharana* and are part of the community evidenced by being part of the union.

Thus, embodying *gharana*, mobilising place and enacting collective community can be understood to be processes that underpin the accumulation of alternative forms of capital that accrue as dimensions of practice. In other words, elements of past tradition, relations and spatiality, are used to adapt to and manage uncertain futures. These processes also offer some insights as to how, despite the influence of non-local environments on the prevailing institutional contexts, practices endure. The findings also provide insights into how institutions are not just constrictive of human agency. Rather agency here is layered across *gharana*, place and community and is not surrendered to institutional orders; creativity thrives in the relational, spatial and historical situatedness of practices.

Corresponding to increasing commodification of festivals, these practices have arguably become untethered from their normative contexts. The younger generation in Kumortuli is progressively moving away from this profession, which is seen as involving 'dirty work', to professions that involve less manual labour. Further, skilled seasonal labourers find lucrative alternatives that do not necessarily utilise their artisanal skills. With art school graduates who do not fall within the Pal community entering a realm that was the mainstay of a hereditary, lineage-driven practice, community relations are ruptured. With mushrooming of studios outside Kumortuli and other prominent clusters such as the ones in Behala and Ultadanga gaining fame, the signifying function of Kumortuli also stands threatened. One can also postulate that a disruption of *gharana*, place and community relations may present a threat to the durability of the practices, a rupture of institutional contexts making way for new contexts and practices.

In sum, in this study, I seek to develop an alternative account of organising that illuminates an unconventional context characterised by seasonal work in a neighbourhood that is simultaneously a site of craftsmanship, residence, and commerce. By focusing on occupational practices and the realised institutional orders, I contribute to developing more situated accounts of work and occupations that are side-stepped in dominant organisational narratives. I illustrate how the institutional realm and its social practices are mediated by scripts such as embodying *gharana*, mobilising place, and enacting community, which enable the artisans to consciously, inadvertently, or intuitively derive meanings and representations in the reproduction of their social world. I thus respond to calls to more closely examine institutional maintenance and to 'bring work back in' to organisational studies, by describing the institutional texture of the social life of the *mritshilpis* within which their practices endure.

Appendix 3A

Table 3.1: Festivals in Bengal that involve idols

Bengali calendar	Roman calendar	Activities/Festivals
Chaitra	March – April	Basanti Durga Puja Shitala Puja Poila Boishakh
Baishakh	April – May	Buddha Purnima
Jaishtha	May – June	
Ashar	June – July	Rath Jatra Manasa Devi Puja
Shraban	July – August	Manasa Devi Puja
Bhadra	August – September	Janmashtami Vishwakarma Puja* Ganesh Chaturthi
Ashwin	September – October	Mahalaya Durga Puja Sherawali Kojagori Lakshmi Puja Dhanteras Kali Puja/Diwali
Kartik	October – November	Durga Puja Kojagori Lakshmi Puja Kali Puja/Diwali Kartik Puja Jagaddhatri Puja
Aghran	November – December	Jagadhatri Puja
Poush	December – January	
Magh	January – February	Saraswati Puja
Falgun	February – March	Maha Shivratri Shiv-Durga Dol Purnima or Holi Gopal Puja (Pal community) Kali Puja (Pal community)

* Season begins with Vishwakarma Puja and ends with Saraswati Puja, although orders reduce after Jagaddhatri Puja

Appendix 3B

Table 3.2: Glossary of commonly used terms

Vernacular term	Meaning in English
Bhakti	Devotion
Dhyaan	Meditation
Ekchala	Images of Gods (typically Durga and her family) within one structural frame
Epar Bangal or *Ghotis*	People belonging to West Bengal
Gharana	Style or school of thought
Karigar	Craftsman, artisan; in Kumortuli *karigar* is used to identify the labourers
Mritshilpis or *Protima Shilpis*	*Mrit* refers to clay; *protima* refers to idols This translates to clay image-makers or idol-makers. Both are used interchangeably
Murti	Form or solid object, often refers to image, idol or statue
Opar Bangal	People belonging to what is now Bangladesh
Puja	Worship, homage
Shilpa	Art, craft
Thakur	God

Endnotes

1   I would like to thank Sritama Mandal Dasgupta without whose able research assistance this project would not have moved beyond the point of casual curiosity. Rohit Varman generously provided criticism and encouragement from the earliest stages of this project. Uma Malhotra lent valuable research assistance, particularly in the later stages. The project was enabled by research funding from the Indian Institute of Management Calcutta.

2   Roop poripurna korche.

Devi Vijay
91

References

Agnihotri, Anita. 2001. *Kolkatar Pratima-Shilpi*. Kolkata: Prabandha.

Anteby, Michel and Beth A. Bechky. 2016. 'Editorial Essay: How Workplace Ethnographies Can Inform the Study of Work and Employment Relations.' *ILR Review* 69(2): 501–05.

Asad, Talal. 1993. *Genealogies of Religion: Discipline and Reasons of Power in Christianity and Islam*. Maryland, USA: Johns Hopkins University Press.

Bamberger, Peter A. and Michael G. Pratt. 2010. 'Moving Forward by Looking Back: Reclaiming Unconventional Research Contexts and Samples in Organisational Scholarship.' *Academy of Management Journal* 53(4): 665–71.

Barley, Stephen R. 1986. 'Technology as an Occasion for Structuring: Evidence from Observations of CT scanners and the Social Order of Radiology Departments.' *Administrative Science Quarterly* 31(1): 78–108.

Barley, Stephen R. and Gideon Kunda. 2001. 'Bringing Work Back In.' *Organisation Science* 12(1): 76–95.

Barley, Stephen R. and Pamela S. Tolbert. 1997. 'Institutionalization and Structuration: Studying the Links between Action and Institution.' *Organisation Studies* 18(1): 93–117.

Barley, Stephen R. 2008. 'Coalface Institutionalism.' In *The Sage Handbook of Organisational Institutionalism*, edited by Royston Greenwood, Christine Oliver, Roy Suddaby and Kerstin Sahlin-Andersson, 491–518. London: Sage.

Barnes, Barry. 2001. 'Practice as Collective Action.' In *The Practice Turn in Contemporary Theory*, edited by Theodore R. Schatzki, Karin Knorr-Cetina and Eike Von Savigny, 17–28. London, UK: Routledge.

Bechky, Beth A. 2006. 'Gaffers, Gofers, and Grips: Role-based Coordination in Temporary Organizations.' *Organization Science* 17(1): 3–21

———. 2011. 'Making Organisational Theory Work: Institutions, Occupations, and Negotiated Orders.' *Organisation Science* 22(5): 1157–67.

Becker, Howard. S. 1978. 'Arts and Crafts.' *American Journal of Sociology* 83(4): 862–89.

Bhattacharya, Saswati. 2008. 'Murtikaras (Idol-Makers) of Bengal: A Sociological Study of Their Craft Occupational Mobility and Market.' PhD thesis, Jawaharlal Nehru University, New Delhi.

Bhattacharya, Tithi. 2007. 'Tracking the Goddess: Religion, Community, and Identity in the Durga Puja Ceremonies of Nineteenth-century Calcutta.' *The Journal of Asian Studies* 66(4): 919–62.

Bielby, Denise D., Molly Moloney and Bob Q. Ngo. 2005. 'Aesthetics of Television Criticism: Mapping Critics' Reviews in an Era of Industry Transformation.' *Research in the Sociology of Organisations* 23(1): 1–43.

Bourdieu, Pierre *et al*. 1999. *The Weight of the World: Social Suffering in Contemporary Society*. Translated by Priscilla P. Ferguson, Susan Emanuel, Joe Johnson and Shoggy T. Waryn. Stanford: Stanford University Press.

Boyacigiller, Nakiye Avdan and Nancy J. Adler. 1991. 'The Parochial Dinosaur: Organisational Science in a Global Context.' *Academy of Management Review* 16(2): 262–90.

Brown, John Seely and Paul Duguid. 1991. 'Organisational Learning and Communities-of-

Practice: Toward a Unified View of Working, Learning, and Innovation.' *Organisation Science* 2(1): 40–57.

Christopherson, Susan and Michael Storper. 1989. 'The Effects of Flexible Specialization on Industrial Politics and the Labor Market: The Motion Picture Industry.' *Industrial and Labor Relations Review* 42(3): 331–47.

Coomaraswamy, Ananda. 1909. *The Indian Craftsman*. London: Probsthain & Company.

Coser, Lewis A., Charles Kadushin and Walter Powell. 1982. *Books: The Culture and Commerce of Publishing*. New York: Basic Books.

Davis, Gerald F. and Christopher Marquis. 2005. 'Prospects for Organisation Theory in the Early Twenty-first Century: Institutional Fields and Mechanisms.' *Organisation Science* 16(4): 332–43.

Dutta, Krishna. 2003. *Calcutta: A Cultural and Literary History*. Oxford: Signal Books.

Eccles, Robert G. 1981. 'Bureaucratic versus Craft Administration: The Relationship of Market structure to the Construction Firm.' *Administrative Science Quarterly* 26(3): 449–69.

Faulkner, Robert R. and Andy B. Anderson. 1987. 'Short-term Projects and Emergent Careers: Evidence from Hollywood.' *American Journal of Sociology* 92(4): 879–909.

Friedland, Roger and Robert R. Alford. 1991. 'Bringing Society Back in: Symbols, Practices and Institutional Contradictions.' In *The New Institutionalism in Organisational Analysis*, edited by Paul J. DiMaggio and Walter W. Powell, 232–63. Chicago, IL: University of Chicago Press.

Ghosh, Anjan. 2000. 'Spaces of Recognition: Puja and Power in Contemporary Calcutta.' *Journal of Southern African Studies* 26(2): 289–99.

Giddens, Anthony. 1984. *The Constitution of Society: Outline of the Theory of Structuration*. Cambridge, UK: Polity Press.

Goldblatt, Beth. 1979. 'Government Aid to Small-scale Industries and the Self-employed: A Case Study from Calcutta.' *Ethnos* 44(3–4): 192–216.

————. 1981. 'The Erosion of Caste Monopolies: Examples from West Bengal.' *Social Analysis* 7: 99–113.

————. 1983. 'The Formation of a Labour Union in a Slum Quarter of Calcutta.' *Ethnos* 48(1–2): 46–68.

Goffman, Erving. 1967. *Interactional Ritual*. Garden City: Anchor.

Guha-Thakurta, Tapati. 1992. *The Making of a New "Indian" Art: Artists, Aesthetics, and Nationalism in Bengal, c. 1850–1920*. Cambridge, U.K.: Cambridge University Press.

————. 2014. 'Conceits of the Copy: Travelling Replicas of the Past and Present.' In *New Cultural Histories of India: Materiality and Practices*, edited by Partha Chatterjee, Tapati Guha-Thakurta and Bodhisattva Kar, 180–220. New Delhi: Oxford University Press.

————. 2015. *In the Name of the Goddess: The Durga Pujas of Contemporary Kolkata*. Kolkata: Primus Books.

Hallett, Tim, and Marc J. Ventresca. 2006. 'Inhabited institutions: Social Interactions and Organisational Forms in Gouldner's Patterns of Industrial Bureaucracy.' *Theory and Society* 35(2): 213–36.

Hughes, Everett C. 1936. 'The Ecological Aspect of Institutions.' *American Sociological Review* 1(2): 180–89.

Jones, Candace and Robert J. DeFillippi. 1996. 'Back to the Future in Film: Combining Industry and Self-knowledge to Meet the Career Challenges of the 21st century.' *The Academy of Management Executive* 10(4): 89–103.

Kunda, Gideon, Stephen R. Barley and James Evans. 2002. 'Why do Contractors Contract? The Experience of Highly Skilled Technical Professionals in a Contingent Labor Market.' *Industrial and Labor Relations Review* 55(2): 234–61.

Langley, Ann. 1999. 'Strategies for Theorizing from Process Data.' *Academy of Management Review* 24(4): 691–710.

Lawrence, Thomas, Roy Suddaby and Bernard Leca. 2009. 'Introduction: Theorizing and Studying Institutional Work.' In *Institutional Work: Actors and Agency in Institutional Studies of Organisations*, edited by Thomas Lawrence, Roy Suddaby and Bernard Leca, 1–27. Cambridge, UK: Cambridge University Press.

Leblebici, Huseyin, Gerald R. Salancik, Anne Copay and Tom King. 1991. 'Institutional Change and the Transformation of Interorganisational Fields: An Organisational History of the US Radio Broadcasting Industry.' *Administrative Science Quarterly* 36(3): 333–63.

Lincoln, Yvonna. S. and Egon Guba. 1985. *Naturalistic Inquiry*. Beverly Hills, CA: Sage.

Meyerson, Debra, Karl E. Weick and Roderick M. Kramer. 1996. 'Swift Trust and Temporary Groups.'. In *Trust in organisations: Frontiers of Theory and Research*, edited by Roderick M. Kramer and Thomas R. Tyler, 166–95. Thousand Oaks, CA: Sage Publications.

McDermott, Rachel. F. 2010. 'Playing with Durga: Ritual Levity in Bengali Goddess Religion.' In *Sacred Play: Ritual Levity and Humor in South Asian Religions*, edited by Selva J. Raj and Corinne Dempsey, 143–59. Albany: State University of New York Press.

Nicholas, R. 2013. *Night of the Gods: Durga Puja and the Legitimation of Power in Rural Bengal.* New Delhi: Orient Black Swan

Perrow, Charles. 1967. 'A Framework for the Comparative Analysis of Organisations.' *American Sociological Review* 32(2): 194–208.

Powell, Walter W. 1990. 'Neither Markets nor Hierarchy: Network Forms of Organisation.' *Research in Organisational* Behavior, edited by B. M. Staw and L. L. Cummings, 12: 295–336. Greenwich, CT: JAI Press.

Samra-Fredericks, Dalvir and Francesca Bargiela-Chiappini. 2008. 'Introduction to the Symposium on the Foundations of Organizing: The Contribution from Garfinkel, Goffman and Sacks.' *Organisation Studies* 29(5): 653–75.

Scott, W. Richard. 2001. *Institutions and Organisations*. Stanford, USA: Sage.

Scrase, T. J. 2003. 'Precarious Production: Globalisation and Artisan Labour in the Third World.' *Third World Quarterly* 24(3): 449–61.

Strauss, Ansell and Juliet M. Corbin. 1990. *Basics of Qualitative Research: Grounded Theory, Procedures and Techniques*. Newbury Park, CA: Sage Publications, Inc.

Stinchcombe, Arthur L. 1959. 'Bureaucratic and Craft Administration of Production: A Comparative Study.' *Administrative Science Quarterly* 4(2): 168–87.

Swidler, Ann. 1995. 'Cultural Power and Social Movements.' In *Social Movements and Culture*, edited by Hank Johnston and Bert Klandermans, 25–40. Minneapolis: University of Minnesota Press.

Tolbert, Pamela and Lynne G. Zucker. 1996. 'The Institutionalization of Institution Theory.' In *A Handbook of Organisation Studies*, edited by Stewart. R. Clegg, Cynthia Hardy, and Walter R. Nord, 175–90. London: Sage.

Thornton, Patricia H., William Ocasio and Michael Lounsbury. 2012. *The Institutional Logics Perspective: A New Approach to Culture, Structure, and Process*. Oxford: Oxford University Press.

Weber, Max. 1946. 'The Social Psychology of the World Religions.' In *From Max Weber,* edited by H. H. Gerth and C. W. Mills. New York: Oxford University Press.

Whittington, Richard. 2006. 'Completing the Practice Turn in Strategy Research.' *Organisation Studies* 27(5): 613–34.

Zelizer, Viviana A. 2010. *Economic Lives: How Culture Shapes the Economy*. Princeton University Press.

4

Shelter for Homeless
Ethnography of Invisibility and Self-exclusion

Ram Manohar Vikas

> That invisibility to which I refer occurs because of a peculiar disposition of the eyes of those with whom I come in contact (Ellison, 1947, 1).

In *The Invisible Man*, Thomas Ellison's narrator contends that he is 'invisible' and argues that his invisibility is not because of a physical condition but is the result of others refusing to see him. It is a refusal to acknowledge humanity (Nussbaum, 1999). In the novel, the narrator also contends that he has purposefully remained invisible to society as a mark of protest. Similar invisibility, though in a different context, has been portrayed by the protagonist in Mahasweta Devi's *Bashai Tudu* (1990) who is always killed in police encounters and yet Tudu never dies. Tudu is invisible. Ellison's narrator is a homeless black American. Tudu is a tribal. *The Invisible Man* and *Bashai Tudu* are stories of individuals. What happens when invisibility refers to the disposition of state and the affected are a group of vulnerable people? How does state structure invisibility against its own citizen? And finally, how do vulnerable people respond?

The idea of invisibility is widely discussed in social sciences. Robinson (2000) contends that there are two kinds of invisibility – invisibility of those who are on the margin and of those who are in the centre of cultural and political power. She argues that non-dominant individuals and groups are 'hidden from history' i.e., excluded from the narratives of history. The powerful enjoy the invisibility behind the mask of universality (Robinson, 2000), similar to the person sitting inside the light emitting central tower of the Panopticon or Bentham's idea of a jail. For the vulnerable, invisibility is both a cause and effect of social and political exclusion (Phelan, 1993). This chapter is about the homeless who are on the margins and are socio-politically excluded.

Invisibility is physical and non-physical absence. The latter may be either absence in idea or absence of stimuli, such as the silence or even absence in the ability to experience. Sen (1999) interprets physical absence as missing. He contends that discrimination against women in South Asia is responsible for low women to men ratio. Even though biology favours women, the ratio is not in their favour. The difference in the number of women to maintain adequate ratio are 'missing women' (Sen, 1999, 104–07). March (1982, 99), from a feminist point of view, argues that females are invisible in the androcentric sociological theories. She contends that the social theories of Durkheim, Weber and Marx rendered women invisible because 'the center from which the theories are elaborated, the implicit experience and interest on which they are based, are male'. The invisibility of women theorised by March (1982) is the absence of women from the central focus and women appear as powerless subjects. In her typology of women's invisibility, she identified three forms of invisibility: exclusion, pseudo-inclusion and alienation. In the first, women are completely excluded and the subjects are exclusively men. In pseudo-inclusion, the account of women is taken but their voice is marginalised. In the third, women's experience is analysed from men's perspective. For example, domestic labour in the Marxist tradition was seen as non-productive. The third type of non-physical absence is the inability to register things in the surrounding in spite of their presence. Haraway (2008, 4) contends that she has grown with innumerable bacteria without realising it. She says 'to be one is always to become with many'. The realisation of 'become with many' is akin to visibility.

Latour (2010) contends that invisibility is neither mere social construction, such as racism or caste-based discrimination, nor distant autonomous realities, such as God. It is real and operates through 'regimes of invisibility', which is a set of practices and actors. His 'regimes of invisibility' is akin to the Focauldian terminology of governmentality, which is a tool of control and governance through an ensemble formed by institutions, tendencies and processes. Varman, Skålén and Belk (2012, 20) contend that 'Governmentalities are discourses that promote certain rationalities (ways of knowing) and further specific mentalities (ways of thinking) that inform particular types of governing'. Latour (2010) argues that governmentality exerts violence through silence. I argue that violence may be exerted through invisibility. Looking away or denial to see is a strategy of governance. Berger (1972, 8) contends 'We only see what we look at. To look at is an act of choice'. The Government of India (GoI) refuses to see (recognise) the homeless in its planning and policies. The academia, primarily funded by GoI, also refuses to see homeless by not including homelessness into academic discourse.

0.78 million persons in India were homeless in urban areas in 2001 and the number increased to 0.938 million in 2011 (Jha, 2013). The Government of India has constructed shelters, also called *Rain Basera* (literal translation is Night Shelter) for the homeless in cities. During a pre-ethnographical study, I observed that the government officials interpret the service offered by them to the homeless as 'free service'. I also noted that most of the shelters for homeless were empty though a large number of visible homeless persons live on footpaths and under flyovers. The urban local bodies cite data on utilisation of shelters to argue that there is more than enough number of shelters. On the contrary, there are too many homeless outside these shelters. The state expresses invisibility towards the homeless. It refuses their presence. The signs of invisibility start at the definitional level. Census defines homelessness as absence of 'census house', which makes homelessness so ubiquitous that it becomes invisible. This is similar to Gupta's (2012) question 'Does the ubiquity of state makes it invisible?' It also questions the interpretation of governmentality as state control through 'immersion of details and minutiae of people's life'. The state does not maintain details of population of homeless persons and is ignorant of the minutiae of the daily needs of the homeless. The former is expressed through conflicting numbers reported by various agencies and the latter is confirmed by the absence of standard operating procedures for shelter operation.

The night shelter appears to offer visibility to the homeless but it reinforces their invisibility. In March's (1982) typology, this is pseudo-inclusion as shelters are not constructed to meet the need of the homeless. Shelters are there to meet a Supreme Court order. The operational processes further alienate the homeless, as the third form of invisibility (March, 1982). The homeless refuse to live in shelters. Should we construe their absence as a boycott, mark of protest, a silent protest? Hirschman (1970) contends that members of an organisation (citizens of nation in this case) respond in two possible ways if they perceive that the organisation is not offering any value – exit and voice. Exit is silent while voice is confrontational. Gaventa (1980) contends that the powerless do not raise their voices. They 'cannot speak' (Spivak, 1988). Gaventa (1980) also highlights the combination of invisibility and the silence of powerless as he quotes Mohiyan, 'The American poor are not only invisible..., but they are also silent'. The powerless maintain silence and refuse to participate either because of barriers created by the powerful or an anticipation of defeat (Gaventa, 1980). Scott (1985) argues that the weak protest through silence. He offers the example of people turning their back during an inflammatory speech by Indira Gandhi. Low caste Hindus protest against the high caste by avoiding visits to their houses (Vikas *et al.*, 2015).

In this chapter, I offer insights into the functioning of shelters by studying the plans and policies of the Indian state, academic discourse on the homeless in India and by interviewing the officials of the Municipal Corporation (MC) of Lucknow and Varanasi, NGOs, shelter operators and homeless persons. I also base my findings on my voluntary work at charity homes for the destitute. The data were collected using qualitative research tools of participant observation and interviewing. The locations of study were Lucknow and Varanasi. However, data of shelters and the homeless from Delhi have also been included. This chapter helps understand how the homeless continue to be invisible to the state.

Absence of the homeless in plans, policies and academic discourse

The Indian state adopted a five-year plan model of development and as of date has released twelve five-year plans. These plans lay financial provisions for various state interventions. My study of these plans offers insights into the state's initiative to tackle the case of the homeless. In the section titled 'Social Welfare' in almost all the plans, the state mentions its intention to deal with marginalised groups including the homeless. The plans also contain the topic of homelessness in sections titled 'Housing', 'Urban Development' and 'Urban Poverty Alleviation'.

The absence of the homeless in the plans excludes them from receiving state resources. Until the third five-year plan no fund was allocated for the homeless. Between the Third and Eighth Five-year Plans there is no reference of shelters for the homeless. The plan document segregates welfare expenditure into social defence and social welfare. The provision for shelter in the form of institutional homes in the plan documents was for persons in conflict with law under the social defence category. Shelter for the poor and vulnerable was conceived in the Night Shelter Scheme (NSS) in 1988–89. The shelter in previous plans was for old and infirm beggars who were allowed concession in the Beggary Abolition Act. In the Eighth Plan, there is a mention of shelters against an outlay of INR 20 million made in the Seventh Plan against 'International Year of Shelter for Homeless'.

Table 4.1: Homeless in Five Year Plans

Sl. no.	Plan Number	Specifics on homelessness
1	First (1951–56)	• Institutional homes for persons in conflict with law • Shelter for homeless provided by charity organisation appreciated

Sl. no.	Plan Number	Specifics on homelessness
2	Second (1956–61)	• Institutional homes for persons in conflict with law • Provision laid for one home for old, infirm and disabled beggars in each state
3	Third (1961–66)	• INR 28.6 crore provisioned for night shelters
4	Fourth(1969–74)	• No provision laid for operation and maintenance of shelter
5	Fifth (1974–78)	• No reference of shelters
6	Sixth (1980–85)	• No reference of shelters
7	Seventh (1985–90)	• No reference of shelters • INR 2 crore was allocated for 'International Year of Shelter for Homeless and International Cooperation'
8	Eighth (1992–97)	• Footpath Dwellers Night Shelter Scheme was introduced in 1988–89 • It is mentioned that the NSS impact was limited with outlay of only INR 2.27 crores for two years
9	Ninth (1997–2002)	• No reference of shelters • Voluntary organisations should be encouraged to set up 'Homes for the Aged/Homes for the Destitute/Homes for the Dying'
10	Tenth (2002–07)	• It is recognised that the urban shelter-less and pavement dwellers have not been offered necessary assistance by the state • It is declared that there is a need to rejuvenate scheme for night shelter
11	Eleventh (2007–12)	• The Eleventh Plan mentions that right to shelter is a fundamental right
12	Twelfth (2012–17)	• The Twelfth Plan offers to promote creation of the night shelters • It also mentions about night shelters for beggars and recognises that there is a need for shelter for elderly persons • The plan contends that the Development Plan (DP) of city should include provision of old age homes, orphanages, working hostels, and night shelters

Source: Planning Commission, Government of India.

The second level of invisibility in the plan documents is portrayed through absence of implementation details. In the Third Plan, details of night shelters were not laid out except the number of night shelters and the budgetary outlay. It was not mentioned how these shelters would be operated as no outlay was made for operation and management (O&M) of the night shelters. In absence of O&M fund, the NSS could not pick up. Plan documents mentions that the NSS was unsuccessful and could not provide shelter and the homeless were left to the vagaries of nature. However, plan documents do not offer any remedy or hold anybody accountable for the same.

Homeless persons die every year due to extreme weather condition during summer and winter. Mander (2010) contends that between 1 January 2005 and 31 December 2009 seven homeless persons died daily in Delhi. He argues that not a single death of homeless was recorded by the police. The crematorium or burial ground used by the police to dispose dead bodies does not maintain records of a homeless person's death. Dr Padmesh, a physician who worked in a governmental hospital in Delhi before joining a primary health centre in Uttar Pradesh, informed me:

> The usual norm of reporting the cause of a death of an unidentified person on the post-mortem report is 'Death due to circulatory and respiratory failure'. Anything additional would become a matter of investigation for the police. The physician's role is to only mention biological reasons of death.

This corroborates Foucault's (2007, 16) idea of biopower, which is a 'set of mechanisms through which the basic biological features of the human species became the object of a political strategy'. The doctor mentioned that a third person who has only access to post-mortem reports cannot know about the habitation condition of the deceased, for example death due to exposure to extreme cold or heat conditions in the absence of a shelter.

The Office of Supreme Court Commissioner (OSCC) brought the plight of the homeless to the Supreme Court of India (SCI) and argued that lack of shelter is the primary reason for the death of the homeless. SCI in its order dated 20 January 2010 mandated construction of both temporary and permanent shelter homes in Delhi. SCI also mandated that all states and urban local bodies (ULBs) for cities with population of more than five lakhs should establish one 24X7 shelter for the homeless with a capacity of 100 persons for every 1 lakh people. The order stated that the shelter for the homeless should contain basic amenities, such as mattress, blanket, potable drinking water, sanitation arrangement, primary health facilities, de-addiction and recreation facilities. 30 per cent of the shelters were to be special shelters for women, old and the infirm. The order of the SCI is still work-in-progress. In the absence of any structure to address the issue of homelessness, the SCI order is being only partly followed.

On 13 December 2013, Ministry of Housing and Urban Poverty Alleviation (MHUPA) issued an operational guideline for the Scheme of Shelter for Urban Homeless (SUH). It is argued that the guideline is an improvement over the previous guidelines of shelters under various schemes. However, the SUH in its background note indicates immigrant workers as homeless, which again renders the homeless invisible as the policy implementers at the field-level prefer immigrant workers over the homeless. Moreover, most of the existing shelters were constructed before the release of the SUH guidelines in which there is a need to provide 60 sq ft for one person. The existing shelters of Delhi calculate the capacity assuming an average requirement for each person as 16.76 sq ft (Sudan, 2014).

The homeless are missing in academic discourses in India. Study of the homeless in India is limited by a lack of clarity and definition (Tipple and Speak, 2009). In the absence of clarity, the number of homeless persons in India is higher than the number reported by the Indian census (Mander and Jacob, 2010). For example, the Delhi Urban Shelter Improvement Board (DUSIB) reported 16,760 homeless persons but the 2011 Census counted 46,724 homeless and OSCC indicated 1.8 lakh homeless in its report titled 'Shelter for Urban Homeless'. The confusion is largely due to the unclear definition of the homeless in Census India and questions have also been raised on their survey technique. In the absence of academic research, homelessness is primarily a news item in India. Literature pertinent to the issue mainly involves reports prepared by the NGOs working on homelessness including the Aashray Adhikar Abhiyan (Campaign for Right of Homeless), Sahari Ashray Adhikar Manch (Forum of Right of Urban Home – SAM) and the OSCC. Unlike Western countries (refer Liebow, 1993; Kozol, 2006) there is a dearth of academic research on the homeless in India.

In summary, the homeless in India are invisible in plan, policy and academia. The invisibility is maintained in the plans by not including homeless in the provisions laid out in the plan documents. Rare cases of inclusion make homeless invisible by not including details for the implementation of the plans. Policy on the homeless does not recognise the presence of homeless and mentions migrant workers as homeless. Finally, the homeless are also invisible in academic discourses.

Methodology

I chose to conduct this research through ethnography for three reasons. The first and foremost was absence of literature on homeless persons in India. I had very little option but to obtain first-hand an idea of homelessness in India. Secondly, I had previously conducted a study of homeless children (Vikas and Varman, 2007) through ethnography and found that it was helpful in understanding the details of the issue. Lastly, some of the well-known studies on the homeless in the West (refer Hill and Stamey, 1990; Liebow, 1993, 2003; Kozol, 1995, 2006) are ethnographic studies. However, my research is not a traditional ethnography of a single site. I conducted this research while I was also teaching and it was not possible to conduct traditional ethnography. I have used multi-locality ethnography (Haney, 2000, 48), which is taking the whole terrain of homeless persons as a 'field' of sites. This means I spent my research time, from July 2013–June 2014, in conducting a survey of homeless persons, visiting shelters, interviewing officials of MC and NGOs, and caretakers of the shelters in Lucknow and Varanasi. I also participated in a workshop, visited a leper's colony, and worked as a volunteer in a charity home for destitute.

I came across several problems before starting my fieldwork. First, the definition of the homeless mentioned in the Census of India includes all categories of homeless. I defined homeless in this research as a person or family without any asset (except minimum personal belongings) and also one who does not have any source of livelihood other than begging. Individuals who have chosen to be voluntarily homeless for religious purposes, such as *sadhus* or *fakirs*, do not qualify as homeless in my definition. Secondly, there is almost no literature on the homeless of Lucknow and Varanasi. The reports prepared by NGOs define homeless according to the convenience of grant-offering institutions. For example, in Lucknow and Varanasi NGOs, which claimed that they work for homeless, were working on immigrant workers and slum dwellers respectively. Third, the local MCs did not provide any record of homeless persons in both the cities. In certain cases, information was obtained by filing a petition under the Right to Information Act (RTI). Fourth, as I started counting homeless in accordance to the method mentioned by the Census India I realised that every person sleeping on the footpath was not homeless. The migrant workers and road-side vendors sleep on footpaths in large numbers. Near hospitals, many patients and their family members sleep on the footpath. Children from nearby villages who come to Lucknow during the weekend to earn money by cleaning vehicles at the road intersections, also sleep on footpaths. Similarly, many pilgrims in Varanasi sleep on footpaths. The other problem was waking up sleeping persons to know if they were homeless according to my definition. Finally, homeless persons keep moving and hence the point in time (PIT) method adopted in the census has limitations. Therefore, I decided to survey homeless persons in all the 110 wards of Lucknow and nine wards in Varanasi and to visit all the shelters.

I visited all twenty three shelters for the homeless in Lucknow and twelve in Varanasi. No shelter in both cities offered space to the homeless. Most of the shelters in Lucknow and Varanasi were empty even though the homeless occupied footpaths close to shelters. However, there were homes for the poor and destitute run by religious charity organisations that contained many homeless persons. As a negative case analysis (Hill and Stamey, 1990), I studied one charity home each in Lucknow and Varanasi and one lepers' settlement in Varanasi. To understand the day-to-day working of charity homes, I worked as a volunteer in a charity home (Hill and Stamey, 1990). Working as a volunteer offered an opportunity to meet caretakers of the charity homes and to talk to inmates. The study of the leper's settlement helped me understand how once homeless and stigmatised live as a community. The leper's settlement included thirty families.

To understand the functioning of state-operated institutional homes I visited institutions under both social defence and social welfare. The transit homes for juveniles and women come under social defence and old age home come under social welfare. I found that institutional homes under social defence have laid down processes, albeit inadequate, for operation. The relevant Act provides norms for organisation structure and various actors' respective roles and responsibilities are defined. Similarly, institutional homes established under social welfare acts, for example, Section 19.1 of Chapter III of the Maintenance and Welfare of Parents and Senior Citizens Act 2007, lays provision to establish one old age home in every district of a state, and also offers structural clarity. I studied one old age home for women in Varanasi.

I participated in workshops conducted by Human Settlement Management Institute (HSMI) in Delhi for the officials of urban and local bodies to address problems of the homeless. The discussion with the officials and middle-level social development programme officials during workshops offered an opportunity to understand their perspectives. I shared my observation during the seminars and led a transit walk for a group of the officials to the Lodhi Road intersection to explain qualitative research techniques to them. Visits to two shelters in Nizamuddin, New Delhi were also a part of the transit walk. I also interviewed homeless in

Delhi who live in Nizamuddin area that contains shelters in the vicinity. The list of participants is included in Table 4.2.

Table 4.2: List of participants

Sl. no.	Name of participant	Age	Gender	Description	Duration of interview (in minutes)
1	Manoj	21	M	NGO worker	60
2	Sarfaraz	40	M	MC official	60
3	Manju	35	F	NGO chairperson/ chairwoman	45
4	Dr Padmesh	25	M	Physician	90
5	Mahesh	55	M	Chief engineer	45
6	Ramesh	55	M	Executive engineer	30
7	Sambhu	57	M	Caretaker of shelter	120
8	Nawab	35	M	Engineer	45
9	Sanjay	45	M	Engineer	60
10	Mustafa	32	M	Homeless	60
11	Suraj	57	M	Caretaker of shelter	90
12	Jalim	40	M	Homeless	60
13	Santosh	45	M	Homeless	45
14	Purno	60	M	Homeless	60
15	Bacchu	18	M	Homeless	90
16	Janam	70	M	Homeless	120
17	Munna	42	M	Homeless	60
18	Ramesh	45	M	Homeless	45
19	Suresh	50	M	Homeless	60
20	Janam	70	M	Homeless	60
21	Puja	17	F	Homeless	30
22	Salim	25	M	Homeless	60

Sl. no.	Name of participant	Age	Gender	Description	Duration of interview (in minutes)
23	Sahida Khatoon	30	F	Homeless	60
24	Ram	65	M	Homeless	60
25	Sita	64	F	Homeless	60
26	Muhammad	30	M	Homeless	60
27	Mahabirji	65	M	Lives in a charity home	480

Source: Author.

Findings: Invisible shelters and absent inmates

My study of shelters further explains the invisibility of homeless. During discursive analysis of the data, two themes emerged: (a) invisible shelters; and (b) absent homeless. The first theme explains the structure of invisibility created at the local government through the elements of spatiality and operation of shelters. The first theme highlights that shelters become invisible because of their inaccessible location, inferior architecture and poor layout. Shelters are invisible to both the homeless and common citizens. The second theme highlights that the homeless are absent from shelters, which reinforces their invisibility. Poor quality of infrastructure is one of the reasons for the homeless to remain absent. However, the homeless also refuse to live in shelters because these inhibit the freedom of the homeless by restricting mobility, not addressing livelihood issues, restricting family and friends, and by not allowing basic routine activities such as cooking of food.

Invisible shelters

To comply with the SCI order, the Uttar Pradesh government has constructed twenty three shelters in Lucknow and twelve shelters in Varanasi. The structure of the shelter is in place but almost all of them, except three in Lucknow, were empty. I found that shelters were empty because of spatial and operational reasons.

Spatial elements of invisibility: Location, architecture and layout

Foucault (2007) argues that discipline is exercised through spatial division of territory. He uses the architectural metaphor of foundation, common part, and noble part to explain constitution of the state. Peasants are the foundation, artisans are the common part and the noble part contains sovereign and officers of the sovereign. In his explanation of spatial terms, country-side is foundation, small towns are common part and capital is the noble part. Similarly, I find that the state uses three components of location, architecture and building layout to make shelters invisible. Location is invisible because of remoteness, inaccessibility, physical barriers of boundary wall, legal issues of ownership, identity of structure and design of structure. It took three days (or 30 hours) to find all the twenty three shelters in Lucknow and two days (or 16 hours) to find twelve shelters in Varanasi as the addresses provided by the MC office neither contained building numbers nor street names. It only contained area names. The shelters, especially in Lucknow, have poor access and are located in areas with a low density of homeless people. In some cases, the shelter was constructed within gated premises, out of sight of the homeless and common citizens. The response to the question raised under provisions of RTI on the selection of locations for setting up of the shelters was that:

> the selection of sites for the construction of permanent night shelter (shelter home) was in accordance to the various orders of the Honourable Supreme Court on the writ petition (civil) number 196/2001 filed by People's Union for Civil Liberties and Others and orders issued by the chief secretary, City Development Department, Government of Uttar Pradesh on 28th January 2011, for providing one shelter home for one lakh population. In response to the same, Municipal Corporation identified land and constructed shelter home.

The subsequent question in the RTI was whether any survey was conducted to identify shelter locations. The corporation responded curtly 'as above'. It indicates that the MC did not conduct any scientific study and all its actions on providing shelter to the homeless were driven by the SCI's order.

The total lack of awareness of shelters, as well as someone trying to take benefit of the opaqueness, perpetuates the invisibility. Suraj, the caretaker of a shelter, told me:

> It was a winter morning and there was fog all around. A person came to the shelter. He was accompanied by two or three persons who were carrying a bundle. Incidentally, I was present in the hall where the homeless sleep. I was recollecting quilts from the homeless persons. I asked what was the purpose and why were they bringing the bundle inside. When they saw me, the leader of the

group came to me and mentioned that there was a dead body of a worker in the bundle. The worker fell from height and died. The person offered money and said that no one will suspect the cause of death in the shelter, which has record of death of unidentified homeless. I refused.

The anecdote supports Mander's (2010) argument that police do not investigate the death of a homeless person. The disposal mechanism of a dead body found in a shelter is generally recorded under unidentified.

Shelters in Varanasi are located adjoining to a police *chowki* (post) and MC office. The local residents were generally not aware of the shelters. However, the invisibility increased when shelters were adjoining the police *chowki* or MC office. There were small boards with '*Rain Basera*' written by black paint on these building and yet local people perceived these buildings as an extension of either the police post or the MC office. During a field visit, I observed a policeman sitting in the verandah of the shelter at Gumti No 2, Lahartara in Varanasi and junior engineers in the Beniabagh shelter.

Shelters are also associated with previous identities of tax collection office, worker's rest house and community centre. The previous occupants do not allow the homeless to use the shelter. The local community refuses to accept the changed identity of the buildings. Ramesh said:

> In the evening when we cook in the verandah of the building the local residents come and threaten us. They say that we are creating smoke and making noise. In the morning when we bathe they threaten to beat us. They argue that the water will become a breeding site for mosquitoes. People in the neighbourhood are rich and powerful. They often discover reasons to fight with us.

The building which was a worker's rest house was occupied by immigrant workers. Similarly, the caste-based community centres in Lucknow that have been converted into shelters by the government are still occupied by the caste leaders. The caretakers and officials of the MCs at Lucknow and Varanasi mentioned that shelters are for immigrant workers and pilgrims respectively.

The architecture of the shelters is similar to the surrounding buildings. There is no differentiation in shape, size, or exterior finish. Most of the homeless are illiterate and cannot read signage written in text. The interior layout of the shelter furthers the invisibility. The rooms are too small and there is no furniture inside. The only pieces of furniture inside the building are the table and chair of the caretaker. To an outsider it appears that the building is either abandoned or not ready for living. In many shelters, cycles and fogging machines were stored in the rooms. These shelters offered perceptions of store houses. The kitchen layout appears as if it is a private residential building. The provision for toilet and bathrooms are not adequate. The MC's engineer informed that in the absence of specific norms, the buildings were designed like any other residential duplex in Lucknow. The older buildings that are converted into shelters have not been altered, for example, presence of car garage and elevated stage in community hall. There is a common verandah in the shelter building that also shares the space with another organisation. The ground floor of a school building has been converted into a shelter near the Lucknow railway station. There is a common entrance for the shelter and the school.

In summary, I found that locating shelters at a disadvantaged location creates the invisibility of the brick mortar structure. The incompatible architecture and poor layout add to the invisibility of shelters. Invisibility is furthered by the absence of operational policy and standard operating procedures.

Operational opaqueness: Absence of administrative structure, budget and human resources

Proper operation might have pulled many homeless persons to the shelter. The homeless who are also afflicted by mobility problems prefer to live on footpaths as they are not confident about how shelters operate. I informed Purno, a homeless person who was standing with the support of a walker, about shelters in Varanasi. He repeatedly enquired 'Are you sure that shelters will be open?' and then added *'Jodi okhaney...*if there is nobody I will be ruined. You can observe that I walk with lot of difficulty. If I leave my place at Dasashwamedh and go there I will lose my place here. Somebody else will occupy'. I noted that many homeless persons in Varanasi were aware about the hotels that provide food for free at Dasahswamedh Ghat. Almost no homeless knew about shelters. Figure 4.1 shows an empty shelter.

Operational opaqueness is created by the absence of an operational strategy. Who will operate? And how will it be operated? The first question refers to issues of operating shelters by directly engaging MC staff or by outsourcing the operations to NGOs. Even after three years of the court order, permanent shelters were not fully commissioned (this study was conducted in 2013–14). There was a lack of clarity among senior officials of the MC. Sarfaraz, an MC official said:

Initially for a few months, some of the shelters were operated by the NGOs but off-late it was decided that the corporation will operate these shelters. It is possible that once again the corporation would hand over the shelters to the NGO.

Figure 4.1: Picture of an empty shelter

Source: Author.

The confusion in Varanasi was much more as no caretaker was assigned duty until December 2013. In a shelter near the railway station in Lucknow, caretakers mentioned that they were on contract and never received their salaries on time. At all other locations, wherever I could find in Lucknow, caretakers were fourth-grade employees of the MC.

The operational opaqueness is further compounded by the definition of homeless provided by the Census of India. In the absence of a definition, anybody who is without a shelter occupies it. For example, the shelter near Lucknow railway station was occupied by passengers, some on transit, and some were students who had come to Lucknow to write competitive examinations. In Lucknow, both government officials and NGOs argued that the night shelters were for immigrant workers. Manoj, who works for an NGO as a community mobiliser and also lives in the Indranagar shelter in Lucknow said, 'Every city is dependent on immigrant workers. They are the providers of cleanliness and they construct the city. The night shelters are for the immigrant workers'. On the contrary, provisions of The Building and Other Construction Workers (Regulation and

Employment and Conditions of Service) Act, 1996 contend that employers
should provide accommodation to workers. A significant proportion of workers
of *naka* (checkpoints) reported that they were into construction activities.
I observed NGO officials at these *nakas* filling registration forms under the
Act. The registered workers are eligible for financial support from the labour
department from the cess collected under the Act. 'The grant that we receive
from the donor agency is based on the number of registrations that we complete.
There is a separate grant for conducting awareness campaigns. All our grants are
activity based,' said Manoj. The NGOs have selected activities that are easier to
accomplish, as enforcing real estate developers to provide housing to immigrant
workers is almost impossible.

Out of the twenty three shelters in Lucknow, three shelters were found locked
and among the remaining twenty shelters, thirteen are close to the *naka* sites where
workers stand in the morning to get hired. This has created a general perception
in Lucknow that night shelters are for migrant workers and not for the homeless.
In Varanasi, the perception was different. The officials and NGOs argued that the
night shelters were for pilgrims. Manju, chairman of an NGO that was operating
a shelter in Varanasi said:

> We were offered contract to operate this shelter during the Kumbha
> fair last year. Many pilgrims came to Varanasi on their way to
> Sangam, the site of Kumbha. The district magistrate office asked
> us to make arrangements for the accommodation of pilgrims. This
> year during bathing ritual of Sankranti, many pilgrims stayed here.
> We do not allow the homeless inside the shelter. This is not for
> them. The officials informed us not to allow any homeless person.
> They will make the shelter dirty.

The second important question under the operational opaqueness trope is
'How to operate shelters?' This includes issues of standard operating procedures,
budgetary provisions for cleaning the shelter premises, toilets, bathrooms and
maintenance works, procurement of furniture, bedding, operating kitchen,
training caretakers and payment of caretakers. Mahesh, engineer-in-charge of
MC said:

> No separate financial provisions have been made for the shelters.
> The buildings were constructed to comply with the SCI's order.
> The present caretakers are staff members of the MC. They were
> anyway being paid while they were in the office here. We have only

transferred them. For repair work, for example, change of bulbs, cost
is booked against the general building repair head.

The shelter is absent in the budget of the MC. The SCI mentions that three
caretakers should be engaged in one shelter with one supervisor. However, the SCI
does not mention who should be engaged as caretakers and what qualifications
a supervisor should have. The MCs of Lucknow and Varanasi have engaged
orderlies, Class IV employees, as caretakers. Sambhu said:

> I was working in the main office of the corporation. I was serving
> water and shifting file from one table to another. All of a sudden they
> transferred me here. The head clerk was not happy with me. He had
> threatened to teach a lesson to me. I am suffering now. This place
> requires a person who can write. I am an orderly and my job is to
> serve water. How can I write the occupant's details in the register'?

Sambhu is an elderly person and was recruited as an orderly almost three
decades back. The job requirement was offering water and carrying files. His
educational qualification was not taken into account. In the new posting, he
is expected to enter details of the person who is offered a place in the shelter.
Sambhu finds it difficult. I also observed that caretakers in Lucknow are elderly
and almost on the verge of retirement. Some of them are also suffering from
physical and mental health problems. It is assumed that working in shelters is
easy compared to the main office and hence elderly orderlies were transferred to
the shelters. The caretakers were not informed about their role. They were also
not consulted. The municipal corporation did not even train them for their new
roles. In the MC, there is a general understanding that there is no requirement of
any qualification for a caretaker. The engineer, Nawab, said, 'What is so special
about shelters? Anybody can operate it'.

The supervisors of shelters are junior engineers who report to the executive
engineer of the concerned zone of the municipal corporation. The supervisors
of shelters complained that the day-to-day operation of the shelter is too trivial
for them. The supervisors had no empathy for the poor and homeless. Sanjay
contended that:

> The homeless are dramatists (*dramebaaz*). If you want to observe
> their drama you should go to the Dasashwamedh Ghat. As soon
> as they know that somebody has come to feed the poor they start
> behaving peculiarly. They will refuse to take the food if it is not in

accordance to their liking. They refuse simple food. I have witnessed how one person whose relative had died and he was conducting *Daridra Narayan Bhoj* (God of Poor's feast) was troubled by these crooks. He was on the verge of crying. The beggars were demanding *kheer* and *puri*.

The phrase '*kheer* and *puri*' literally means rice pudding and deep-fried Indian bread but metaphorically it signifies a rich person's food. Sanjay intended to say that beggars were demanding more than they deserved.

In summary, shelters are invisible because of spatial and operational reasons. Shelters are spatially invisible because of inaccessible location, camouflaged architecture and poor layouts of the interiors of these buildings. The operational opaqueness, which is created by the absence of operational strategy, budgetary provisions and appropriate human resources, reinforces the invisibility.

Absent homeless persons

In spite of seemingly tough conditions of road-side dwelling, homeless persons refuse to live in shelters. At Lucknow and Varanasi, I noticed that the homeless were living on the road-side though there was a shelter nearby. In some cases, the homeless were not aware about shelters but in many cases they knew and yet they avoided these settings. Hill and Stamey (1990, 311) argue that 'Governmental authorities as well as general public often wonder why homeless individuals opt for the streets over the shelters that are available in many communities'.

I found that the homeless maintain certain perceptions about shelters and many of them have been there at least once. Most have subsequently chosen to live on road-side as they did not find enough value to remain in shelters. The homeless argue that shelters are unkempt and dirty. They are correct as all the shelters' toilets and washrooms were dirty. The homeless argue that the sanitation level in a shelter is inferior to the road-side sanitation level (See Figure 4.2 and 4.3). Mustafa said:

> Shelters are very dirty. You cannot enter their toilets. At least here there is lot more fresh air. The mattresses of shelters are very dirty (*nongra* in Bengali) and infested with bed bugs (*udish* in Bengali). There is no control on sanitation. One person sleeps on a bed and the same bed is transferred to another without cleaning it. How can you sleep on the bed used by others? Every person should have his own bed. My bed is very clean.

Figure 4.2: Entrance to a shelter

Source: Author.

Figure 4.3: Conditions outside a shelter in Varanasi

Source: Author.

A homeless person has to return the bedding every morning. The location of sleeping place also changes every night. This leads to a sense of loss. There is no sense of ownership. Unlike the personal bed that Mustafa is describing, the bed in a shelter does not invoke ownership. His own bed, which is quite unclean, is his possession and the bed provided in a shelter is an alien object. The number of toilets is less. I noticed that the toilets were dark and also lacked ventilation (See Figure 4.4). Broken doors and leaking taps offered micro-version of Broken Window Theory that contends that relatively minor unattended problems indicate disorder (Kellig and Wilson, 1982). In the Nizamuddin shelter, there was a long queue in front of the toilet. As highlighted in the previous section, MC official mentioned that there is no budgetary allocation for operation and maintenance activity. This hinders cleanliness that in turn keeps homeless away from the shelter. Mustafa's argument contests Hill and Stamey's (1990, 314) observation that 'the constant search for the basic necessities of life and the everyday struggle for survival reduce the importance of hygiene to the trivial'. Mustafa sees the importance of cleanliness. He has set a personal level of sanitation and in his opinion the shelter is unclean.

Figure 4.4: Poor sanitation facilities at a shelter
Source: Author.

The poor sanitation level of a shelter is one of the factors that keeps the homeless away. The homeless are not comfortable with the living conditions as well. The homeless often associate shelters with drug addicts who keep fighting all the time and thieves who steal anything. Jalim said,

> Last year I went to live in a shelter. I could not even live for a week. There are so many drug addicts there. They are under the influence of drug and pick up fight easily. They will beat you if you do not

give them money to buy smack or they will steal your money. One person who was living there lost his money. Somebody stole his money while he was sleeping.

Jalim finds road-side living safer. During a visit to Nizamuddin shelter, I noticed that there were too many persons in the room. Most of them were lying on the ground close to each other. There were no cupboards or provisions to deposit money.

The homeless also perceive the shelter as a violent space where inmates pick up fights without any reason. Santosh told me:

> It was a winter night and was difficult to sleep on the *Pucca Pool* (bridge over River Gomti). I ate dinner in the Hanuman temple and tried to sleep. I lit plastic scrap and covered myself with blanket. I was still feeling cold. There was chilliness in the atmosphere (said *galan* for chilliness in Awadhi). I tried to sleep for an hour or two but could not. I went to the shelter near the court. It was around 10 pm. It was crowded. As soon as I tried to sleep *smackiyas* (drug addicts) started fighting with me without any reason. The caretaker was helpless. With some difficulty he was able to bring the situation under control. I decided not to go there again. I sleep peacefully here.

Wolf *et al.* (2008) have mentioned that safety of accommodation is one of the parameters to decide the quality of a shelter. Santosh's experience also highlights that clubbing all the homeless in one group is not correct. It alienates homeless from a shelter.

Freedom from the homeless perspective

The homeless are vulnerable but they value their freedom. Most of the homeless who choose to live on the road informed me that they felt claustrophobic in a shelter because of poor infrastructure and bad behaviour of shelter officials. The narrative of freedom was also heard during interviews with the homeless who were living in charity homes but voluntarily left after some time. The meaning of freedom was diverse across the group.

Mobility and livelihood as freedom

Freedom is highly valued by the homeless. They want to move around. Roaming around is an important source of recreation. Bacchu said:

> I live on the road, but I often go to the railway station and sit on

the platform for the entire day. I have made friends there but what interests me more is that the time passes quickly (*samay kat jata hai*). There will be some train or other passing by. There are lot of people and some or the other activity keeps happening. It is fascinating (*bahut accha lagta hai*). Moreover when I come to the station I also earn money. It is enough for *gutka* (betel nut masala).

Freedom to move around also offers scope for earning livelihood. Shelters do not offer such opportunities. While walking on the road in Varanasi I met Janam. His beard was white and he was wearing a thick glass with broken frame precariously perched on his nose. He said:

I do not have any other source of livelihood. A few years back I was pulling rickshaw. Begging is my source of livelihood. If I will live all day in a shelter, how will I earn? I cannot live in one place. Moving around also keeps me busy.

Mobility provides livelihood and also recreation. Munna was affected by polio since childhood and now his tricycle is his home. I found him near Nizamuddin crossing. He said:

I go far off places on my tri-cycle. I returned from the *Urs* (birthday) of Kwaja Moinuddin Chisti of Ajmer last week. I will live in Delhi for a few months and then I will go to some other city. I have roamed across India on my tricycle. I like to travel. Who will carry me or buy me train ticket? My tri-cycle is my train.

He patted the tri-cycle as he looked into the mirror and combed his beard. The homeless also use mobility as a strategy for livelihood. Suresh said:

During winters I sleep on the footpath of a busy road. A lot of people donate blankets during winters. People come in cars and put blankets on people sleeping on the road. Last year in one night I collected 58 blankets. I sold all of them. On all the cold nights, I slept at different locations and collected blankets. If I sleep in a shelter what would I get?

Suresh was squatting in the Jhandewala Park near Aminabad shelter in Lucknow. The park was full of the homeless and the shelter was empty.

I also came across cases in which the homeless chose to live on footpaths instead of charity homes. Figure 4.5 shows a bus stop in Lucknow occupied by the homeless. Janam lived in a charity home in Varanasi for one year and then left it. He accepts food from the charity home but refuses to live there. Janam said, 'Entire day you have to sleep. You wake up eat and then sleep. The cycle continues. The home is for sick. I am not. I came out. Now, I walk on the road. I go to the Ghat. I am free. I feel good'. Incidentally, the charity home refers its inmates as patients.

Figure 4.5: Bus stop in Lucknow occupied by the homeless
Source: Author.

Living with friends and family

In the absence of common space and in the closed atmosphere it is difficult to develop relationships. In Neezamuddin shelter, I observed that there were around sixty persons in the room and very few of them were talking to each other. The TV was on. Some inmates were looking at it squatting and some were sleeping. In the open, it is easy to develop relationships and at times developing relationships is needed for survival. Puja said:

> We do not fight with each other. We sell flowers at the road intersection as vehicles stop at the red sign. Sometimes if a particular customer requires yellow rose and I do not have it I take it from my friend and sell it to the customer.

In shelters, opportunities of interaction are primarily gossip for a limited time.

In the absence of a real-life situation, shelter inmates do not get opportunities to test the strength of their ties.

Ram who lives with his wife Sita on the footpath near Neezamuddin shelters told me:

> We went to the shelter but they refused entry to us. The person said that the shelter is for men and suggested that Sita should go to the women's shelter. He added that there is a shelter for women on the other side of the road at a distance. We are too old now and cannot live separately. We preferred roadside. Here, we can eat together whatever we get.

In public policy, the idea of homeless in India is similar to the idea of homelessness in the Unites States. In the United States, a homeless person is defined as a person without a family (Jencks, 1995). In India, a sizeable number of homeless in urban landscape live with families. This indicates a disconnect between public policy and the structure of homelessness in India.

Cooking and eating food together

The other important aspect that most of the homeless emphasised was the ability to eat food in accordance to their choice and eat together. I found that right next to the road crossing signal at Lodhi Road in Delhi a homeless woman was cooking fish curry. The smell of mustard and the sound of frying fish were drawing attention of the people passing by. A person was sitting on a wheelchair and observing the spatter of oil as turmeric coated piece of fish touched the hot oil. Another person was squatting near the woman and was slowly nibbling fried fish. 'We cook and eat together. It is a joy. I cannot do the same if I have to live in the shelter. There is no cooking space. Even if someone can offer food to me I will prefer to cook', said Sahida Khatoon. Cooking and eating together are considered as a mark of freedom. All the men who eat at Sahida's place are not her family members but she loves to cook for them.

In the newly constructed shelters at Lucknow there is a kitchen but is not operational. It has been constructed as a community kitchen and individuals are not allowed to cook food. The MC officials informed that the kitchen may be operated by an NGO in future. The inmates cooked food outside the shelter by using bricks as *chulha* (hearth). The shelter building of Varanasi does not include kitchen. None of the shelters at Lucknow and Varanasi has provision for families. It is the same in Delhi.

Possessions as mark of freedom

Most of the homeless refuse to live in the shelter because it does not offer any space for personal possessions. Muhammad said:

> They provide no place to keep our possessions. Where should I keep my personal belongings? I went to the shelter near station with my bag. The caretaker rudely said that it was trash and he will not allow me to bring it inside the shelter. He said that my bag will make his shelter dirty. I was upset. I argued that the bag contained my necessary belongings. He further argued that there is no provision to keep the bag and added that if someone steals the bag I should not complain. I left the shelter without much thought.

The shelters at both Lucknow and Varanasi do not offer space for keeping possessions. In Lucknow, Lakshman Mela shelter contained metallic cabinets and was the only shelter with such provisions. Incidentally, this shelter was previously a rest house for migrant workers and the homeless are not allowed to live there.

The inability to keep possessions was also expressed by the inmates living in charity homes. Mahabirji said:

> I am fond of reading but I cannot keep books here. They clean beds regularly and change the bed sheet. All you have here is your bed. Nothing other than a pillow is allowed on the bed. Caretakers argue that books and newspapers on the bed are signs of uncleanliness and are forbidden. Even if I keep a book under the pillow they take it away. Now I have stopped thinking of keeping anything.

The homeless maintain a strong desire for personal belongings but they are not allowed to keep any. Shelters lack amenities and their norms construe personal belongings of the homeless as dirt (Douglas, 2002). Mahabirji after some time compromises with his personal identity and slowly learns to live without personal possessions. However, Muhammad is not ready to change. He prefers to live on the road than in a shelter because his possessions are not allowed. As compared to Mahabirji's charity home, the shelter that Muhammad approached only offered a living space. Mahabirji is privy to many facilities, for example, cleanliness and better sanitation, regular food, security from violence and medical care. A shelter does not provide such facilities. Thus, the cost of not living in a shelter for Muhammad is not high.

Conclusion and discussion

Invisibility as absence: Strategy of governance by reverting processes of governmentality

In this chapter, I have explained how the state addresses the issue of homelessness. I have used the concept of invisibility to explain the metaphor of 'not seeing' homeless by the state. Seeing here refers to governing or control. Foucault (1975) has used seeing the metaphor to argue how medical science takes control of human body by increasing its ability to see. Foucault (1975, ix) contends 'it is about act of seeing, the gaze'. He argues that with the help of technology, as gazing apparatus and institutional processes of medical sciences the human body has become increasingly 'transparent'. For homeless, it is the other way round, and the state refuses to see them. The gaze is absent. On the contrary, the state apparatus works to make the homeless opaque. Plans and policies do not take note of the homeless. The homeless have been almost excluded from plans and policies. In a few cases, where plan and policy refer to the homeless it is either in the form of pseudo-inclusion or alienation. For example, the plan allocates money for shelters construction but provides no provision for operation and maintenance. The homeless are further distanced from the gaze by constructing shelters at locations unknown to many or difficult to find. The homeless not only avoid going to shelters, but those who visit once, rarely return back. They spread negative word-of-mouth about shelters.

One of the important features of Foucault's idea of seeing is seeing through detail. Biopower is explained as use of biological details to control people. Invisibility is created by not giving attention to details or providing irrelevant details. Biopower in invisibility is used to create confusion. For example, post-mortem reports of unidentified bodies contain only vague biological reasons for death. I observed an absence of details at the plan level as well. There is no detailing of categories of the homeless; various types of homeless, such as men, women, children, single, family, old, young, drug addict, diseased and physically challenged fall under only one category of the homeless. There is no agreement on the number of homeless. The state creates ubiquity as a tool for bureaucratic production of indifference (Herzfeld, 1992). It is 'denial of identity' (Herzfeld 1992, 1) of the homeless. The shelter is for everybody who does not have a house on that fateful day, for example, a traveller. This creates confusion and fear among the homeless, whether she is entering into the wrong building. The absence of operational details makes shelters opaque. The room size, amenities, and capacity of shelter are not designed adequately. Agamben (2005) argues that exclusion is a basis for violence in states of exception (also refer to Gupta, 2012). He refers to the example of killing of Jews and gypsies in Nazi Germany as a state of exception. India, a democratic country, is using exclusion as a strategy to make the homeless invisible. Gupta (2012, 6) in his study on the Indian state's policies on poverty eradication makes a contra-Agamben argument that 'the poor are killed despite their inclusion in projects of national sovereignty and despite their centrality to democratic politics and state legitimacy'. For the homeless, there is no 'projects of sovereignty'. Homeless are excluded. They die because of harsh weather condition. These deaths may not appear to be killing as in the case of the state of exception, but the deaths of the homeless on road side are indirect killings by a democratic state.

Foucault (1991) contends that the state controls people by taking control of knowledge. He argues that it is not about sovereign power but about epistemic power. In Foucault's argument on power there is directionality in discourse or regimen of knowledge. For example, when Foucault mentions positive and negative knowledge. Positive knowledge is a discourse aligning people with dominant power and negative knowledge is misaligning people from dominant power. In the case of the homeless, there is an absence of any form of academic discourse. I argue that the state avoids seeing the homeless. Intellectuals avoid them though they should not have because intellectuals speak 'truth to those who had yet to see it' (Foucault and Deleuze, 1977, 207). The absence of homeless from academic discourse reinforces the invisibility of the homeless.

Absence as invisibility: Freedom from alienation and semi-exclusion to self-exclusion

The homeless are perceived as a group though the various types of homelessness also make it a specific type of group or collection of persons. The differences and distinctions among the homeless do not qualify them to be in 'autonomous domain of subaltern classes and groups' (Guha, 1982, 4). This almost disqualifies them from developing a collective consciousness to resist subordination. The theories of resistance do not explain the reasons of absence of the homeless from shelters for two reasons. First, the binary of governance and resistance cannot apply in this case as governance has been replaced by non-governance. Second, the affected group cannot be categorised as a class. The powerless peasants of Scott (1985, 240) raise 'everyday forms of peasant resistance' against 'elite-created social order'. Peasants resist because they were excluded as a class from access to economic benefits of production. The case of the homeless does not qualify for any of the conditions of peasants. However, Scott's idea of intention may be useful here. Scott (1985, 290) contends that acts of peasants are 'intended either to mitigate or deny claims'. The homeless prefer to live outside shelters. The intention here is not of resistance. It is self-exclusion. The state is not concerned. I could not find any attempt by the state to convince the homeless to live in shelters. MCs do not even attempt to inform the homeless about shelter homes.

When the homeless avoid living in shelters, there is no negative consequence for shelter officials. They still exist. Caretakers do not bother to come and open shelters. Even if they do, they are there during the office hours and return back home at stipulated time. Supervisors and higher officials' are also not affected either. There is no accountability. The infrastructure and other operating conditions are too bad for the homeless to motivate them to live in shelter. The quotidian resistance, for example working slowly, of the powerless peasants of Scott (1985) negatively affected landlords. There is no loss to shelter officials if the homeless do not live in a shelter. Therefore, the idea of resistance fails to explain the reason of the homeless refusing to live in shelters, and only self-exclusion does.

In summary, I argue that the homeless have been neglected by the state. To explain the negligence, I have used the framework of invisibility that explains the structure of negligence. The ideas of governance and control of governmentality exist in the invisibility though the elements that facilitate governmentality, gaze, detail, and knowledge are inverted. The homeless also remain out of vision because they refuse to occupy shelters. The refusal is obviously affected by the poor quality of shelter design and operational processes. The unobvious component is their quest for freedom. Public policymakers can use the insights offered in this chapter on mobility, livelihood, and freedom to improve the effectiveness of these shelters.

This chapter also raises questions at two levels for future public policy researchers. First, at a macro level, some of the relevant questions are: How do we identify a group that is invisible? What all public policy level interventions should be made to increase visibility? And what happened during the period when the state could not see? Second, and at a micro level, some of the relevant questions are: What should be the basis of designing buildings for the homeless? How much area, both carpet and utility, should be allocated to each person? What mechanism should be adopted to incorporate experiences of the homeless into the standard operating document? Some of the answers to these questions will help us create alternatives that can provide some support to the most under-privileged members of our society.

References

Agamben, Giorgio. 2005. *State of Exception*. Translated by Kevin Attell. Chicago: University of Chicago Press.

Berger, John. 1972. *Ways of Seeing*. London: British Broadcasting Corporation and Penguin.

Devi, Mahasweta.1990. *Bashai Tudu*. Translated by Samik Bandhopadhyay. Calcutta: Thema.

Douglas, Mary. 2002. *Purity and Danger*. London: Routledge.

Ellison, Ralph. 1947. *The Invisible Man*. New York: Signet Books.

Foucault, Michel. 1975. *Birth of the Clinic: an Archaeology of Medical Perception*. Translated by A. M. Sheridan Smith. New York: Vintage Books.

_____. 1977. *Power/Knowledge*. Edited by Colin Bordon. New York: Pantheon Books.

_____. 1991. 'Governmentality.' Translated by Rosi Braidotti and revised by Colin Gordon. In *The Foucault Effect: Studies in Governmentality*, edited by Graham Burchell, Colin Gordon and Peter Miller, 87–104. Chicago: University of Chicago Press.

_____. 2007. *Security, Territory, Population: Lectures at the College de France 1977–78*. Basingstoke: Palgrave Macmillian.

Foucault, Michel and Giles Deleuze. 1977. 'Intellectuals and Power.' In *Language, Counter-Memory, Practice: Selected Essays and Interviews*, edited by D. F. Bouchard, 205–17. Ithaca: Cornell University Press.

Gaventa, John. 1980. *Power and Powerlessness*. Oxford: Clarendon Press.

Guha, Ranajit. 1982. 'On Some Aspects of the Historiography of Colonial India.' In *Subaltern Studies 1*, edited by Ranajit Guha, 1–8. Delhi: Oxford University Press.

Gupta, Akhil. 2012. *Red Tape*. London: Duke University Press.

Haney, Lynne. 2000. 'Global Discourses of Need: Mythologizing and Pathologizing Welfare in Hungary'. In *Global Ethnography: Forces, Connections, And Imaginations in a Postmodern World*, edited by Michael Burawoy, Joseph A. Blum, Sheba George, Zsuzsa Gille, Teresa Gowan, Lynne Haney, Maren Klawitter, Stephen H. Lopez, Seán Ó Riain and Millie Thayer, 48–73. London: University of California Press.

Haraway, Donna J. 2008. *When Species Meet*. Minneapolis: University of Minnesota Press.

Herzfeld, Michael. 1992. *The Social Production of Indifference: Exploring the Symbolic Roots of Western Bureaucracy*. Chicago: University of Chicago Press.

Hill, Ronald P. and Mark Stamey. 1990. 'The Homeless in America: An Examination of Possessions and Consumption Behaviours.' *Journal of Consumer Research* 17(3): 303–21.

Hirschman, Albert O. 1970. *Exit, Voice and Loyalty: Responses to Decline in Firms, Organisations, and state*. Cambridge: Harvard University Press.

Jencks, Christopher. 1995. *The Homeless*. London: Harvard University Press.

Jha, Somesh. 2013. '1.77 Million People Live Without Shelter, Albeit the Number Decline Over a Decade.' *Business Standard*, 6 December.

Kellig, George L and James Q Wilson. 1982. 'Broken Windows', *The Atlantic*. Accessed on 10 April 2017. Available at https://www.theatlantic.com/magazine/archive/1982/03/broken-windows/304465/.

Kozol, Jonathan. 1995. *Amazing Grace: The Lives of Children and the Conscience of a Nation.* New York: Broadway Paperbacks.

_____. 2006. *Rachel and Her Children: Homeless Families in America.* New York: Three Nation Press.

Latour, Bruno. 2010. *On the Modern Cult of Factish Gods.* London: Duke University Press.

Liebow, Elliot. 1993. *Tell Them Who I Am: The Lives of Homeless Woman.* New Delhi: Penguin Books.

_____. 2003. *Tally's Corner.* New York: Rowman & Littlefield Publishers, INC.

Mander, Harsh. 2010. 'Barefoot: Deaths on the Street.' *The Hindu,* 2 October.

Mander, Harsh and Smita Jacob. 2010. *Homeless Deaths on the Street.* New Delhi: Centre of Equity Studies. Accessed on 10 February 2015. Available at http://centreforequitystudies. org/wp-content/uploads/2012/08/Homeless-deaths-on-the-streets.pdf.

March, Artemis. 1982. 'Review Essay: Female Invisibility in Androcentric Sociological Theory.' *Critical Sociology* 11(2): 99–107.

Nussbaum, Martha. 1999. 'Invisibility and Recognition: Sophocles' *Philoctetes* and Ellison's *Invisible Man.*' *Philosophy and Literature* 23(2): 257–83.

Phelan, Peggy. 1993. *Unmarked.* London: Routledge.

Robinson, Sally. 2000. *Marked Men.* New York: Columbia University Press.

Scott, James C. 1985. *Weapons of the Weak.* New Haven and London: Yale University Press.

Sen, Amartya. 1999. *Development as Freedom.* New York: Anchor Books.

Spivak, Gayatri. 1988. 'Can the Subaltern Speak?' In *Marxism and the Interpretation of Culture,* edited by Cary Nelson and Lawrence Grossberg, 271–313. Urbana: University of Illinois Press.

Sudan, Avinash S. 2014. 'Who Cares for City's Homeless?' *Deccan Herald,* 12 April.

Tipple, Graham and Suzanne Speak. 2009. *The Hidden Millions: Homeless in Developing Countries.* London: Routledge.

Varman, Rohit, Per Skålén and Russell W Belk. 2012. 'Conflicts at the Bottom of the Pyramid: Profitability, Poverty Alleviation, and Neoliberal Governmentality.' *Journal of Public Policy and Marketing* 31(1): 19–35.

Vikas, Ram M. and Rohit Varman. 2007. 'Erasing Futures: Ethics of Marketing Intoxicants to Homeless Children.' *Consumption, Markets and Culture* 10(2): 189–202.

Vikas, Ram M., Rohit Varman and Russell W Belk. 2015. 'Status, Caste, and Market in a Changing Indian Village.' *Journal of Consumer Research* 42(3): 472–98.

Wolf, Judith, Maurice van Luijtelaar, Carinda Jansen and Strid Altena. 2008. 'Measuring Client Satisfaction in Shelters and Housing Projects for Homeless People.' *European Journal of Homelessness* 2: 335–38.

5

Alternative Spaces of Employment Generation in India

Informal Rules, Structures and Conflicting Organisational Requirements

Joydeep Guha and Bhaskar Chakrabarti

This chapter is about how panchayats, institutions of rural local government in India, cope with conflicting organisational requirements. These requirements arise from the need to harmonise the organisation's internal processes with constraints imposed by the other organisations involved in rural development projects and the electoral necessity of satisfying popular aspirations. Using ethnographic methods like participant observations and unstructured interviews we analyse implementation of the Mahatma Gandhi National Rural Employment Guarantee Act (MGNREGA) in three districts of the eastern Indian state of West Bengal. Our study reveals that conflicting organisational requirements and stakeholder interests necessitate deviations from prescribed procedures. In such a situation a panchayat's success depends on its ability to camouflage deviations by formulation and enforcement of informal rules with the active support of different stakeholders.

The present three-tier panchayats[1] in West Bengal came into existence in 1978. During its prolonged and uninterrupted existence, it has been entrusted with the responsibility of providing all services required by the rural citizens (Robinson, 2005). This not only makes it an important institution for rural citizens but also imparts considerable political importance to it. It is acknowledged that winning the panchayat elections is the first step towards forming a government at the state level (Chakrabarti, 2016). While a panchayat's political importance makes it prone to perils of partisan politics (Kundu, 2009), inadequate fiscal decentralisation makes it dependent on external funding agencies (Robinson, 2005). Thus, panchayats not only have to deal with their internal processes formulated by the Panchayati Raj Department, but have to abide by funding agencies' guidelines. Moreover, the presence of different political combinations at different tiers of panchayat and dynamics of politician-bureaucracy relationship make partisan politics integral to their functioning.

The MGNREGA, with a dual focus on providing guaranteed employment and creating rural assets, is the flagship rural development initiative of the Indian government. While the financial liability of the MGNREGA is shared by the union and state governments in 75:25 ratio, panchayats are responsible for identifying works, framing projects, selecting beneficiaries, executing projects and paying wages. However, panchayats have to perform the above functions after complying with the guidelines issued by the union and state governments (MoRD, 2008). The MGNREGA's relationship with rural livelihood also makes it a politically important programme.

Our study covers eight village panchayats in three districts of West Bengal. Using a decentred approach (Davies, 2009) by employing ethnographic methods like participant observation and study of artefacts like government orders, implementation guidelines, management information systems (MIS) reports, in-depth interview with bureaucrats, politicians and other actors associated with MGNREGA implementation, we find that deviations become necessary for a variety of stated and unstated reasons. In order to ensure sustained funding, it also becomes necessary to camouflage such deviations through record keeping and enforcement of locally arrived decisions with the active support of different stakeholders.

The rest of the chapter is organised as follows. We begin with a brief description of the structure and importance of panchayats in West Bengal. This is followed by an overview of the MGNREGA implementation process. The methodology and site selection are taken up in the next section. Key findings from fieldwork and thematic analysis of the data are presented in the fifth section, followed by our concluding remarks in the sixth section.

Panchayats in West Bengal

West Bengal is one of the pioneers in rural decentralisation. While history of West Bengal's rural decentralisation starts with the enactment of West Bengal Panchayat Act in 1957, the three-tier panchayats came into existence in 1978. All the three tiers are constituted through regular electoral process where political parties contest elections. The village, block and district panchayats are headed by Gram Pradhan, Sabhapati and Sabhadhipati, respectively. They enjoy greater power compared to other members because all decisions of panchayats have to be approved by them and they are accountable for decisions of a panchayat.

Although political decentralisation and a better implementation of developmental plans were the ostensible reasons for instituting panchayats, it also had a strong political rationale. The Left Front (LF), which came to power in 1977, wanted to create a permanent support base among rural landless and marginal farmers by introducing radical land reforms (Webster, 1992). The panchayat was the vehicle through which this was sought to be achieved (Chakrabarti, 2016). While party activists mobilised masses, panchayats implemented radical reforms like redistribution of ceiling surplus land and providing security of tenure to tenant farmers (Kundu, 2009). These did not have a smooth sailing and encountered stiff bureaucratic resistance. As district bureaucracy was reluctant to share power with panchayats, the LF-controlled panchayats considered bureaucracy as the biggest obstacle to implementation of radical land reforms. Thus, senior officials like Block Development Officers (BDOs) and District Magistrates became targets of political agitations like sit-in demonstrations, blockades and protests (Webster, 1992, 137). However, the ruling LF government's political will resulted in an ever-increasing role of panchayats. This led to a gradual acceptance of panchayat's role by bureaucratic apparatuses at district and block levels and a decreasing animosity between politicians and bureaucrats.

Subsequently, the West Bengal Panchayati Raj Act was amended in 1992[2] – the year when constitutional amendments took place in India in recognition of the Panchayati Raj Institutions by including provisions like mandatory elections after every five years, protection against arbitrary dissolution and transfer of functions to panchayats concerning the day-to-day life of rural citizens. Functions transferred to panchayats included land reforms, minor irrigation, agricultural development, education, health services, supply of drinking water, social forestry, cottage industry, animal husbandry and so on (MoPRD, 2009, 6). Panchayats are also responsible for planning, beneficiary selection and implementation of all developmental schemes sponsored by the central and state governments. However, a firm establishment of political party-controlled panchayats brought about significant changes in rural society as people realised that traditional sources of power like caste and economic status were replaced by political affiliation. However, such a realignment of population on party lines also made panchayats vulnerable to politics of patronage and partisan politics started influencing beneficiary selection. While 'politicisation of development' was reported way back in 1989 (Webster, 1992), gradually it metamorphosed into exclusion based on political considerations (Bardhan et al., 2008) and created a situation where party functionaries exercise effective power and critical decisions are taken at party offices (Kundu, 2009). While this was evident in the working of the LF government which was in power in the state of West Bengal from 1977 to 2011, the present ruling party in the state, the Trinamool Congress (TMC), which came to power with a massive victory in 2011, and won most elections in the state panchayat elections in 2013, is also keen to exercise political control over the panchayats.

Politics is not the only factor affecting functioning of panchayats. While they have been made responsible for a large number of functions and decentralisation of financial powers, transfer of personnel needed for discharge of these functions have lagged behind (Robinson, 2005). As a result, panchayats have to depend on different government departments for funding and execution of different activities falling under their jurisdiction. These organisations, though not part of Panchayati Raj Institutions, are indispensable for the effective functioning of panchayats. This results in the coexistence of a number of organisations such as elected panchayats, district administration, and different line departments (Figure 5.1).

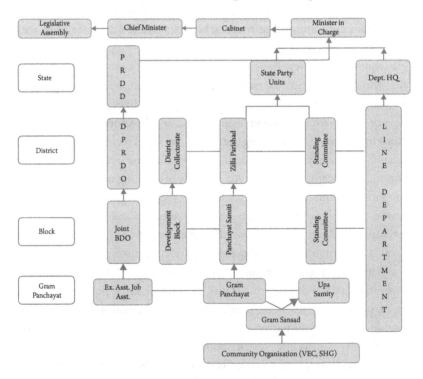

Figure 5.1: Organisation of panchayats

Source: SRD Cell, MoPRD, Govt. of West Bengal.

As is evident from this structure, while elected representatives in panchayats are responsible for implementation of schemes, they have to rely on the line departments of state administration for technical expertise and on district administration for staffing and other forms of support. Thus, successful implementation of any scheme requires cooperation and coordination among a large number of agencies. Moreover, with limited revenue, panchayats have to depend on the central and state governments for funds. These funding difficulties constrain the functioning of panchayats (Bardhan and Mookherjee, 2006) and most elected representatives blame irregular fund flow for delayed execution of projects (Ghatak and Ghatak 2002).

The MGNREGA

The MGNREGA, 2005 is a flagship rural development initiative of the Indian government that seeks to provide 100 days of guaranteed employment to every registered rural household by employing them in rural asset creation projects (MoRD, 2005, 1). Early studies indicate that the MGNREGA has been successful in targeting the most marginalised households (Jha, Gahia and Shankar. 2008), acting as a source of hunger alleviation and preventing rural-urban migration (Khera and Nayak, 2009), and is leading to women empowerment (Narayanan, 2008). There are also reports of misuse of funds for unauthorised activities (Gopal, 2009) and corruption (Vanaik, 2008). However, our interest in the MGNREGA lies in finding out how the complex organisational structure of panchayats and the quagmire of rules and procedures impact its implementation.

MGNREGA implementation involves close coordination among different tiers of government. While the Gram Panchayats[3] have been assigned the most important functions like registration of rural households, providing employment to job-seekers within stipulated time and planning and execution of projects, the block and district offices play critical role in fund allotment, technical vetting of projects and monitoring MGNREGA implementation (MoRD, 2008).

As per MGNREGA guidelines, intending beneficiaries register themselves with the Gram Panchayat and are provided with job-cards. Any registered household can demand employment by applying in the prescribed form. The inability to provide an employment within fifteen days from the demand makes the beneficiary eligible for an unemployment allowance. The daily attendance of labourers, amount of work done and wage payable are recorded in project-specific muster rolls (MR). Supervisors[4] responsible for monitoring individual projects complete MRs and submit them to a Gram Panchayat office for payment. The

wage payment information is entered in a dedicated software called NREGASoft and uploaded on the MGNREGA website (www.mgnrega.nic.in).

The MGNREGA implementation starts with the preparation of an Annual Action Plan (AAP) containing the complete list of projects likely to be implemented in the next financial year. The AAP prepared by a panchayat and approved by the Gram Sabha[5] is forwarded to the District Nodal Officer through the Block Programme Officer. However, before implementing any of these projects a panchayat is required to frame project estimates, get it technically vetted and approved by a competent authority.[6] Funds for new and on-going projects are allotted on the basis of a periodic fund requisition and utilisation certificate submitted by panchayats.

The allotment of funds is dependent on two criteria. First, 60 per cent of funds already allotted must be utilised before the next allotment takes place. Second, expenditure reported in the utilisation certificate must be reflected on the website. Quantum of fund allotted is regulated by the average quarterly utilisation and funds available with the district office. Fund allotment proposals prepared by the district MGNREGA cell is forwarded to the District Magistrate for approval. A schematic representation of the fund allotment process is given in Figure 5.2.

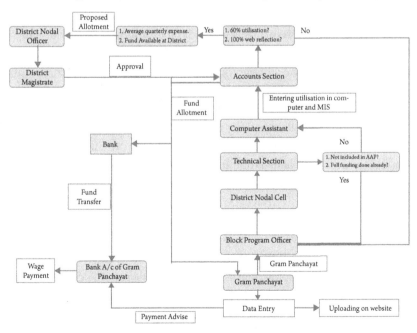

Figure 5.2. Allotment and utilisation of MGNREGA fund

As may be evident from the above description, a successful implementation of MGNREGA hinges upon panchayat's ability to navigate different constraints associated with funding and project formulation. Moreover, its linkage with rural livelihood makes MGNREGA important for political survival of elected panchayats.

Methods

The aim of our enquiry was to examine how MGNREGA implementation gets shaped by the complex organisational structure of panchayats and conflicting rules and regulations. The data pertaining to MGNREGA were collected by conducting in-depth interviews with decision-makers and officials associated with key activities, examining government orders and reports pertaining to MGNREGA implementation and information available on the MGNREGA website.

The two major criteria used for the selection of research site were role of politics in panchayats and political conditions prevailing in different districts and villages. Burdwan, South 24 Parganas and Murshidabad districts were selected as they presented contrasting political realities. Burdwan is one of the three districts (the other two are Jalpaiguri and Bankura) where the LF has won more than 90 per cent of the panchayats at the district level in the last three panchayat elections. Murshidabad is a district that has witnessed frequent changes in political power. While the LF came to power in 1998, the Indian National Congress (INC) regained power in 2003 but lost out narrowly to LF in 2008. South 24 Parganas, another LF bastion, was captured by TMC in the 2008 panchayat elections.

Our fieldwork was conducted in eight panchayats, three each in Murshidabad (Haridevpur, Hukumpur, Chalsa) and South 24 Parganas (Ramnagar, Govinndapur, Shyamnagar) and two in Burdwan (Kalsi, Palashpur) having different political environment. Haridevpur, Ramnagar and Kalsi present instances where all three tiers of panchayat are under the control of same political formation. However, the political formation in question is not the same. Haridevpur and Kalsi are controlled by the LF and Ramnagar is under the control of TMC.[7] Hukumpur, Govinndapur and Palashpur represent instances where the Gram Panchayat is under the control of a political formation which is the political opponent to the party in power at the two higher levels. Thus, while INC and TMC are controlling Hukumpur and Palashpur respectively, the upper two tiers are under the control of the LF. Similarly, Govindapur is under the control of the LF while the upper two tiers are ruled by the TMC.[8] Chalsa under the LF and Shyamnagar under TMC are Gram Panchayats where the ruling and opposition parties are present in more or less equal strengths. These political configurations are represented schematically in

Table 5.1 below. The fieldwork was conducted in two phases. The first phase of the fieldwork, covering Burdwan (December 2010 to February 2011) and South 24 Parganas (March–April 2011) was conducted before the 2011 Assembly elections that resulted in the electoral decimation of the LF at the hands of the TMC-INC alliance (eventually TMC, once they broke the alliance). The continuation of the fieldwork was not possible after the second week of April 2011 as the entire government machinery was engaged in the Assembly elections. The fieldwork in Murshidabad district was conducted in April-May 2012 after allowing some time for the new ruling dispensation to settle down.

Table 5.1: Political configuration of Gram Panchayats

District	Gram Panchayat	Political configuration
Murshidabad	Haridevpur	All three tiers of panchayat under control of LF
	Hukumpur	Gram Panchayat controlled by INC while upper two tiers under LF
	Chalsa	Gram Panchayat controlled by LF but INC present in equal strength
South 24 Parganas	Ramnagar	All three tiers under control of TMC
	Govindapur	Gram Panchayat under LF control while upper two tiers under TMC
	Shyamnagar	TMC-controlled Gram Panchayat having equal representation as combined opposition strength (LF and INC)
Burdwan	Kalsi	All three tiers controlled by LF
	Palashpur	Gram Panchayat under TMC while upper two tiers under LF

Source: Authors, prepared during the time of the study.

Findings

The fieldwork in Burdwan was conducted at a time when the assembly elections' dates were about to be announced and the winds of an imminent political change were palpable. Burdwan is one of the best performing districts in terms of MGNREGA implementation. However, there is a perception in the district-level bureaucracy that the amount being spent is not getting reflected in the rural asset creation. Although district-level bureaucrats did not elaborate much on this issue but the reasons became evident during our fieldwork and are presented in the next section. The Kalsi and Palashpur Gram Panchayats have little in common. Kalsi is a part of the electoral constituency of one of the powerful cabinet ministers and has no opposition member. It enjoys excellent transport and communication facilities. It is highly urbanised and the majority of people is engaged in non-agricultural activities. It is one of the best-performing panchayats in terms of the utilisation of MGNREGA funds.

In contrast, Palashpur is the only TMC-controlled panchayat in this block. The physical distance from the block office and the absence of internet or fax facility result in a considerable delay in the flow of information. During our fieldwork, an allotment was held up because the expenditure reported by the panchayat was not available on the website (http://nrega.nic.in). Two features common in both panchayats were the political roles played by supervisors responsible for monitoring projects and the general reluctance of people to work for a full day's wage. Villagers by and large have construed MGNREGA as a scheme that guarantees 100 days of wage and not as 100 days of guaranteed employment. As a result, they are unwilling to work for what they consider as their entitlement. The extent to which this is permitted depends on the supervisor responsible for monitoring a project and her or his political allegiance. Since supervisors owe allegiance to the ruling party, citizens loyal to opposition parties are discriminated against. They either get lesser days of employment or are entrusted with duties involving hard labour. This issue has been elaborated in greater detail in the next section.

The fieldwork in South 24 Parganas was conducted after the announcement of the 2011 Assembly election schedule and the electoral Model Code of Conduct[9] had come into force. The power to run a panchayat gets transferred to bureaucracy when the Model Code of Conduct is in force as panchayats cannot commence implementation of any new project without the prior approval of the district nodal office. Thus, the underlying power struggle between politicians and bureaucrats come into open as politicians are not willing to comply with bureaucratic diktats while bureaucracy is not ready to loosen its control over project implementation. The fieldwork was conducted in Ramnagar, Govindapur and Shyamnagar Gram Panchayats having contrasting political environment and located in the southernmost block of the district. Being located in the Sunderban delta region, tidal waves form a part of daily life in all the three Gram Panchayats. Tidal waves can strike at any location at any time causing immense loss of property and livelihood. Thus, embankments have to be erected and repaired at short notice to safeguard life and property of villagers. However, the MGNREGA operating procedure requires advance planning and is not suited to deal with such natural uncertainties. Thus, all three panchayats are forced to deviate from MGNREGA guidelines in order to cope with the constant threat of tidal waves. However, the bureaucracy-politician power tussle made such deviations difficult and the MGNREGA implementation had come to a grinding halt at the time of our fieldwork.

The fieldwork in the three panchayats of Murshidabad was conducted in April and May 2012. They fall under the same block[10] but have contrasting political realities. Haridevpur is the LF's stronghold and the present Gram Pradhan has been in office for the last twenty years. In contrast, the INC came to power in Hukumpur in 2008. The Chalsa panchayat contains an equal number of representatives from both the LF and the INC. The presence of political rivals in equal strength has resulted in frequent political defections and three different persons have become Gram Pradhans during the last four years. An intense political rivalry had vitiated the atmosphere to such an extent that in 2011–12 they were unable to arrive at a consensus about locations where projects would be implemented.

One interesting feature of MGNREGA's implementation is that the scope of computerisation extends far beyond that of the other two districts. The MGNREGA software is used for generation of payment advice being sent to banks for crediting bank account of wage earners. It has also tried to simplify fund allotment process by doing away with fund requisition process. Instead, details of expenditure are entered in NREGASoft and uploaded on the website even before payment is actually released. This enables the district office to ascertain quantum of funds required by different Gram Panchayats and release funds accordingly. However, as the discussion in the next section shows, extensive computerisation and process simplification have failed to ensure smooth flow of funds, and, as a result, delayed wage payment is quite common. At the time of our fieldwork, all three panchayats were having huge carried forward liability from the previous financial year. The prominent role of Panchayat Samiti (an intermediate institution at the block level) in MGNREGA implementation is another distinguishing feature of this district. However, as the subsequent discussion shows, the opposition party-controlled panchayats challenge the legitimacy of projects implemented by Panchayat Samiti and create hurdles for future implementation.

We found that deviation from the prescribed procedure is a feature common to MGNREGA implementation in all the eight Gram Panchayats where we conducted our fieldwork. We now examine different types of deviations and the underlying reasons that make them necessary.

Decoupling everyday practices from formal rules

The MGNREGA guidelines framed by the Ministry of Rural Development (MoRD) do not take into account the requirements of all sections of people. For example, construction of concrete roads is not permissible under MGNREGA. However, the people of the highly urbanised Kalsi panchayat demand better roads. The panchayat obliges them by constructing all-weather concrete roads in contravention to MGNREGA guidelines (Figure 5.3). However, in doing so they have to somehow maintain the mandatory 60:40 wage to material ratio. The following incident gives us a hint about the mechanism through which this is achieved. At one of the pond re-excavation projects in this panchayat, 354 workers were engaged. However, less than 100 people were present during our visit (Figure 5.4). The supervisor[11] explained that only 100–120 people are engaged every week so that everyone gets an opportunity to work. Although work had started one week back in most places the pond had been dug 1–2 ft and the work was yet to begin in many parts. The Nirman Sahayak, the permanent employee of a panchayat responsible for framing estimates and supervising all technical projects, informed that the pond is supposed to be dug 6 ft deep. However, the supervisor immediately responded that this would not be possible this year and will be taken up in subsequent years. The labour–material ratio is maintained within the stipulated

Figure 5.3: All-weather concrete road in B1
Source: Photos taken by the first author.

Figure 5.4: Re-excavation of pond at B1 Gram Panchayat
Source: Photos taken by the first author.

limit by implementing a large number of projects and by employing more than the required manpower. People do not complain as they get paid more than what they had worked for.

Towards the end of our fieldwork, a high-level inspection by MoRD objected to this blatant violation of the MGNREGA norms. Interestingly, instead of issuing orders for not sanctioning such projects the District Administration issued an order requesting the BDOs to instruct Pradhans 'not to take up any of those schemes further under MGNREGA'. The question which came to our mind was that why did it require inspection by MoRD team? The project should not have been approved in the first place. A district-level officer commented that MGNREGA implementation would be stopped if projects are scrutinised too meticulously. This would be unacceptable to both panchayats as well as District Magistrates as MGNREGA implementation is one of the most important evaluation criteria for both. Thus, the bureaucratic apparatus and politicians collude to decouple everyday practices from procedural guidelines so that popular aspirations can be addressed and their core concerns are safeguarded.

Cooperation in a network

Tackling the damage caused by tidal waves is a part of the daily life in the three panchayats of South 24 Parganas. Since MGNREGA guidelines, involving advance planning, are not suited for dealing with uncertainties of nature's fury the panchayats are forced to deviate from the prescribed procedure to safeguard life and property of residents.

The fragile mud embankments erected along the entire coastline get damaged by tidal waves and require repairs at a short notice. To deal with such emergencies, panchayats have sub-divided embankments into smaller segments and prepare AAPs covering all segments. Such a division ensures that the projected expenditure is within the Nirman Sahayak's sanctioning power because projects requiring vetting by the Executive Engineer involve a longer processing time. Since the same embankment can be damaged more than once, two estimates – one for the riverfront and the second for the earth-front – are prepared for each segment. If needed, both estimates can be used for repairing the same embankment. Even this may be insufficient due to a repeated damage of the same embankment. In such a case, project pertaining to an adjacent segment is utilised. Another way of tackling the problem is by keeping the status of projects 'on-going' so that they can be utilised in case of an emergency because no expenditure can be incurred on closed projects.

Since this is an issue of overwhelming public interest, elected representatives are forced to adopt this course of action. However, it requires the active cooperation of the Nirman Sahayak. A Nirman Sahayak has to measure the volume of work done under a particular project and certify each MR before wages are paid. Thus, whenever an embankment is repaired using an estimate pertaining to another site, the Nirman Sahayak has to certify the work done having full knowledge of the deviation. The BDO is also kept informed because there are situations when technical vetting is done after the work has been completed. Bureaucrats cooperate as long as proper paperwork is maintained. Thus, special care is taken for the preparation of error-free MRs and supporting documents. Since muster rolls prepared by supervisors are full of errors, Ramnagar and Shyamnagar panchayats do not hand over MRs to them. Supervisors submit records of daily attendance and final measurement to panchayat offices. The contractual persons hired by panchayats prepare MRs and subsidiary records in the panchayat offices. The payment to these contractual employees is made from MGNREGA funds in an ingenious way. Each project has a provision of about INR 2,000 for purposes like water jug, shed, temporary boards, etc. The actual spending on these items is curtailed and the resultant savings are used for making payments to persons engaged in the preparation of proper documentation. This again requires the cooperation of the Nirman Sahayak because he has to certify inflated bills related to permissible items on which money can be spent.

An accurate measurement of work done is another problem associated with these projects. Since tidal waves wash away freshly created embankments and deposit silt into pits dug for excavating earth, an accurate measurement of work is impossible. This creates the possibility of misuse of public funds by way of inflated wage bills. Nirman Sahayaks of the three panchayats deal with this problem in their own ways. While the Nirman Sahayak of Ramnagar certifies measurement taken by supervisors if it is within 10 per cent of the measurement done by him, the official at Shyamnagar insists that the final measurements should be done in his presence. The official at Govindapur does not bother to verify the measurement. However, as the following incident narrated by an official of Shyamnagar shows, there is an inherent safeguard against a gross misuse of public money.

Residents of another Gram Sansad[12] were employed to repair an embankment. Since the workers were not residents of the village where the embankment was located,[13] they were primarily interested in getting paid with a minimum effort. As a result, the quality of work was poor and tidal waves damaged the embankment. Local residents were furious and they sent a message with their protest that when it comes to matters relating to life and property quality of work should not suffer. After this incident the panchayat always provided employment to local residents for embankment work. Thus, quality of work is assured as long as local workers are employed.

In summary, it is known that actors in a network are willing to cooperate to achieve network goals as long as their core interests are satisfied (Klijn, 2005). Since MGNREGA guidelines do not take care of the special needs of this area, panchayats have to find local solutions for dealing with their problem but this requires cooperation of all actors involved in the process. Panchayats are forced to deviate from the prescribed practice because protecting citizens from vagaries of tidal waves is a political compulsion of those elected in panchayats. The state bureaucracy is willing to cooperate as long as such deviations are not detected. Since an error-free MR makes detection of irregularities extremely difficult and ensures that the data requirement of NREGASoft are met, extra caution is taken for preparing MRs. A timely uploading of expenditure on the website leads to allotment of greater funds and future work is not jeopardised.

Conflicts between politicians and the bureaucracy

An intermittent flow of funds and delayed payment of wages are chronic problems faced by most of the panchayats. This has led to the adoption of different measures for streamlining flow of funds. However, as the following critical incidents show, results obtained are not always satisfactory.

Panchayats in South 24 Parganas resort to pressure tactics wherein panchayats start projects without waiting for funds and send agitated labourers to block offices in the case of a delay in fund allotment. At times they send applications demanding work to the block office to prove that demand for work is there but work cannot be started due to the non-availability of funds. Some of the panchayats have entered into a strategic alliance with a local NGO. The NGO mobilises people to submit demand for work in times when the panchayat is facing fund shortage. The panchayat finds itself in a difficult situation. If it provides employment, then wage payment will get delayed due to non-availability of funds. If it fails to provide work within fifteen days, then it has to pay an unemployment allowance as per the MGNREGA guidelines. This would in turn attract an adverse attention of the district office and the BDO would have to explain reasons for such a payment. Moreover, political opponents would try to discredit the panchayat by highlighting its failure to provide employment.

Unlike South 24 Parganas, where the bureaucracy-politician relationship is mired in a power struggle, officials of Kalsi panchayat share an extremely cordial relationship with the district bureaucracy and have the right political connections. As a result, they have the information on the district office's funds in advance. Armed with this advance information, officials in Kalsi panchayat start a parallel planning of different activities. The work on projects starts as soon as the fund requisition is sent. Estimates for fresh projects are also processed simultaneously. Since MR data are ready by the time fund is received, wage payment and uploading payment information are done immediately on receipt of funds. As a result, the next fund requisition alongwith a utilisation certificate is ready in three to four days.

In contrast, panchayats in Murshidabad try to get over the problem by introducing process re-engineering. After a fund requisition has been dispensed, panchayats upload MR data on the MGNREGA website before payment. Thus, the district cell knows the financial liabilities of different panchayats and is able to allocate funds accordingly. However, this has failed to solve the problem and the three Gram Panchayats had accumulated liabilities of INR 7.51 million, 3.22 million and 3.34 million at the time of our fieldwork.

On examining the past two years' fund flow information (Table 5.2) we could see that the flow of funds dries up during the first few months of a financial year. This is because the union budget is placed before the Parliament in February and the parliamentary approval is obtained in the month of May. The allotment and disbursement of funds starts from June onwards. Thus, during these first

Table 5.2: Fund allotment during 2011–12 and 2012–13

Fund allotment for 2011–12 (in million rupees)						Fund allotment for 2012–13 (in million rupees)					
M1		M2		M3		M1		M2		M3	
Date received	Amount	Date received	Amount	Date received	Amount	Date received	Amount	Date received	Amount	Date received	Amount
19/04/2011	1.50	15/09/2011	0.50	01/04/2012	0.10	18/04/2012	0.8	18/04/2012	0.4	18/04/2012	0.4
27/05/2011	1.00	27/10/2011	0.15	01/10/2012	0.10	25/04/2012	2	25/04/2012	1.5	25/04/2012	1.5
29/08/2011	0.50	18/11/2011	0.90	01/11/2012	0.10	05/05/2012	1	05/05/2012	0.8	05/05/2012	0.4
29/09/2011	0.80	28/12/2011	0.30	27/01/2012	0.20	06/11/2012	0.35				
21/10/2011	3.00	01/10/2012	0.20	30/01/2012	0.20	14/06/2012	0.7				
13/03/2012	1.00	30/01/2012	0.30	21/02/2012	0.20						
16/03/2012	0.70	21/02/2012	0.50	03/01/2012	0.20						
		03/12/2012	0.40	03/07/2012	0.30						
		16/03/2012	0.80	16/03/2012	0.40						
		22/03/2012	0.80								

Source: http://www.nrega.nic.in (downloaded on 07/07/2012)

Source: http://nrega.nic.in.

three months of the financial year limited funds are available with departments. However, less agricultural activity and conditions favourable for manual labour make December to March the most active period for MGNREGA implementation. Moreover, panchayats are in a hurry to commence projects before the end of March because funds lapse at end of a financial year. March being the peak season for MGNREGA work, the financial year begins with a backlog of unpaid wages. Inadequate funding during the first few months results in wages remaining unpaid when the next phase of activities begins.

In summary, Kalsi has overcome the funding problem by utilising its harmonious relationship with the district bureaucracy that allows it to do a parallel planning of different activities. A hostile bureaucracy-politician relationship has forced panchayats in South 24 Parganas to resort to pressure tactics resulting in mixed results. Murshidabad's attempt to re-engineer process has run into obstacles created by a mismatch between the fund flow from the top and MGNREGA activities.

Overcoming restrictions imposed by the software

NREGASoft, the dedicated software for recording MGNREGA-related information, forms a very important part of MGNREGA implementation because the data entered in it get reflected on the website. While the software is designed for monitoring by higher-level users, it has been put to innovative use by different Gram Panchayats. For example, in Palashpur panchayat MR data are entered in the software before wage payment to ensure that wage payment data pertain only to the registered workers. The village-level entrepreneur, the contractual employee responsible for the data entry, informed us that uploading of MR data takes a long time as they contained many workers whose names were not available in the database. Such a situation arose because names of family members were entered without coming to the panchayat office. A considerable amount of time was spent in updating the database and this resulted in delayed allotment of funds.

However, the most innovative use of the software has been made in Murshidabad. A direct involvement of Panchayat Samiti in the MGNREGA implementation is a distinguishing feature of this district. This has been necessitated by two reasons. First, panchayats' inability to implement projects due to political fragmentation prompted the Block Programme Officer to implement projects of the Panchayat Samiti (an intermediate institution functioning at the block level) to provide employment to people living in those villages. Second, since employment is often related to political affiliation, Panchayat Samiti is particularly active in the opposition-controlled Gram Panchayats.

However, this creates problem in data entry. This is because the NREGASoft database is created Gram Panchayat wise and the MR data for projects executed by Panchayat Samiti have to be entered by Gram Panchayats. However, Gram Panchayats are reluctant to enter such data due to political rivalry. To overcome this problem, the district MIS coordinator has appended different tables of the database and has created a combined database. However, as the following critical incident shows, this has not solved the problem fully and Gram Panchayats strike back at an opportune moment.

The Pradhan of Hukumpur panchayat narrated an incident that occurred when the panchayat was in the process of issuing new job-cards.[14] An applicant was not eligible for the renewal of a job-card because no employment was recorded in the employment register maintained at the panchayat.[15] However, his job-card showed that Panchayat Samiti provided him employment. The applicant was told to approach the authority that had provided him employment for renewing the job-card. Since Panchayat Samiti cannot issue a job-card so the applicant gave a written application to the BDO. The BDO returned the application to the applicant with an endorsement to the Pradhan, without giving any specific instruction. The applicant returned to panchayat. However, the panchayat refused to accept the endorsement, because it did not come through the official channel.

In summary, restrictions imposed by the logic of the centralised software come in the way of meeting the needs of local implementation. Software modifications removing these restrictions fail to provide a lasting solution as the underlying political factors remain unaddressed. In contrast, the smooth working relationship between politicians and bureaucrats working at different tiers of panchayat in Burdwan facilitates flow of information and ensures a continuous supply of funds.

Divergent social construction of the MGNREGA

In all three districts, people conceive the MGNREGA as a scheme that guarantees 100 days of wage payment and not as 100 days of guaranteed employment. This feeling of entitlement translates into a general reluctance for a full day's wage.[16] The incident from Kalsi panchayat where the number of persons present is far less than the number of persons who should be present shows that inflated wage bills are not uncommon. Is this phenomenon restricted to the ruling party controlled panchayats only? Hukumpur panchayat's Pradhan informed us that, Panchayat Samiti employs workers who are loyal to the ruling party and the yardstick used for wage payment is different from that used by the panchayat. This creates a problem because people want to know why some people get paid for lesser work. Similarly, the Palashpur panchayat Pradhan told us that villagers complain that for the same wage they work more compared to people in neighbouring villages. The Pradhan and an influential TMC leader explained how they have to explain to villagers that they need to be more careful as this is an opposition-controlled panchayat.

However, the following incident challenges the validity of this claim. On our way to the panchayat office, Nirman Sahayak suddenly stopped and paid a surprise visit to one of the projects. He found that ninety eight were present though the attendance board declared the presence of 117 workers. The supervisor, who was absent during our visit, came to meet the Nirman Sahayak in the panchayat office. He demanded to know why he was not informed about the visit and claimed that only he can ascertain the exact number of workers. From his narration it became clear that the number of workers is ascertained indirectly. Workers are divided into groups and each group has a leader. If a particular leader responds when his/her name is called out, then all members of that group are deemed to be present. The meaning of being 'more careful' mentioned by the Pradhan became clear when the Assistant Nirman Sahayak explained how people's expectations can be met without getting caught. Workers need to stay at the site between 8 am to 1 pm to earn a full day's wage, the most common period when inspections take place. If an inspection takes place later then it can be explained that work had started early and workers had left.

An incident from Govindapur panchayat in South 24 Parganas reveals difficulties in accurate measurements and the complete inaction of village-level bureaucracy facilitates this process. During one of our visits a supervisor came to the panchayat office with a bundle of MRs. We found that two days' wages for every day's attendance was noted against each name but the amount of work done was not noted. Nirman Sahayak asked him to multiply the number of male man-day by 176 and female man-day by 150 to arrive at the amount of earth excavated (male and female workers are required to excavate 88 and 75 cubic ft earth respectively to earn full wages) and to record the measurement accordingly.

The role of street-level bureaucrats in shaping policy outcomes (Lipsky, 1980) by applying discretion to bridge gap between policy guidelines and popular expectations (Winter, 2012) is well known. Evidence also suggests that application of such discretionary powers often has the tacit approval of the higher levels of authority (Kathryn, 2011). Social construction of the MGNREGA as a scheme that guarantees 100 days of wage (and not 100 days of employment) creates a gap between policy prescription and popular perception. The formulation and enforcement of local rules become necessary for bridging this gap. This is done through the agency of supervisor. Thus, application of discretionary powers is not the only way in which street-level bureaucrats influence policy outcomes. They can also have a significant impact on policy outcomes by way of formulation and enforcement of locally arrived at rules that seek to bridge the gap between a policy prescription and popular perception.

The political panchayat and bureaucratic apparatus involved in MGNREGA implementation are two parallel hierarchies having different goals and priorities. As the following incidents show, outcomes of these differences depend on the bureaucracy-politician relationship.

During one of our visits to the South 24 Parganas district nodal office, a key official associated with the fund allotment process received a call from executive assistant of one of the panchayats. He was enquiring about a fund allotment. He was informed that the fund was not allotted because they were yet to utilise 60 per cent of already allotted funds. The panchayat official informed that the work had already started and funds were needed for payment. The district official told him that he had come to know that employment was provided within three days of application. This was unnecessary because work needs to be provided within fifteen days. They would have spent 60 per cent of funds if they had waited for fifteen days. Thus, the problem had been created because of a deviation from the prescribed procedure.

On another occasion, the same officer received a frantic call from one of the Block Program Officers. Activists of a local NGO that mobilises villagers to demand work in times of fund scarcity had laid siege to his office and were demanding an unemployment allowance. He asked the officer to ascertain the number of households who demanded work. If less than fifty households demanded work, then they should be accommodated in the on-going projects in other villages. If the number of households exceeds fifty then he should wait for fifteen days before starting a new work. This is because MGNREGA stipulates that 100 days employment is to be given to each registered household and not to every registered person.

However, this interpretation is not acceptable to panchayats because every registered worker is a voter and they try to provide employment to anyone who demands work. Moreover, the seasonal nature of MGNREGA activities implies that work can be done only in specific periods. Thus, the modus operandi recommended by bureaucrats will lead to very low employment generation, which is not acceptable to panchayats.

In contrast to the hostile bureaucracy in South 24 Parganas, Burdwan presents a picture of cooperation. The district MGNREGA cell has published a booklet of model estimates that is extremely useful to panchayats. Furthermore, the district cell prepares estimates for projects involving higher level of technical inputs. For example, estimates for the Rajiv Gandhi Seva Kendra have been prepared and sanctioned at the district MGNREGA cell. Similarly, the district office has issued a letter to all panchayats listing the common mistakes committed by them in preparing fund requisitions in the past.

The bureaucratic cooperation is not only restricted to a facilitative role and there are ways in which they actively collaborate with panchayats. For example, monthly progress report (MPR) is one of the most important reports relating to MGNREGA implementation. It is checked thoroughly by officials before forwarding to the state headquarter. Although there is no prescribed checklist, the official responsible for checking MPR has prepared a guideline on the basis of his interactions with state officials. Accordingly, the main issues which are checked are (a) per day wage should be in the range of INR 85 to INR 110; (b) expenditure per person-day (labour, material and contingency) should be about INR 167; (c) employment per household should show an increasing trend; (d) wage to non-wage ratio should be around 60:40; and (e) administrative expenditure should be around 6 per cent of the total expenditure. Although this information is not passed on to panchayats, if their reports do not conform to these standards, then they are asked to revise. These measures are in bureaucratic interest as they help in hiding blatant violation of rules and create a picture of normalcy to an external user.

It is known that depending on the circumstances, political executive and bureaucracy develop collaborative, adverserial, or submissive relationships. An adverserial relation develops when the two compete for power, a collaborative relation develops when their interests converge, and incompetence of politicians leads to transfer of effective power to bureaucrats and a prolonged rule by a single party leads to politicisation of bureaucracy (Peters, 2007). The above examples show that there are significant differences between how bureaucrats and politicians understand different provisions of the implementation guidelines. However, the impact of such differences depends on bureaucracy-politician relationship. While a submissive bureaucracy in Burdwan does not question politician's interpretation, an adversarial relationship in South 24 Parganas leads to a coordination failure.

Until now we have concentrated on deviations that are necessitated by explicit reasons. However, during our fieldwork we found that many of these deviations were also linked to the hidden agenda of political actors. For example, until very late in our fieldwork we were unable to explain why panchayats in South 24 Parganas meet after receipt of funds to decide which projects to start when they have already executed projects long back. The village level officials did not provide a satisfactory answer. A district-level official gave an enigmatic answer that panchayats want a lump sum amount so that they can spend it at their will. During one of our visits to a panchayat we found the Secretary to panchayat busy in signing MRs for work executed three months ago. This delay in the preparation of the MR is inexplicable; the least they could do is to keep MRs ready so that payment could be made immediately on receipt of funds. The Assistant Nirman Sahayak provided the answer during our way back from panchayat office when seeing no one around he elaborated on how the system works. Panchayats execute work without sanctioning projects. On receipt of funds they decide which projects should be processed. Antedated estimates are processed and sanctioned at the panchayat level with the cooperation of the Nirman Sahayak and MRs are prepared accordingly. Thus, politicians are able to exercise greater control over funds. The resulting delay in wage payment is used as a pressure tactic against bureaucracy. If bureaucrats succumb to the pressure, panchayats get greater funds. If bureaucrats stand their ground then political motive is attributed to bureaucratic action and is used to political advantage by politicians.

Similarly, Murshidabad's panchayats' tendency to execute most of the work towards March end when funds are about to dry up is inexplicable. Why can they not execute most of the work in January–February when funds are available? The district nodal officer provided an enigmatic answer that panchayats are not philanthropists. They have to arrange participants for political rallies, entertain visitors, and spend most of their time in panchayat and party offices. In return they get negligible honorarium and are never sure how long they would be in power. He refused to elaborate any further and said that answers would be apparent once we visit the field. We got the answer from a block-level official involved in the computer cell towards the fag end our fieldwork. The execution of a large number of projects in March ensures a delay in payment to a time when everyone is busy in agricultural activities. The preparation of false MRs is easier as people do not recall whether beneficiaries are genuine or not. Moreover, since inspections are done for projects implemented during the financial year so projects executed in March are never inspected. Thus, there is a remote chance of irregularities getting detected.

In summary, the above discussion highlights the importance of hidden agenda (Bruijn and Heuvelhof, 2008) of political actors and the bureaucratic inability to confront the political challenge (Davies, 2009) leading to a weakening of institutional safeguards against opportunistic behaviour (Schrank and Whitford, 2011). While public interest is the ostensible cause for necessitating deviations from the prescribed procedure, many of the deviations are linked to the hidden agenda of political actors. Public interest in invoked to elicit bureaucratic cooperation to deviation from the prescribed procedure. This creates a space for political actor to break free from bureaucratic control and to fulfil her hidden agenda. The relationship between the two gets strained whenever bureaucracy tries to resist fulfilment of hidden agenda of political actors and a harmonious relationship prevails when bureaucratic cooperation is available.

Conclusion

Our three district study on MGNREGA implementation in West Bengal reveals widespread deviation from the prescribed procedure. Since centrally formulated procedural guidelines are inadequate to meet the daily and aspirational needs of people belonging to diverse geographical locations and social strata, panchayats are forced to de-couple everyday practises from the prescribed procedure. Thus, panchayats of South 24 Parganas have devised ways for dealing with the constant threat of tidal waves and all weather concrete roads have been constructed in Kalsi Gram Panchayat Murshidabad's attempt at overcoming restrictions imposed by NREGASoft has met with only a partial success because the underlying political factors remain unaddressed. Some deviations also become necessary for ensuring a smooth flow of funds. As the critical incident from Kalsi shows, such attempts bear fruit when the information about fund availability is available in advance. However, an absence of advance information leads to the failure of extensive process re-engineering in Murshidabad. The funding in South 24 Parganas becomes an arena where panchayats and bureaucrats fight each other for securing greater control. They resort to conflicting interpretation of rules and procedures to justify their stands and the relationship gets mired in strategic games that lead to a complete deadlock. While officials invoke public interest to explain deviations, we often found hidden political agenda and vested interests shaping these outcomes.

The existence of locally arrived at rules and active cooperation of a large number of stakeholders in covering up deviations is a feature common across panchayats. For example, in Burdwan bureaucrats cooperate to construct concrete roads and collaborate with panchayats in preparation of reports that present a picture of normalcy to external observers. The opposition-controlled Palashpur panchayat has devised informal rules that ensure overpayments are not detected.

The solution to tidal waves created by panchayats of South 24 Parganas involves active cooperation of the village and block-level bureaucracy. Since proper documentation is necessary for non-detection of such deviations, special care is taken in the preparation of error free documents. Although this involves wrong classification of expenditure but bureaucrats do not object because it satisfies their core interests.

Through this chapter we have attempted to capture how conflicting organisational requirements, balancing interests and objectives of diverse stakeholders introduce deviations in implementation of the MGNREGA. However, the study suffers from a number of limitations. First, the study was conducted before and after a watershed election. The study needs to be continued after sufficient time has elapsed for stabilisation of the new political regime. Second, it provides a snapshot of implementation of the MGNREGA and does not capture the longitudinal aspect. A more detailed longitudinal study would be necessary in view of some of the changes being introduced in the MGNREGA.[17]

Endnotes

1   District-level Zilla Parishad at the top followed by block-level Panchayat Samiti as the intermediate level and village-level Gram Panchayat forming the lowest tier are the three tiers of panchayat. All the three tiers are constituted through electoral process in which political parties can contest.

2   The first Prime Minister of India, Jawaharlal Nehru, supported the suggestions of the Balwantrai Mehta Committee (set up in 1957) that suggested an establishment of elected local bodies and devolution to them of necessary resources, and power, which should not be constrained by too much control by government or government agencies, but constituted for five years by election, with an aim to developing agriculture with special attention to irrigation, as well as the promotion of other services. During Nehru's time, the jurisdiction regarding the panchayats was given to the states. Different states thereof undertook the process of implementing the Panchayati Raj system. Elections to the village panchayat and the higher, 'area Panchayat' started happening. Panchayats in various states did not at this time, however, develop the requisite democratic momentum since there was resistance at the state level to the sharing of power. The Ajanta government established at the centre in 1977 instituted a committee headed by Asoka Mehta. The report of this committee, once again, argued in favour of devolution of power to the villages. The committee's recommendations included that the district be made the administrative unit for which planning coordination and resource allocation are feasible and technical expertise available, the panchayats be made capable of planning for themselves, and regular elections through participation of political parties happen. Finally, in 1992, through a constitutional amendment, these powers were devolved to the panchayats.

3   The lowest tier of the three tier system of rural local government corresponding to the village.

4   Rural citizens having certain minimum educational qualifications are appointed as supervisors for monitoring implementation of projects executed under MGNREGA. They are paid daily wages from MGNREGA funds.

5   Village assembly.

6   Authority competent for technical vetting and approval depends on the estimated value of the project.

7   Hereafter, referred to as ruling party-controlled panchayats

8   Hereafter referred to as opposition-controlled panchayats

9   Model Code of Conduct (MCC) is a set of guidelines regarding conduct of political functionaries and bureaucrats. It remains in force from date of announcement of election dates and continues till results are declared.

10   Block is the intermediate level in the three tier district administration. It plays a very-important role in functioning of panchayats. It is a vital link in the communication channel between village and district. Expenditure incurred by Gram Panchayats needs to be approved by the BDO. In most cases the BDO also doubles up as the Block Programme Officer for MGNREGA implementation.

11   The panchayat appoints a supervisor for each village for monitoring implementation of individual projects.

12   Each Gram Panchayat is sub-divided into a number of Gram Sansads. Each Gram Sansad elects one representative to the Gram Panchayat.

13   MGNREGA guidelines permit providing employment in nearby Gram Sansads if there is no on-going project in the gram sansad where the labourers are residing. The panchayats generally resort to this practice when labourers press for work in expectation of unemployment allowance, fully aware of the fact that there is no on-going project in their Gram Sansad.

14   As per MGNREGA guidelines, fresh job-cards are to be issued after five years.

15   It was decided that job-card will not be renewed if a person had not done any work during the past five years.

16   Amount of work that needs to be done to claim full days wage is specified in MGNREGA guidelines. Proportionate wage is paid in case of deviation from standard.

17   We would like to acknowledge the assistance provided by a large number of officials associated with the MGNREGA in the three study districts. The first author would also like to thank his employer, the Department of Telecommunications, for granting him a study leave for pursuing this research.

References

Bardhan, P. and D. Mookherjee. 2006. 'Pro-poor Targeting and Accountability of Local Governments in West Bengal.' *Journal of development Economics* 79(2): 303–27.

Bardhan, Pranab, Sandip Mitra, Dilip Mookherjee and Abhirup Sarkar. 2008. 'Political Participation, Clientelism and Targeting of Local Government Programs: Analysis of Survey Results from Rural West Bengal, India.' Institute for Economic Development Working Paper dp-171. Boston: Department of Economics, Boston University.

Chakrabarti, Bhaskar. 2016. *Participation at the Crossroads: Decentralisation and Water Politics in West Bengal.* New Delhi: Orient Blackswan.

Davies, S. Jonathan. 2009. 'The Limits of Joined-up Government: Towards a Political Analysis.' *Public Administration* 87(1) : 80–96.

de Bruijn, Hans and Ernst ten Heuvelhof. 2008. *Management in Networks.* London, NY: Routledge.

Ghatak, Maitreesh and Maitreya Ghatak. 2002. 'Recent Reforms in the Panchayat System in West Bengal.' *Economic and Political Weekly* 37(1): 45–57.

Gopal, K. 2009. 'NREGA Social Audit: Myths and Reality.' *Economic and Political Weekly* 44 (3): 70–71.

Jha, R., R. Gahia and S. Shankar. 2008. 'Reviewing the National Rural Employment Guarantee Programme.' *Economic and Political Weekly* 43(11): 44–48.

Kathryn, Eliis. 2011. 'Street-level Bureaucracy' Revisited: The Changing Face of Frontline Discretion in Adult Social Care in Englandspol.' *Social Policy and Administration* 45(3): 221–44.

Khera, R. and N. Nayak. 2009. 'Women Workers and Perceptions of the National Rural Employment Guarantee Act.' *Economic and Political Weekly* 44(43): 49–57.

Klijn, E. H. 2005. 'Networks and Interorganizational Management: Challenging, Steering, Evaluation, and the Role of Public Actors in Public Management'. In *The Oxford Handbook of Public Administration*, edited by E. Ferlie, 257–80. Oxford: E. H. Klijn.

Kundu, M. 2009. 'Panchayati Raj or Party Raj? Understanding the Nature of Local Government in West Bengal'. In *Inclusion and Exclusion in Local Governance*, edited by B. S. Baviskar and G. Mathew, 107–36. New Delhi: Sage, .

Lipsky, Michael. 1980. *Street-Level Bureaucracy: The Dillemas of the Individual in Public Services.* New York: Russel Sage Foundation.

MoPRD. 2009. *Roadmap for the Panchayats in West Bengal: A Vision Document.* Kolkata: Government of West Bengal.

MoRD. 2005. *The National Rural Employment Guarantee Act-Operational Guidelines.* New Delhi: Government of India.

———. 2008. *The National Rural Employment Guarantee Act-Operational Guidelines.* New Delhi: Government of India.

———. www.rural.nic.in. Accessed on 27 January 2017.

Narayanan, S. 2008. 'Employment Guarantee, Women's Work and Childcare.' *Economic and Political Weekly* 43(9): 10–13.

Peters, B. Guy. 2007. 'Politicians and Bureaucrats in the Politics of Pilicy-Making'. In *Public Governance*, volume 3, edited by Mark Bevir, 37–61. London, Thousand Oaks, New Delhi: Sage.

Robinson, Mark. 2005. 'A Decade of Panchayati Raj Reforms: The Challenge of Democratic Decentralisation in India'. In *Decentralization and Local Governance*, edited by L. C. Jain, 10–30. Delhi: Orient Longman.

Schrank, Andrew and Josh Whitford. 2011. 'The Anatomy of Network Failure.' *Sociological Theory* 29(3): 151–77.

Vanaik, A. 2008. 'NREGA and the Death of Tapas Soren.' *Economic and Political Weekly* 43 (30): 8–10.

Webster, Neil. 1992. 'Panchayati Raj in West Bengal: Popular Participation for the People or the Party?' *Development and Change* 23(4): 129–63.

Winter, Søren C. 2012. 'Implementation Perspectives: Status and Reconsideration'. In *Handbook of Public Administration*, edited by B. G. Peter and J. Pierre, 265–78. Los Angeles: Sage.

6

Shaheed Hospital
Alternative Organisation, Ideology and Social Movement

Apoorv Khare and Rohit Varman

Ideology is an essential feature of any society, and stable social systems draw upon it to cultivate beliefs in their legitimacy and to suppress contradictory beliefs (Eagleton, 1991; Habermas, 1976). However, marketing theory has paid limited attention to the role of ideology in the functioning of markets (exceptions include Kozinets and Handelman, 2004; Thompson and Arsel, 2004). This oversight is surprising because market-based exchanges and consumption as essential features of capitalism build on supporting ideologies for their acceptance (O'Reilly, 2006; Sklair, 1994). Similarly, oppositional social movements within capitalism use counter-ideologies to countervail and oppose the dominant system (Beuchler, 2000; Touraine, 1981). Marketing theory has under-examined the role of social movements in shaping alternative institutions that challenge market-based offerings. We offer a corrective to these lacunae by presenting insights into a healthcare initiative that is shaped by a workers' movement impelled by Marxist-Leninist ideology.

In this chapter, we examine Shaheed Hospital at Dalli Rajhara in the central Indian state of Chattisgarh. Shaheed Hospital (SH) was set up in 1983 and offers low-cost healthcare to subaltern consumers living in the region. This chapter helps understand how a counter-ideology and social movement are necessary for the creation of alternatives to market-based offerings. SH further helps us refine our understanding of how a counter-ideology is used to challenge prevailing market-based norms and to denaturalise existing social relations. A health facility also materialised the counter-ideology of Marxism-Leninism and created a broader participation that was necessary for the movement in its early years. Paradoxically, SH also reflects the limitations of an isolated alternative institution, whose survival became dependent on a few heroic individuals as the social movement and ideology that created it declined.

In the following section, we examine the theoretical ideas of ideology and social movement. We follow this review with the presentation of the findings on SH. We conclude the chapter with a discussion of the theoretical ramifications of our study.

Ideology and social movements

Ideology

Drawing from Eagleton (1991) we describe ideology as ideas, which can be false and deceptive, that arise out of the material structure of society. In this interpretation of the term, we do not attribute ideology to any one particular group or a class of actors. Instead, we interpret ideology as the systemic necessity of a particular socio-economic order. Furthermore, from a social movement perspective, we use the term counter-ideology to suggest that activists challenge the dominant ideology and attempt to uncover 'false and deceptive ideas' in any given socio-economic context.

The critical perspective on ideology can be traced to the works of Karl Marx and specifically his celebrated critique in 'The German Ideology'. Marx's (1968) interpretation of ideology was a significant theoretical breakthrough from the social movement perspective because of the importance it attached to systemic forces and to unravelling the relationship of ideology to the economic structures of capitalism. While most of the earlier social commentators were concerned about the overt usage of coercion, Marx (1968) saw in capitalism, a form of control that was hidden and more rampant. In a similar vein, and in the tradition of Marxist thought, Lukacs (1971) related ideology to the problem of reification under the capitalist system and interpreted it as a structurally constrained thought, which was closely tied with the reality of existence in a capitalist society. Similarly, Gramsci (1971) realised that the socio-economic systems create a hegemonic culture in which ideology is a necessary kernel that is employed to justify and hide oppressive social relationships.

Much of the work on ideology emanating from the Frankfurt School draws upon some of these Marxist interpretations. This critical school places considerable emphasis on the deterministic role of ideology in the contemporary world (Marcuse, 1968). The constitutive feature of ideology has also been highlighted by several theorists inspired by the Frankfurt School's emphases on the social control of thought and the commercial-cultural nexus (for example, Ewen, 1976; Horkhiemer and Adorno, 1944; Jhally, 1987).

More recently, scholars have argued that for ideology to be successful, it has to relate to a certain material reality and cannot merely create distortions in the ideational domain as critical theorists, such as Marcuse (1968) and Horkhiemer and Adorno (1944) argued (Eagleton, 1991). Adding to this argument, Althusser (1971, 173) holds that ideology 'interpellates' individuals and creates them as subjects to function as productive parts of a socio-economic system. It is important to add that Althusser's seminal contribution is in systematically highlighting ideology as a structural feature of a lived reality by emphasising lived features of our daily existence, such as voting and saluting, that constitute the materiality of ideology.

Summing up, ideological analyses, have on the one hand, overemphasised the ideational domain and false consciousness. On the other hand, the rationalist emphasis on ideology as a simple representation of ideas is equally problematic. Instead, we have drawn on ideology and its relationship with the material reality and situated it in the realm of lived experience. Furthermore, we do not interpret ideology as a set of distortions attributable to a specific class, but have emphasised its systemic requirements to legitimise social relationships. These relationships can be unjust and oppressive as is the case with capitalism. It is these unjust and oppressive relationships under capitalism that become central to social movements, as in the case of the movement studied in this chapter, in which attempts are made to sharpen contradictions and precipitate conflicts by attacking the dominant ideology.

Social movements

In recent years, the socio-political space in India has been dotted with social movements (for example, environmental movements such as Chipko Movement and Narmada Bachao Andolan; agricultural reform movements such as Shramik Sangathana Movement and Sarvodaya; and Maoist movements such as Naxalite Movement and People's War). The pro-business policies and the integration of the Indian economy into the global capitalist economy after independence created conditions of inequity and injustice for the vast population of subalterns in the country. The workers' movement that created SH was shaped by such conditions of inequity and exploitation in the mining sector in central India.

Social movements have a rich history of theorisation in social sciences. Touraine (1981, 77) defines a social movement as the, 'organized collective behaviour of a class actor struggling against his class adversary for the social control of his historicity in a concrete community'. Social movement theory has been divided into 'old' and 'new' forms based on the role given to the working class in social struggles (Melucci, 1995). Offe (1999) and Melucci (1995) further explain that new social movements increasingly rely on social alliances involving a diverse set of actors. This is particularly relevant because the 'old' social movement theory in the Marxist tradition puts considerable emphasis on the role of the proletariat in the process of social resistance and transformation (Buechler, 2000). Touraine (1981) contends that the various forms of social movements have proliferated in modernity because the meta-social guarantees that held the pre-modern social order together have lessened relevance. This position is also supported by Eder (1995) and Offe (1999), who observe that the defining values of new social movements are the quests for identity and autonomy as compared to just economic redistribution as emphasised in the older movements. Disagreeing with this approach and critiquing the new social movement theory, Olofsson (1988) raises concerns about labelling new forms of protests as social movements and is critical of glorification in the extant theorisation of small and transitory struggles as agents of social change. Significantly, many new social movement theorists acknowledge these concerns, but highlight the role of new forms of incompatibilities within the universe of modern values and realise that the shift is a continuation and is linked with the earlier interpretation of social movements (for example, Offe, 1999; Touraine, 1981). Several critical theorists also support this turn in social movement theorisation and contend that new social movements are increasingly becoming vehicles of social transformation (for example, Habermas, 1976). However, this support does not imply the ascendancy of the cultural over the economic, but instead suggests their meaningful synthesis into a series of contradictions and conflicts.

Bhaskar (1993, 93) observes that a contradiction, 'specifies any situation which allows the satisfaction of one end only at the cost of another, i.e., a bind or constraint'. Ideology plays a critical role in determining or revealing these social cleavages and it is necessary to add that for the avoidance of conflicts and for the creation of opacities that hide societal contradictions, ideology becomes a systemic necessity (Giddens, 1979; Habermas, 1976). Defining conflict as a 'struggle between actors or collectivities expressed as definite social practices', Giddens (1979, 131) suggests that conflict is often a result of contradictions in a system, but their co-occurrence is not necessary. Habermas agrees with Giddens that conflict often remains latent and contradictions do not always result in an open antagonism between actors and 'recognition by participants' is one of the fundamental moving forces in any situation of a systemic contradiction and a social movement. Thus, ideology is particularly critical in maintaining the distance between contradictions and conflicts because these conflicts endanger the stability of any socio-economic system and can often result in a state of crisis. Habermas (1976) further argues that by translating contradictions into conflicts, social movements have an important role to play in precipitating legitimation deficiencies.

In summary, social movement theory is a contested terrain, with a divide between 'old' and 'new' forms of theory. This divide stems from divergent interpretations of the role of economic and cultural factors in the current capitalist system. These varying interpretations, however, converge on the role of ideology and its significance in social movements. This helps attend to the relationship between ideology and social movement in the context of SH. Our review further suggests that contradictions do not necessarily result in conflicts in a society. This separation is achieved through the use of force and ideology and contributes to systemic stability. Social movements, however, try to enhance the crisis tendencies in a system by reducing the distance between these contradictions by further attempting to raise the consciousness of their stakeholders. Thus, it becomes necessary to understand how SH and the workers' movement in Dalli Rajhara raise the consciousness of subaltern groups and challenge the hegemony of capital.

Methodology

To understand the roles of ideology and social movement in the creation and sustenance of an alternative institution, we chose to examine SH. SH is situated at Dalli Rajhara in the state of Chhattisgarh (see Figure 6.1). Dalli Rajhara has captive

Figure 6.1: Shaheed Hospital at Dalli Rajhara

Source: Taken by one of the authors during a field visit to Shaheed Hospital in April 2014.

iron ore mines owned by Bhilai Steel Plant, a Government of India enterprise and one of the largest steel producers in the country. The population of the town is nearly 40,000. Dalli Rajhara is a part of Dondi Lohara legislative seat and comes under Balod district. SH is a 120-bed hospital with a staff of nearly 120 personnel. There are six full-time doctors and thirty six nurses working in the hospital. SH is one of the biggest hospitals in the region. The hospital is reputed for providing affordable and quality healthcare services in the entire region. Patients from as far as 150 km come to the hospital for treatment.

We collected data in various forms and used a number of methods. We began the study by examining and analysing information brochures, media articles and websites giving news about SH. This helped us in identifying the key people involved in managing the hospital. In the next phase of the study, we visited the hospital and observed its functioning. Additionally, we conducted phenomenological interviews with some of the key functionaries at the hospital. Overall, we conducted sixteen interviews, giving representation to doctors, nurses, health workers, hospital staff, general public and patients at the hospital. A participant profile is presented in Table 6.1. Following qualitative research conventions, our sample plan was purposeful, and we utilised within-case sampling and a nested approach, looking at various relevant actors in the organisation. Our objective was to look for variance in the extent of their immersion in the organisation (Thompson and Troester, 2002). We broadly questioned these activists about the functioning of the hospital and their understandings of the state of the workers' movement in the region. We also interviewed three patients. In these interviews, we primarily questioned these patients about their reason for choosing SH, the total cost incurred in the treatment, and their experiences at the hospital.

Table 6.1: A list of key participants

S no	Name	Description	Remarks
1	Saibal Jana	Doctor	Doctor, since the start of the Hospital
2	Sachin	Doctor	Young doctor from Maharashtra
3	Dhaneshwari	Doctor	Young doctor from Maharashtra
4	Dipankar Sen Gupta	Doctor	Doctor (anaesthesia), Batch mate of Dr Jana

S no	Name	Description	Remarks
5	Jaggu Ram	Health worker	Voluntary health worker (retired)
6	Khiv Lal	Health worker	Voluntary health worker (retired)
7	Puran Lal	Health worker	Store in-charge
8	Puna Ram	Health worker	Accounts in-charge
9	Ganesh Ram	CMSS official	President CMSS
10	Durga Prasad	CMSS official	General Secretary (GS) CMSS
11	Hiral Lal Sahu	CMSS official	GS, CMSS
12	Janak Lal	CMSS official	Ex MLA CMM
13	Sahu ji	CMSS official	Office assistant CMSS
14	Mrs Alpana Jana	Head Nurse	In-charge of nursing, wife of Dr Jana
15	Sujata	Nurse	Old timer, volunteer
16	Kuleshwari	Nurse	Old timer, volunteer
17	Sunita	Nurse	Regular staff
18	Wilson	Pharmacist	Regular staff
19	Dewlu Mandavi	Pharmacist	Regular staff
20	Dilip Yadav	Pathologist	Regular staff
21	Dheludas	Ambulance driver	Regular staff
22	Patient from Birsinghtola	Villager	Village Birsinghtola
23	Patient's son	Villager	Village Birsinghtola
24	Veer Sigh Verma	Dresser, Primary Health Centre (PHC) Gotatola	Village Gotatola

Source: One of the authors met these participants during field visit to Shaheed hospital in April 2014.

Our database comprises media articles, material downloaded from websites, field notes and verbatim interview transcripts. This contributed to methodological triangulation necessary for the trustworthiness of our data (Erlandson *et al.*, 1993). Our interpretation of the articles, interview texts and the field notes was conducted through a hermeneutical process. The process involved a continuous movement between individual notes and transcripts and the emerging understanding of the entire dataset (Thompson and Troester, 2002). In the process, the theoretical understanding presented here reflects the final stages of the analysis in which linkages are developed between participant meanings and a broader set of theoretical questions.

Findings

This section is organised into three themes. In the first trope, divided into two sub-themes, we discuss the workers' movement and ideology that gave birth to SH. In the next theme, we analyse how SH challenges market forces. In the final trope, we offer insights into the challenges faced by the hospital as an alternative institution.

Genesis of SH in a workers' movement

SH has its roots in a workers' movement of the 1970s at Dalli Rajhara mines in Chhattisgarh. The 1970s was an epoch of social and political movements in India. The country was witnessing widespread protests against the National Emergency, declared in 1975 by the incumbent Prime Minister Indira Gandhi, that resulted in a suspension of constitutional rights. A popular upsurge in 1977 against the Emergency resulted in its termination, and through a national election people threw out the Indira Gandhi government. Dr Saibal Jana, a key founding figure of the hospital and its head, who has been serving for more than thirty years, recalled:

> 1977 was an interesting year. People were protesting everywhere. The Emergency was over and people had thrown Indira Gandhi out of power. A new Janata Government came to power at the centre. At that time in Dalli Rajhara mines, the captive mines of Bhilai Steel Plant (BSP), most of the workers were contractual workers. Some parts of the mines were mechanised but most of it was non-mechanised. The contractual workers were ill paid, but the regular workers in mechanised mines were well paid. The living conditions of contract workers were also very poor. Moreover, their trade unions did not raise these concerns in front of the management.

Jana refers to the conditions that led to the foundation of Chhattisgarh Mines Shramik Sangathan (CMSS). He refers to the divide between more privileged workers with permanent jobs, who were guaranteed different employment benefits and contractual workers with temporary jobs and lower wages. Accordingly, contractual workers faced high levels of exploitation and did not get proper representation from their unions. This exploitation was unfolding in the backdrop of the suspension of constitutional rights with the declaration of the National Emergency and a popular upsurge against it. Khiv Lal, a retired mine worker, and one of the first voluntary health workers of SH also shared with us the harsh work conditions of contractual workers in that period. He told us:

> We used to start the work in the morning at 4 o'clock and come back by 9 in the night. We could not spend any time with our families, children. On Sunday, we had to work extra for the contractor to get the week's payment.

Such exploitative conditions led to protests by workers that culminated in the formation of CMSS.

The agitation in 1977 started with contractual workers demanding a hike in their bonus. These contractual workers were paid a meagre amount of INR 2 per day for fifteen-sixteen hours of daily work (Sethi, 2011). All the contractual workers belonged to two unions, All India Trade Union Congress (AITUC) controlled by the Communist Party of India and Indian National Trade Union Congress (INTUC) controlled by the Indian National Congress (INC). Around 10,000 contractual workers were denied equal bonus because the unions refused to raise their concerns. In contemporary India, we often find trade unions affiliated to political parties have their vested interests, corrupt leadership, and fail to adequately represent workers. Jana further informed us, 'The union leaders said, "It is not possible. We can't tell the management that the union is demanding equal bonus". This led to an agitation by workers, and they quit their unions (i.e., AITUC and INTUC)'. There was a deep sense of injustice and anger among these mine workers. After quitting the two unions, the workers agitated for fifteen days on their own and demanded an equal bonus. This agitation initially continued without any formal leader or organisation. In March 1977, Shankar Guha Niyogi (originally Dhiresh Guha Niyogi), a trade union activist on his release after thirteen months of imprisonment under the draconian laws passed under the national emergency, provided the mine workers leadership. They formed CMSS as their representative union. The union's demands were met after an agitation for two months. During this period, eleven mine workers were shot dead by the police and Niyogi was again arrested and put in police custody for two months.

Marxist–Leninist ideals and the workers' movement

Shankar Guha Niyogi believed in Marxist–Leninist ideology and wished to develop a new social arrangement that was suitable and attuned to the specific social, economic, and political conditions of India. Niyogi (1993, 2) described Marxism–Leninism as:

> Marxism–Leninism is a theoretical principle for class-struggle and class-struggle does not happen in books. It happens in real life. When a struggle starts between exploited and exploiting class, the first lesson people get is that they are in a class struggle. And this is their Marxism, connected to life. Then Marxism has another form, the scientific development of society. To inform people about the forces which would lead them and which would help them during a struggle.

He believed and propagated the idea of *sangharsh aur nirmaan* (revolution and construction). Lenin (1902) had famously observed:

> not only must Social-Democrats not confine themselves exclusively to the economic struggle, but that they must not allow the organisation of economic exposures to become the predominant part of their activities. We must take up actively the political education of the working class and the development of its political consciousness.

Drawing upon Lenin's writings, Niyogi had a broader view of Marxism and did not interpret the struggle of mine workers only as an economic battle. He observed:

> We never fought on economic matters. We fought for our respect... They (elites, senior managers) said, 'Who are you to tell us about work conditions?...Our fight was about respect and equality. They transformed it into the economic demands (Niyogi 1993, 3).

Niyogi was a very popular figure in the area and Singh (1977) reports:

> Shanker Guha Niyogi has become a household name in this industrial area of Chhattisgarh. Everyone talks about him, many with reverence and affection and some with hatred and fear, but they all – contractors, police, administration, trade union leaders, and the people of Rajhara – seem to agree on two points: Niyogi is the undisputed leader of about 8,000 workers of Rajhara and his honesty, integrity and dedication is beyond question.

Niyogi was not only a charismatic leader but also a person of high integrity and dedication to his ideals. He was originally from a lower middle-class family

in West Bengal and went to schools in Jalpaigudi and Kolkata. After his stint in
the local politics in Bengal and membership of Communist Party of India, Niyogi
moved to Chhattisgarh in the early 1960s to work at BSP. In 1967, Niyogi and
his colleagues organised one of the first strikes at BSP because of which he was
fired. To further understand working conditions, Niyogi changed his name from
Dhiresh to Shankar and worked as a daily-wage worker in a Dani Tola mine, near
Rajhara breaking stones in a quarry. Before the formation of CMSS, Niyogi had
also worked as a farm worker and organised farm workers against exploitative
working conditions. Niyogi was continuously targeted by the local elite and the
government for these actions and was arrested on several occasions (Singh, 1977).
He also got married to a fellow tribal worker Asha, who continued to work in one
of the mines after their marriage.

Janak Lal Thakur, a two-time member of the legislative assembly (MLA) from
the political wing of CMSS, Chhattisgarh Mukti Morcha (CMM) and a devout
worker of CMSS further explained:

> There has to be constructive work associated with the struggle in
> any movement. The way on which Niyogi ji led us was both a fight
> (against capitalism) along with the constructive work. We worked
> in the areas of education, health, anti-alcohol campaign, sports, etc.
> He was clear that a struggle without any constructive work would
> not work. Community participation was extremely important.

It was clear to those leading the movement from the very beginning, that there
was a need to not only challenge existing structures but also to build alternative
institutions. This was drawing upon Lenin's (1902, emphasis in original) insightful
observation that:

> agitation must be conducted with regard to every concrete example
> of *this* oppression (as we have begun to carry on agitation round
> concrete examples of economic oppression). In as much as this
> oppression affects the most diverse classes of society, in as much
> as it manifests itself in the most varied spheres of life and activity
> – vocational, civic, personal, family, religious, scientific, etc. – is it
> not evident that *we shall not be fulfilling our task* of developing the
> political consciousness of the workers if we do not *undertake* the
> organisation of the *political exposure* of the autocracy in *all its
> aspects*? In order to carry on agitation round concrete instances of

oppression, these instances must be exposed (as it is necessary to expose factory abuses in order to carry on economic agitation).

Despite this broad understanding, many of the specific institutions and arrangements within CMSS emerged as the movement started grappling with different problems. In the movement, Niyogi became a central figure and people started rallying around him. Khiv Lal added:

> Workers used to come to him (Niyogi) with various types of problems, e.g., problem related to the children's education, problem related to alcohol consumption by men, water related problems, etc. Niyogi ji made seventeen departments for integrated and wholesome resolution of problems related to workers' lives.

Niyogi and CMSS leadership understood that it would be limiting to circumscribe the movement to an economic domain. They started encountering several social and cultural problems that required attention. As a result, Niyogi and CMSS decided to broaden the economic struggle and tried to create a social movement that could alter the lives of the underprivileged in the region. For example, CMSS succeeded in banning alcohol consumption among its members. Niyogi (1993, 18) observed:

> We are also taking up other issues. Alcohol consumption is a major problem here among workers. It seems that there are more illegal liquor shops than water taps in workers' colonies. Tribals become addicted to it and it is happening because of instability and tension in their lives. Workers slowly lose their confidence and their power to unite and think diminishes. As a result, unions keep revolving around economic matters.

Niyogi saw culture, economy and health as connected domains and wanted to create a wider notion of social struggle. This not only helped in broadening the movement but also earned them the support of women. As theorists have observed, new social movements are impelled by multiple struggles (Eder, 1995; Offe, 1999). Analysing the work done by Niyogi and CMSS, Dogra (1991, 2457) reported:

> Niyogi was first and foremost, a leading activist of the worldwide movement to search for new development paths and a new society based on justice, equality and human values. He struggled relentlessly in this direction for nearly three decades in the course of which he not only innovated a lot but also implemented his

programme in the most difficult situations. In particular, he and his movement fought for (1) removing the exploitation of workers and peasants, (2) bringing women into the mainstream of social change and struggles, (3) implementation of a health programme for the people by the people, (4) eradicating social evils like liquor and gambling, (5) checking ecological ruin, occupational hazards, displacement and linking these issues with the struggles of weaker sections, (6) an appropriate technology which avoids unemployment/retrenchment of workers while meeting production needs, and (7) above all, the creation of a new outlook, a new thinking, that believes in struggles and change beyond the immediate economic interests.

In 1982 to broaden the scope of the union, CMSS formed CMM as a political outfit to jointly represent the interests of workers and peasants in the region. As new social movement theorists have observed, social struggles try to broaden their horizons beyond the domain of class struggle to create wider social coalitions and to create greater resonance (Offe, 1999; Snow and Benford, 1988). Thus, the idea of *sangharsh aur nirmaan* became the founding ideal of CMSS to create a broad social coalition that shaped the emergence of SH.

Creating SH as an alternative institution

Although CMSS was mulling over a possible health initiative, it was the death of Kusum Bai, a CMSS member in 1979 that triggered the opening of a dispensary. Kusum Bai was pregnant and died of a ruptured fallopian tube because her family and fellow workers could not take her to a doctor in time. As a result, CMSS decided to start a dispensary that was to develop later into SH. CMSS constituted a health committee to further the ideals of revolution and construction. A total of 109 mine workers joined the committee. The committee was given the responsibility of setting up a dispensary. The dispensary was an outpatient facility that offered some medical care to its members.

The dispensary started when doctors Anil Sadgopal and Binayak Sen, who were already associated with such initiatives in the region, came to Dalli Rajhara to help CMSS. The involvement of doctors in the movement started getting media attention, and some other doctors who were broadly sympathetic to left politics were influenced. Jana, who graduated from a medical school in Kolkata in 1977, recalled:

We heard about the health initiative from the Sunday magazine of Anand Bazar Group. We read an article that a hospital is coming.

Then we (Dr Saibal Jana and Dr Ashis Kundu) decided to come here. We did not have any knowledge about Chhatisgarh. I had just completed my MBBS from National Medical College Calcutta at that time. Ashis is also my classmate. Dr Pabitra Guha is also my batch mate from another college. So, we decided to come here.

The initial set of doctors came from Bengal because the Naxalite movement mobilised students and created a political consciousness in the late 1960s and 70s. It created an anti-capitalist fervour that encouraged middle-class students to give up their lucrative career paths and devote themselves to the cause of equity and justice that Marxism and revolutionary ideals represented. These doctors took up such positions despite being offered poor monetary compensation and having to live in tough conditions away from the comforts of life in cities. The voluntary healthcare workers, who joined at the beginning of the initiative were given no compensation and stayed with the hospital because of their belief in the movement.

According to Jana, the initial years were rather difficult. Initially, Jana and other doctors ran some health campaigns through exhibitions and posters to inform workers and their families about heath-related issues. These campaigns were also used to make workers aware of exploitative working conditions and for a need to challenge the dominant ideology. This helped the doctors explain several health problems faced by workers as class-based phenomena. Thus, Jana and others tried to create a legitimation deficiency for the mine-owners and upper classes that could challenge the hold of the dominant capitalist ideology and its dissimulation (Beuchler, 2000; Habermas, 1976).

In 1982, CMSS started a small dispensary within the premises of the union office. The union gave INR 2,000 to an internal committee with doctors as its members to manage the facility. The dispensary was started in an abandoned garage. Apart from the problem of meagre resources, the dispensary had a limited supply of doctors and lacked in a trained nursing staff. To overcome this problem, mine workers were trained to function as health workers. Jana and others provided the basic medical skills and training to these workers to support them in the functioning of the dispensary. Jana further added:

We recruited some local girls as nurses. At that time, it was very difficult to get girls to work in a hospital. We were looking for educated girls even up to class 5. But, we did not get many. We took help from workers for recruitment. We went searching house

to house. At that time, there were four doctors. Apart from the
dispensary, we gave very high importance to health education.
We educated workers as well as other people in the region about
health issues.

Low literacy levels in the region made it difficult to recruit health workers and
nurses. With some difficulty, Jana and others assembled a small team to create a
functioning dispensary. They also understood that in a setting marked by high
levels of poverty and ignorance about health issues, it was necessary for them to
focus their attention on educating people about matters related to health.

On 3 June 1983, SH with ten beds was inaugurated after a struggle of four
years. It was on 3 June 1977 that eleven workers fighting for their rights under the
banner of CMSS were shot dead by the state police. The name *shaheed* or martyr
was in memory of those deceased workers. SH did not receive any external funding
or government grant. The CMSS workers had contributed from their salaries for
the hospital building. They also helped in constructing the building by offering
their services and construction material. Despite these efforts, at the inauguration
Niyogi informed CMSS members that the money that was collected to run the
hospital was spent on the building. He asked each of them to contribute the mine
allowances of INR 30 for running the facility. At that time, a collection was made
of more than INR 3,00,000. However, given the concern for resources and the
need for a steady flow of income to meet the working capital requirements, the
SH committee decided to buy a truck that was leased in the local transport market
to generate funds of INR 5,000 per month. Ironically, an alternative healthcare
offering challenging market forces was dependent, albeit in a limited manner, on
a market for the generation of resources.

The hospital started with two slogans. One was '*Mehnatkashon ke swasthya
ke liye mehnatkashon ka apna karyakram*' or workers' own programme for their
health; and the second, '*Swasthya ke liye sangharsh karo*'or fight for your health.
These formed the founding ideals of SH. It was clear that health was a universal
right, but workers would need to struggle for it. Janak Lal further told us,
'Everything in this hospital came from the contribution of the workers. From
the very beginning the hospital was against taking grants from any institution
or person.' He further added that many agencies came forward to help but they
refused to take any external help and resolved to run the hospital only with the
contribution from workers.

In summary, ideology and social movement played important roles in
the genesis of SH as an alternative institution. The CMSS labour movement

provided the necessary basis for the hospital. The guiding principles of SH that included workers taking responsibility for their health, the policy of taking no contributions from outside, rational treatment were beliefs that were rooted in Marxist–Leninist ideals that impelled the leadership of CMSS and doctors who initially joined SH.

Materialising ideology and challenging dominant norms in everyday practices

SH is a large 120-bed facility that offers an alternative to private and corporate market-based healthcare institutions by providing affordable and good-quality healthcare. It challenges market-based norms and capitalist ideals that valorise private wealth with a focus on profitability. This does not mean that SH compromises with the quality of service and it offers healthcare based on the philosophy of rational treatment. SH has also challenged the dominant norms of the expert-based healthcare system by pioneering the concepts of community health education, emphasising the role of workers trained into health service providers and nurses. Unlike most private practitioners and hospitals, it also uses generic medicines to offer cheaper drugs to patients. In following these everyday practices, SH materialises the Marxist–Leninist ideology that impels it. Such a materialisation is considered necessary by social theorists to make an ideology effective (Althusser, 1971; Eagleton, 1991; Gramsci, 1971).

The founders of CMSS and SH did not want to create an alternative institution that was going to function as a patronising charity. Instead, in line with Marxism–Leninism, the goal was to create a facility founded and run by workers themselves with the help of doctors. SH is an institution, where workers and poor take responsibility for their own healthcare. This is considered the cornerstone of affordable and ethical healthcare services. Jana further explained that ownership by workers created greater accountability among the middle-class doctors towards their under-class patients:

> Workers contributed the money, and they are taking the responsibility of their health. So, the doctors and health workers will investigate properly, they will not harass the patients, they will not collect the money unnecessarily, charges would be minimal and also they will go for rational treatment. Our hospital is a rational drug therapy centre where rational investigation is applied, i.e., investigation which is essential to come to a proper diagnosis. Because the diagnosis should be evidence based, you listen to

the patient, you examine the patient properly, then you do the
investigation properly, you also consult the problems with other
doctors. So, all charges, everything will be less for a patient and
they will get the best treatment.

Jana believes that SH is an alternative institution of healthcare that follows the
right line of rational treatment. He added, 'If you want to do a proper diagnosis,
you need proper history taking, proper examination and justified investigation
for positive and negative side'. Accordingly, this was in contrast to the dominant
market-based model in most other hospitals where the poor were exploited. Jana
further explained:

> If a doctor prescribes essential drugs worth INR 100 and a
> (health supplement) tonic worth INR 300, then INR 300 are
> basically being spent on irrational medicines. Actually, there are
> so many formulations in the market. I think there are nearly one
> lakh formulations. But, the WHO (World Health Organization)
> and Hathi committee have lists of essential medicines (http://
> www.communityhealth.in/~commun26/wiki/images/b/b5/
> Hathi_Committee_report_1975.PDF.pdf). The WHO list has
> 200 essential medicines and the Hathi committee report has 100
> essential medicines.

At SH and in health educational programmes, doctors and health workers
question dominant practices that guide other hospitals in the region. They try
to uncover the profit motive in such practices and hope to expose the dominant
ethos of capitalist healthcare as flawed. Doctors at SH discourage any use of health
supplements because they are not part of rational therapy and have no medical
efficacy (see Figure 6.2). Jana tried to expose the capitalist model of healthcare
by rhetorically asking:

> Where do big pharmaceutical companies earn their money? It
> comes from the things like tonics. If you screen a prescription of
> any reputed doctor and see the diagnosis and the drugs prescribed,
> you will find the non-essential drugs prescribed. If the doctor is
> rational, he or she will restrict himself or herself to four or five
> drugs. Otherwise, they will prescribe ten-fifteen medicines. If you
> compare the price of essential drugs with non-essential drugs, you
> will find a big difference in the price of the drugs.

Figure 6.2: A message on the wall of the outpatient department (OPD)
discouraging the use of health supplements

Source: Taken by one of the authors during a field visit to Shaheed Hospital in April 2014.

Thus, the ideals of taking responsibility for own health and rational treatment form the founding principles of SH. The treatment costs at SH are substantially low (see Table 6.2). In addition, SH offers pathology tests at extremely low prices (see Table 6.3). We interviewed a patient, an old woman from a nearby village suffering from paralysis and her son, who was her caretaker. Her son told us that she was admitted at SH for eight days. When we asked him about the total expenses incurred, he told us it was INR 3,400. We saw the bill and the pathology lab expenses were INR 200, medicines INR 2,995, bed charges INR 35, admission INR 15 and treatment charge INR 175. We found it surprising that the total hospital service charge that included tests, room rent and doctors' fees was just over 10 per cent and nearly 90 per cent was spent on medicines, which was the actual out-of-pocket expense incurred by SH. Thus, SH offers a facility that is low priced to make it accessible to the poorest of the poor.

Table 6.2: Treatment charges at SH

In-patient department	Charges (in INR)
Bed charges per night	5
Other charges (including charges for nursing and doctors) per day	25
Total charges per day	30

Outpatient department	Charges (in INR)
For new patients	20
For patients (Revisit)	10
Child delivery charges (appx) (all inclusive)	
Normal delivery	1,200–500
Caesarean	4,000–500

Source: Collected from the Shaheed Hospital by one of the authors in April 2014.

Table 6.3: Rates of pathology tests at SH as compared to the market rates in the region

Pathology tests	SH (in INR)	Market (in INR)
Haematology		
Haemoglobin	10	50
Grouping	20	80
Platelet count	10	100
Human immunodeficiency virus (HIV)	100	300
Widal Test	50	100
Complete blood count (CBC)	50	200
Electrolyte	120	300
Biochemistry		
Rheumatoid (RA) factor	100	200
C-reactive protein (CRP)	100	250
Total protein	60	100
Calcium	60	150
Acid phosphate	120	250
Alkaline phosphate	60	150
Serum glutamic oxaloacetic transaminase (SGOT)	50	100
Serum glutamic-pyruvic transaminase (SGPT)	50	100
Bilirubin	50	100
Hepatitis B (HBS)	50	150
Sugar	40	60
Uric acid	60	100

Pathology tests	SH (in INR)	Market (in INR)
Triglyceride (TG)	80	150
Cholesterol	60	100
High-density lipoprotein (HDL)	120	100
Low-density lipoprotein (LDL)	120	100
Urea	40	100
Creatinine	40	100
Amylase	120	250
Urine		
Microscopy	10	100 (including albumin and sugar)
Albumin	10	100
Sugar	10	
Pregnancy	40	100
Ketone body	20	50
Micro-albumin	350	500
Urea R/E	30	
Reticulocyte count	40	100
Other		
Stool sugar	10	100 (including occult blood)
Stool occult blood	20	
Peritoneal fluid	80	150
Cerebrospinal fluid (CSF)	80	150
Semen analysis	30	150

Source: Collected from the Shaheed hospital by one of the authors in April 2014. Market rates are prevailing rates at pathology labs in the open market.

Dipankar, a doctor at SH, further questioned the dominant normative order and explained the ideal of affordable and quality healthcare to us. He told us, 'We don't do unnecessary tests. Only those tests would be recommended which are necessary'. Sachin, another young doctor at SH added, 'usually in other hospitals doctors recommend a battery of tests. For example, if bilirubin test is

required, only that will be done. We won't ask for liver function test'. Dipankar
further clarified:

> What does the corporate sector do? If the upper limit of the patient's
> ability to pay is INR 30,000 (facility provided to poor patients by
> the government under National Health Insurance Scheme). It
> would finish it in one hour. Then it would ask the patient to pay
> extra money. There is a term called golden hour. If a patient suffers
> from a heart attack, the first hour is crucial to save the patient. For
> them, the golden hour is to charge more than what a patient can pay.

We found that SH has a well-equipped pathology lab and the prices of
pathology tests are nearly half as compared to the open market. SH outsources
to outside labs certain diagnostic tests, which are not internally available. It is
common for these market-based labs to offer commissions to doctors or hospitals
that recommend patients to them. Instead of keeping the commission, SH passes
it to patients to offer them discounts on tests. Thus, SH provides an alternative
to the market-based hospitals and nursing homes that are often engaged in
profit-oriented healthcare practices. It does so by challenging the dominant
profit-oriented normative order. Social movement theorists have argued that
such normative challenges are necessary to denaturalise dominant institutions
(Eder, 1995; Koopmans, 2004).

A network of institutions working with similar left-leaning ideology helps SH
in getting motivated and pro-poor doctors. For example, Sachin came from an
organisation called Jan Swasthya Sahyog (JSS) at Ganiyari in Bilaspur District
in Chhattisgarh (http://www.jssbilaspur.org/about/). Sachin told us, 'JSS and
Shaheed Hospital (SH) are associated with each other. They have very good
relations with each other. Sir (Jana) was the president of the governing body there.
I got to know about SH from there. So I came here'. JSS has a nursing college and
the hospital has a tie-up with it to get nurses to come and work at SH. After learning
the theoretical part at JSS nursing college, nurses get practical training at SH. Jana,
his team of doctors and old staff try to imbibe the ideological underpinnings of
SH in the new joinees so that they become committed to the ideals of the hospital.
Jana observed, 'We try to make the system where the values of caring and good
healthcare practices are inculcated among the staff. These values are in built in
old timers'. Jana and others understand that if there is an ideological deficit, the
SH will seize to be effective.

On the question of empowerment of subalterns, the founding leadership of

CMSS and SH also understand the linkage between issues of class and health. They realise many healthcare problems are results of living subaltern lives in the current exploitative order. There is a recognition that health service in isolation cannot be changed and there is a need for a wider social change for the under-classes to have healthier lives. Another important ideal at SH that contrasts with the prevailing norms is the emphasis on health workers. SH makes attempts to reduce the dependence on doctors and empowers workers to take care of their own health through better education and training. This helps in not only reducing costs but also in creating a greater sense of equality in the setting. Jana emphasised upon the importance of nursing and healthcare workers to provide quality healthcare services. Jana explained to us,

> It is seen in the National Health Service (of the United Kingdom) that better antenatal clinic and better antenatal care reduce maternal and infant mortality rate. Also, the improvement in economic condition of the people reduces the maternal and infant mortality rate. This is without any doctor. So doctor's intervention comes later only in case of any complication and when surgical intervention is required.

Jana believes that in Indian hospitals, doctors are at the top, and the due attention is not given to nursing. Drawing upon the National Health Service in the UK, Jana explained that a multipronged healthcare structure is needed that empowers subaltern consumers and service providers. As a result of this belief, a greater parity in the status of workers and doctors is another important aspect of SH. Jaggu Ram, a health worker, shared, '(At SH), there is no difference between individuals because of a person's position. We do not treat cleaning staff differently. Everyone is treated with respect. There is a sense of belongingness, a family like environment here'. While it is hard to deny that SH is also a reflection of the social hierarchy as it prevails in the outside world and Jana is at the top of this hierarchy, status relations are far more fluid and loosely defined at SH than what we have observed in most other healthcare establishments in the country. Thus, the sense of belonging that Jaggu Ram experienced was an outcome of being located in an alternative institutional space in which the dominant norms were challenged, if not completely inverted.

In summary, SH is an embodiment of an anti-capitalist ideology. It further materialises the ideology in its everyday practices of dealing with subaltern consumers and workers. SH mounts a challenge to the profit-centric healthcare model by rejecting its normative order and by denaturalising it.

Challenges of sustaining SH in neoliberal India

Until 1991, India broadly witnessed an attempt to balance out requirements of operating as a capitalist economy and a welfare state. It is argued that the project had its inherent limitations and the sluggish growth rate brought about a divide between political and economic development as the economy failed to match the changing aspirations of politically and materially more aware people (Bardhan, 2003). Driven by rising internal discontent and the neoliberal phase of global capitalism, India has witnessed some significant changes in the last two decades as part of the structural adjustment programme started in the country in 1991 (see Bardhan, 2003). The economic liberalisation has allowed multinational corporations to have free access to the Indian market, its natural resources, and its cheap labour (Chandrashekhar and Ghosh, 2000). The structural adjustment programme, mandated by the International Monetary Fund and the World Bank, has also been criticised for reducing spending on social programmes and for eliminating state subsidies and price support programmes (Chossudovsky, 1997; Jha and Negre, 2007; Swaminathan, 2000). Neoliberalism has deepened the reach of markets and capital and has created an ethos of private consumption, commercial interests and commodification (Varman and Belk, 2008; Varman and Vikas, 2007). These changes have negatively impacted workers' movements across the country and have weakened the hold of left leaning ideologies.

In 1991, another momentous event changed the course of SH. Shankar Guha Niyogi was assassinated on 28 September 1991. It is alleged that businessmen in the region hired an assassin to get rid of Niyogi (Sethi, 2011). Niyogi had broadened the movement beyond mine workers and was fighting for the rights of thousands of workers employed in the region's ancillary industries. The death of Niyogi has dealt a body blow to the movement and over the last two decades, there has been a decline in its effectiveness to mobilise and support workers. This has further deepened the ideological deficit that SH faces.

A key challenge that SH faces is rooted in an ideological deficit resulting from the changed socio-economic conditions and decline of CMSS. Jana believes that unlike in the 1960s and 70s the left movement in the country is at the low ebb. He observed:

> This surrounding area is in need of a movement, a movement where peasants, poor participate. Then these younger people can become part of the movement, can help them and provide them healthcare services. This will help them develop also. So, the movement is very essential. So long there is no movement, it will remain a challenge.

A decline in the left movement is one of the key reasons for the dearth of politically motivated doctors. Jana further argues,

> In the late 80s and early 90s, there was a junior doctors' movement. They demanded 24-hour emergency care in hospitals, and the government was forced to accept it. The Supreme Court gave a verdict that no government hospital could refuse a patient. But, now a days there is no movement in the medical community, so doctors are also having the mind set to get a higher degree and earn money.

The ideological deficit is because of a lack of a social movement in the larger socio-economic context in general and in the medical community in particular. This results in a dearth of doctors who are pro-poor and politically motivated. Janak Lal shares this concern and told us,

> No one wants to do such work. After MBBS, they want to join government job, see two-three patients and rest the whole day. They are interested in private practice. We try to recruit doctors who are driven by the sense of social service but it is tough to find such doctors.

Janak Lal refers to the discursive shift in neoliberal India in which medical practice has become highly commercialised (Varman and Vikas, 2007). Under these circumstances, it is difficult to find doctors who are not interested in commercial gains. Ganesh Ram, President of CMSS, also talked about the changing ethos. He lamented that the current ethos was contrarian to that in the 1970s and 80s, when people were much more politically conscious. This makes it difficult to get doctors who are pro-working class and are driven by a sense of community service.

Commercial interests rather than Marxist ideals primarily impel most of the current set of doctors who wish to work for SH. Most of the new doctors who join are keen to improve their skills because the hospital has a vast pool of patients. In the job market, exposure to SH is considered an asset because young doctors get to work on a large number of cases, which is a sign of good training. Once they learn enough, they leave for better paying options or start their clinics or nursing homes. As a result, SH is finding it difficult to provide healthcare services to patients who come to the hospital. It is overcrowded and there is a permanent banner fixed at the entrance mentioning that the admission is closed due to a lack of space (see Figure 6.3).

Figure 6.3: A banner permanently hanging at the entrance of the hospital with
the message that fresh admission is closed due to a lack of space
Source: Taken by one of the authors during a field visit to Shaheed Hospital in April 2014.

There are other challenges that SH is facing because of policy changes as a result
of a neoliberal ethos. These policy changes emphasise deployment of experts in
healthcare services that are often more easily available in large commercial hospitals
and to richer consumers of these services. For example, Sachin discussed about a
new nursing act being implemented by the government. Accordingly, the act makes it
mandatory that all nurses should have a bachelor's degree in nursing. There is fear in
SH that such a rule would increase the healthcare costs and give undue advantage to
large commercial hospitals. This law would also go against their practice of training
workers and their family members to practice as nurses. Similarly, Jana points towards
another change in the law that he finds alarming. He told us:

> According to the latest Supreme Court order only an obstetrician
> would be allowed to do a caesarean section operation. But, there are
> very few obstetricians in India. And in rural areas and small towns,
> the numbers are very less. Earlier any MBBS could do the caesarean
> section if he/she had sufficient training.

Jana further emphasised that very often a decision to do a caesarean section is
taken at the last moment. He informed us that there is no government obstetric
centre in Balod district where a caesarean section can be performed. If this

Supreme Court ruling is implemented, it would give an undue advantage to private nursing homes and would increase healthcare costs for subaltern groups. These changes would also increase the healthcare cost at SH. Thus, policy shifts in neoliberal India pose a challenge to SH in meeting the requirements of the subaltern population that it serves.

Faced with these challenges, SH remains precariously dependent on Jana for its continuation. It is the heroic and selfless leadership of Jana that has helped the hospital to survive for more than thirty years. Other doctors and staff recognise this contribution and Sachin told us:

> He (Jana) is the main person who is almost single-handedly running this 120-bed hospital. Jana sir is dedicated, he is sincere. This hospital would have collapsed in his absence. He was not here for two years. In that period, the hospital was almost on the verge of being closed down. He went to Kolkata during that period.

Jana's heroic contribution also becomes one of the points of future challenges for SH. Despite being an outcome of a large workers' movement, SH remains dependent on Jana as a heroic leader who makes this alternative institution functional. It is similar to the story of CMSS and its dependence on Niyogi as a larger than life figure. Thus, one of the challenges that SH is likely to face in future is to create an alternative to its dependence on an individual.

In summary, we emphasise the roles of Marxist–Leninist ideology and the workers' movement initiated by CMSS in the creation and sustenance of SH. SH helps CMSS to materialise the ideology through its everyday practices. Moreover, SH challenges the dominant capitalist ideology by empowering subaltern groups and by rejecting profit-oriented service. However, the movement and ideology that created the hospital have declined over the last two decades and have left SH in a vulnerable state with high levels of dependence on the heroic leadership of its head. Thus, ideology and social movement play a critical role in the genesis, growth, and challenges that SH faces as an alternative institution.

Discussion and conclusion

This chapter investigates the role of ideology in the context of a workers' movement that has helped create an alternative institution. Our findings provide not only evidence that ideology and social movement play important roles in creating alternatives to capitalist enterprises but also contribute to understanding how the use of ideology takes place within a social movement.

We draw upon our data as well as scholarship inspired by the political economy framework, which has taken a more nuanced and a critical view of ideology (Althusser, 1971; Eagleton, 1991; Gramsci, 1971). In this research, we show that denaturalisation, exposing dissimulation and challenging legitimation are the three fundamental ideological practices that CMSS and SH have used (see also Beuchler, 2000; Eagleton, 1991). Our focus on these three practices helps us in developing a framework for understanding the role of ideology and social movement in the creation of an alternative institution.

A dominant ideology makes its belief system appear natural and self-evident. Eagleton (1991, 58) suggests that successful ideologies are thought to be 'the "common sense" of a society so that nobody could imagine how they might ever be different.' In this research, we show that for an ideology to achieve this status, it has to align closely with and simultaneously transform social norms in society. This property makes the normative order a particularly useful framework of reference for CMSS and SH to invoke to challenge the dominant ideology of capitalism. Ideology draws its strength by deeply penetrating the normative framework of a society. This allows ideology to become part of the taken-for-granted belief system and the cultural rules in a society.

Several theorists (Eagleton, 1991; Gramsci, 1971) have argued that it is preferable for power to remain invisible and naturalised as a spontaneous practice because questioning it as another ideological discourse can lead to questioning the naturalisation necessary for an ideology to remain dominant. Our data show that SH challenges this form of naturalisation of capitalist ideology by invoking an alternative set of norms of equality and justice. These findings further the understanding developed by Eder (1995) and Koopmans (2004) and provide a rich description of how normative frameworks are deployed as arenas for ideological engagements in a social movement. Our analysis of the data suggests that Jana and others associated with SH raise issues about capitalist and market-based exploitation in the healthcare sector. Our research shows that CMSS as a workers' movement invoked the Marxist–Leninist norms of equality to attempt to counter various elements of capitalist relations and market-based ties in the region. These alternative norms offered a framework for activists to bring in moral dimensions in their contra-ideological attack, which helped in critically examining the practices of other healthcare providers in the region. Such a challenge in the lifetime of Niyogi and before the neoliberal turn was effective because of the strength of the workers' movement and greater acceptance of left-leaning ideologies. In more recent years, SH has become dependent on the heroic leadership of Jana in the absence of a larger movement and groundswell of discontent that had initially created this alternative institution.

Dissimulation is another common ideological practice to hide true relations of domination (Beuchler, 2000). Highlighting this feature of ideology and its use within oppositional social movements, Touraine (1981, 99) observes that, 'the ideology of the ruling class does not exalt the struggle and its strategy but rather the rationality of order, and the laws of economics, balance or growth'. It is common to see poor working conditions and inequity justified in the name of economic growth. Moreover, popular media present capitalism as the only possible way of modern life. CMSS opposed this form of dissimulation and set up an alternative discourse of the 'real' capitalism that is fundamentally exploitative and revealed the gap between the actual functioning of a profit-oriented system and its popular representations. According to Beuchler (2000, 202) revelation is used in social movements to challenge the dissimulating effect of dominant ideologies and brings, 'power relations to the surface of social consciousness'. CMSS tried to create this revelation through close inquiry into business actions and by bringing corporate behaviour under public scrutiny. Our data show that SH was an important embodiment of this process of dissimulation. SH helped the CMSS leadership to show that alternative institutions that worked for subaltern groups could be successfully created as a challenge to capitalist enterprises and state inaction in the domain of public service.

To mount a counter-ideological attack, SH's and CMSS' leadership understood that it was necessary to relate Marxist–Leninist ideas to the lived experience of workers and farmers. According to Eagleton (1991, 48), 'ideology must work both practically and theoretically, and discover some way of linking these levels. It must extend from an elaborated system of thought to the minutiae of everyday life, from a scholarly treatise to a shout in the street'.

Similarly, Althusser (1971) and Gramsci (1971) differentiate between theoretical ideology and practical ideology of social life and emphasise the significance of the latter. In creating alternative political, economic and health-related institutions, Niyogi and other CMSS leaders understood that for the counter-ideology of Marxism–Leninism to take an organic hold, it was necessary to make it a part of the lived reality of subaltern groups in the region. Moreover, the leadership of CMSS recognised that health was a salient issue for workers that could help the movement to achieve resonance in a seamless fashion (see also Snow and Benford, 1988). This resonance, in turn, helped the movement to achieve wider and more committed workers' participation. Thus, this chapter enhances our understanding by offering insights into how CMSS tried to create multifaceted practices and how the domains of politics and material existence were woven together to create a web of ideas that could appeal to subaltern groups and move them to participate in a common struggle.

Legitimation is another essential feature of ideology that allows unjust and oppressive social relations to be accepted in a society (Eagleton, 1991; Habermas, 1976). Our findings provide a rich illustration of how the CMSS and SH leadership attempted to create a legitimation deficiency (Habermas, 1976). Habermas (1976, 46) defines legitimation crisis as emerging when, 'the legitimizing system does not succeed in maintaining the requisite levels of mass loyalty while the steering imperatives from the economic system are carried through'. We find that Niyogi, Jana and others emphasised problems with the existing treatment of workers to precipitate a breakdown in the consensual reference points, discursive justification, and thus the legitimacy of capitalist relations (Habermas, 1976; Steffek, 2003).

In conclusion, in examining a workers' movement in this chapter, we have highlighted the significance of ideology in the creation of an alternative institution. Most significantly, we have focused our attention on how an alternative institution becomes an embodiment of a counter-ideology. We have emphasised the importance of naturalisation, legitimation and dissimulation in this ideological process. Our study raises several issues that researchers may wish to address, including how different ideological practices are brought together to appeal to diverse actors in a social movement. In addition, researchers might explore ways in which anti-capitalist ideological practices are sustained or getting transformed, in the face of the onslaught of neoliberalism in India. Moreover, researchers can examine how extra-ideological violence is used and justified as a repressive tool against alternative institutions and subaltern groups. In the face of failing state institutions, lack of accountability of private enterprises, alternative public institutions are of great importance for subaltern groups. It is necessary for management research in India to understand how such institutions are created and sustained. Addressing some of these questions will help management theorists to imagine alternatives to neoliberal capitalism.

References

Althusser, Louis. 1971. *Lenin and Philosophy*. New York: Monthly Review.

Bardhan, Pranab 2003. *Poverty, Agrarian Structure and Political Economy in India: Selected Essays*. New Delhi: Oxford.

Bhaskar, Roy. 1993. *Dialectic: The Pulse of Freedom.* London: Verso.

Buechler, Steven M. 2000. *Social Movements in Advanced Capitalism: The Political Economy and Cultural Construction of Social Activism.* New York: Oxford.

Chandrashekhar, C. P. and Jayati Ghosh. 2000. *The Market That Failed.* New Delhi: Leftword.

Chossudovsky, Michel. 1997. *The Globalization of Poverty Impacts of IMF and World Bank Reforms.* London: Zed Books.

Dogra, Bharat. 1991. 'Chhattisgarh People's Movement after Niyogi.' *Economic and Political Weekly* 26(43) (26 October): 2457.

Eagleton, Terry. 1991. *Ideology: An Introduction.* London: Verso.

Eder, Klaus. 1995. 'Does Social Class Matter in the Study of Social Movements? A Theory of Middle-class Radicalism'. In *Social Movements and Social Classes: The Future of Collective Action*, edited by Louis Maheu, 21–54. London: Sage.

Erlandson, David A., Edward L. Harris, Barbara L. Skipper and Steve D. Allen. 1993. *Doing Naturalistic Inquiry: A Guide to Methods.* Newbury Park, CA: Sage.

Ewen, Stuart B. 1976. *Captains of Consciousness: Advertising and the Social Roots of the Consumer Culture.* New York: McGraw Hill.

Giddens, Anthony. 1979. *Central Problems in Social Theory: Action, Structure and Contradiction in Social Analysis.* Berkeley and Los Angeles: University of California Press.

Gramsci, Antonio. 1971. *Selections from the prison notebooks of Antonio Gramsci.* Translated by Quintin Hoare and Geoffrey Nowell Smith. New York: International Publishers.

Habermas, Jurgen. 1976. *Legitimation Crisis.* London: Heinamann.

Horkheimer, Max and Theodor Adorno. 1944. *Dialectic of Enlightenment.* NY: Continuum.

Jha, Praveen and Mario Negre. 2007. 'Indian Economy in the Era of Contemporary Globalization: Some Core Elements of the Balance Sheet'. Accessed on 15 August 2007. Available at http://www.macroscan.org/anl/may07/pdf/Indian_Economy.pdf.

Jhally, S. 1987. *The Codes of Advertising: Fetishism and the Political Economy of Meaning in the Consumer Society.* New York: St. Martin's Press.

Klein, J. G., N. C. Smith and A. John. 2004. 'Why We Boycott: Consumer Motivations for Boycott Participation.' *Journal of Marketing* 68(3): 92–109.

Kurien, C. T. 1994. *Global capitalism and the Indian economy.* New Delhi: Orient Longman.

Kozinets, R. V. and J. M. Handelman. 2004. 'Adversaries of Consumption: Consumer Movements, Activism, and Ideology.' *Journal of Consumer Research* 31(3): 691–704.

Koopmans, Rudd. 2004. 'Movements and Media: Selection Processes and Evolutionary Dynamics in the Public Sphere', *Theory and Society* 33(3–4) (June): 367–91.

Lenin, Vladimir. 1902. 'What is to be Done?' Accessed on 3 December 2015. Available at https://www.marxists.org/archive/lenin/works/download/what-itd.pdf.

Lukacs, Georg. 1971. *History and Class Consciousness: Studies in Marxist Dialectics.* London: Merlin Press.

Marcuse, Herbert. 1968. *One Dimensional Man.* Boston: Beacon Press.

Marx, Karl. 1968. 'The German Ideology'. Accessed on 3 December 2015. Available at

https://www.marxists.org/archive/marx/works/download/Marx_The_German_
Ideology.pdf.

Melucci, Alberto. 1995. 'The New Social Movements Revisited: Reflections on a Sociological
Misunderstanding'. In *Social Movements and Social Classes: The Future of Collective Action*,
edited by Louis Maheu, 107–19. London: Sage.

Niyogi, Shankar Guha. 1993. *Two Conversations with Comrade Niyogi on Trade Union Movement*
(An interview of Shankar Guha Niyogi by Pankaj Sharma originally published in *Nai
Duniya* on 14 June 1981). Dalli Rajhara, Durg: Lok Sahitya Parishad.

O'Reilly, D. 2006. 'Branding Ideology'. *Marketing Theory* 6(2): 263–71.

Offe, Claus. 1999. 'New Social Movements: Challenging the Boundaries of Institutional
Boundaries'. In *Modernity: Critical Concepts, Volume IV*, edited by Malcolm Waters,
336–72. London: Routledge.

Olofsson, Gunnar. 1988. 'After the Working-class Movement? An Essay on What's "New" and
What's "Social" in the New Social Movements'. *Acta Sociologica* 31(1): 15–34.

Sethi, Aman. 2011. 'The Five Legged Elephant'. *The Hindu*, 30 September. Accessed on 3
December 2015. Available at http://www.thehindu.com/opinion/op-ed/the-fivelegged-
elephant/article2497776.ece.

Singh, N. K. 1977. 'Dalli Rajahara: Trade Unionism with a Difference'. *Economic and Political
Weekly* 12 (29) (16 July). Accessed on on 4 April 2017. Available at http://www.epw.
in/journal/1977/29/our-correspondent-columns/dalli-rajahara-trade-unionism-
difference.html.

Sklair, Leslie. 1994. 'Capitalism and Development in Global Perspective'. In *Capitalism and
Development*, edited by L Sklair, 165–85. London: Routledge.

Snow, David A. and Robert D. Benford. 1988. 'Ideology, Frame Resonance, and Participant
Mobilization'. In *International Social Movement Research, Vol. 1: From Structure to Action*,
edited by B. Klandermans, H. Kriesi and S. Tarrow, 197–218. Greenwich: Jai Press.

Steffek, Jens. 2003. 'The Legitimation of International Governance: A Discourse Approach'.
European Journal of International Relations 9(2): 249–75.

Thompson, C. J. and Z. Arsel. 2004. 'The Starbucks Brandscape and Consumers: Anticorporate
Experiences of Glocalization'. *Journal of Consumer Research* 31(3): 631–42.

Thompson, C. and M. Troester. 2002. 'Consumer Value Systems in the Age of Postmodern
Fragmentation: The Case of Natural Healthcare Microculture'. *Journal of Consumer
Research* 28(March): 550–71.

Touraine, Alain. 1981. *The Voice and the Eye: An Analysis of Social Movements*. London:
Cambridge University Press.

Varman, R. and R. W. Belk. 2008. 'Weaving a Web: Subaltern Consumers, Rising Consumer
Culture, and Television'. *Marketing Theory* 8(3): 227–52.

Varman, R. and R. M. Vikas. 2007. 'Rising Markets and Failing Health: An Inquiry into
Subaltern Health Care Consumption under Neoliberalism'. *Journal of Macromarketing*
27(2): 162–72.

7

Acting for Change

A Circuits of Power Analysis of a Denotified Nomadic Tribe and Budhan Theater's Struggle for Change

Prateek Shah, George Kandathil and Anvika Kapoor

We arrive in an auto-rickshaw; on its three wheels it is far more capable of plying the single narrow road in Chharanagar than a car. It is our first visit and we end up missing the library altogether, instead getting off at a railway crossing at the end of the road, from where we are escorted backwards on foot. We are later told that years ago, renowned writer-activist Mahasweta Devi and noted literary critic and activist G. N. Devy had stood at the same railway crossing when they came to meet the Chharas – a criminalised tribal community that lives in Ahmedabad, Gujarat, India. That particular meeting had heralded the possibility of a different future for the community.

We sit in the library, and over the next two days hear from the Chharas about their history, their circumstances and their recent efforts to change those circumstances. We are taken around Chharanagar as well: while there is only a single road, there are many narrow lanes, accessible only to feet and bicycles, where an entire community lives. Discouraging as the sights of the community's living conditions are, however, it is not in their poverty that the tragedy of their plight lies – such poverty is quite common in this country. What really ails the Chhara community is their powerlessness, their inability to change their plight because the label of 'born criminals' given to them by the British a century ago has stuck on even generations after independence, carrying with it all the social stigma and oppression that it carried then and perhaps more. The stigma denies most opportunities even to those few Chharas who possess some economic capital; for the large majority born without wealth, it is the ocean that separates them from the aspiring youth of modern India.

Our aim in this chapter is to describe the story of the Chharas as they have told it to us, as well as analyse their situation, and their attempts to change it, through theories of power. Specifically, we employ Clegg's (1989) framework of the circuits of power that comprises three different circuits – the episodic, the dispositional and the facilitative – that operate in an interconnected manner to create distributions of power. We explore how these circuits are at play in creating the asymmetries in power relation that so disadvantage the Chhara community, leaving them largely helpless to change their situation. In doing so, we also examine the attempts of the Budhan Theatre – an organisation that uses theatre as well as social and legal activism to improve the situation of the Chharas.

This study is based almost entirely on accounts provided to us by the Chharas. There was little attempt at triangulation of historical facts; besides, it is unlikely that the Chharas' account would be corroborated by official documents. Friedman (2011) has investigated some of the history of the Criminal Tribes Act (CTA), and we will briefly refer to his findings, but our interest is far more in the current-day situation of the Chharas, with history being important only in the discourses it has generated around them. In this respect, it is the accounts more than accurate facts that matter and hence our approach can be described as narrativist rather than realist (Silverman, 2000). Narrativism as an approach is more useful when we want to consider the rich culture in the narratives themselves and when meanings assigned by interviewees to events can be more useful than trying to reconstruct reality (Silverman, 2000). The story of the Chharas, in our view, requires this approach.

Theoretical framework

We chose to use Clegg's (1989) circuits of power framework for our analysis primarily because it seemed to explain very well what we were observing in the case of the Chharas: power asymmetries along multiple interconnected circuits. Clegg's framework, which borrows from both structural and post-structural theories of power, has the advantage of allowing for modes of power beyond what is apparent on the surface, but without resorting to concepts like hidden interest, which can be difficult to operationalise.

Briefly, Clegg conceptualised power as acting along three interconnected circuits: the episodic, the dispositional and the facilitative. The episodic circuit consists of visible acts of power in the sense of making others act as per one's will. However, the possibility of such episodic power arises from the underlying dispositional and facilitative circuits. The dispositional circuit involves flows of power based on meanings and membership, for example the ways in which the use of certain words and categories lead to a certain distribution of power. Finally, the facilitative circuit leads to power distributions based on techniques of discipline and of production.

Act I: The Chharas – a narrative of powerlessness

> On street corners my community members sell maps on which there is no place for them.
>
> Ankur Garange 'Chhara'

The portion of Chhara history that most concerns us can be said to begin with the passing of the Criminal Tribes Act by the British Government in India. The Act was passed in various pieces of legislature, starting 1871, and branded certain communities around the country as 'born criminals'. Purportedly the Act was intended to combat *Thuggees*, a 'cult of professional stranglers' (Roy, as cited by Friedman, 2011, 366). Friedman (2011) contends that 'there is considerable debate today about the extent to which such a phenomenon actually occurred, or to what extent it was a product of the colonial imagination' (366). The result, however, was to allow law enforcement agencies to detain members of these communities based on arbitrary descriptions of how to identify members of these tribes, including details of how they disguised themselves as other communities (Friedman, 2011).

The Chharas have a slightly different version of why the Criminal Tribes Act was passed. As Ankur, one of our interviewees, narrated:

> We were nomadic tribes with no fixed income who did not pay taxes to the British government. We were also jungle *rajas* (kings of the forest) who knew the ins and outs of the forests and so helped the freedom fighters in their (1857) struggle against the British. For these reasons, we were disliked by the British and 192 such communities were put under the Act.
>
> The tribes were captured and kept in open jails, where they also became cheap labour for the British. They were bound and taken to the mills to work, then bound and brought back. They were not paid and were given minimal food in the settlement.

Friedman confirms that while the official reason for registering the Chharas as a criminal tribe in 1933 was that they were a 'menace to the city' (Symington, as cited by Friedman, 2011, 369),

> ...the history of the CTA suggests other possible motives. At a conference held in Southern India in 1916, the Settlement Officer

for Criminal Tribes in Bijapur, O.H.B. Starte, discussed the advantages of building settlements near textile mills, which 'afforded employment for men, women and children alike' (Radhakrishna, 2001, 111); but it was really Ahmedabad's mill owners, suffering from labour shortages and increased labour militancy, who seemed to benefit the most from having a steady supply of labourers (Kamat, 1998, 72; Radhakrishna, 2001, 119).

As mentioned earlier, our interest is not as much in historical fact as in how present-day discourses have been historically framed. It is interesting to note, however, that a counter-history does exist regarding the Chharas' registration as a criminal tribe, of which the Chharas are aware. Foucault considered such counter-histories as a way of exercising the power of knowledge and challenging dominant discourses (Foucault, 1979), as he himself did by putting together counter-histories, for example around the sexual act in Western discourses (Allan, 2011).

While the rest of India became independent on 15 August 1947, the so-called Criminal Tribes remained in their settlements until the Act was repealed in 1949. The day of their liberation remains an important one in Chharas' memory:

> Nehru cut the wire fencing on one of the settlements and declared the tribes not just *mukt* [independent] but *visheshmukt* [specially independent]. We thus celebrate our independence on 31st as well as 15th August (Ankur).

However, much as they celebrate the day of their freedom, liberty was a bitter pill to swallow for these tribes throughout India who were suddenly released into society without any support or attempts at rehabilitation.

> After release, no empowerment, facilities or support were granted to us. We were left to live or die; but we knew no occupation or skill and the criminal stigma prevented us from getting jobs or education. Since the British had taught us to manufacture liquor for their needs, selling this liquor to the public became our sole source of livelihood (Ankur).

For the Chharas, this meant a double blow, since the state of Gujarat has had a continuous prohibition on alcohol production, sale and consumption since its creation as an independent state in 1960. With their primary source of livelihood declared criminal, the label of their community being that of 'born criminals' was only reinforced and the stigma attached with it continues to haunt the Chharas to this day.

This label, and the associated stigma, will be seen to be the primary source of the Chharas' disempowerment, for in Clegg's (1989) model it acts along the dispositional circuit, the circuit of social integration, which determines rules of meaning and of membership, and in Clegg's own words, the circuit that is 'central to the model of circuits of power' (Clegg, 1989, 239). It is this circuit that has closed doors for them economically, politically and socially, denying them legitimacy as citizens of the city of Ahmedabad.

The way the label is maintained and reinforced is an ideal example of a discursive practice, wherein thoughts, words and actions constantly reinforce one another to further a dominant discourse. There is a continuous discourse around Chharanagar being a hub of illicit and criminal activities. Some visitors to Chharanagar were reportedly warned by their auto-rickshaw drivers not to visit the area. Indeed, one Chhara himself experienced this in action:

> I was coming back by an auto to Chharanagar and I was asked whether I was going there to drink liquor. Because I was well-dressed he did not even consider the possibility that I might be a Chhara (Kushal).

The media also play a role in this discourse. According to the Chharas, the media are responsible for constantly generalising crimes in Chharanagar or by Chharas to the entire community to stereotype Chharas as criminals:

> You should not generalise crimes to a community. You never see headlines saying Patels (a wealthy community in Gujarat) were caught thieving but in the case of Chharas it is always generalised (Ankur).

The generalisation works the other way as well, with the Chharas saying they are often assumed to be guilty of crimes they never committed. For example, they were implicated in the communal violence during the 2002 riots in Gujarat even though they only protected those being persecuted:

> We have faced riots and political oppression. Muslim killings during the riots were also blamed on us but the only two surviving Muslim shops were in Chharanagar. 150 Muslims even sheltered in the house of a Chhara: wouldn't we have easily killed them if we

wanted to that night? Few Chharas are still in jail for a crime we did
not commit (Atish).

It quickly becomes apparent that 'born criminals' is a nodal point in the
discourses surrounding the Chharas, and fixes the dispositional circuit in a manner
greatly unfavourable to them. We will continue to see episodic manifestations of
this circuit in the anecdotes through the rest of this chapter.

The economic disempowerment of the Chharas arises from a vicious cycle
between their lack of (legitimate) skills and formal education and their social
unacceptability in the labour market. While there are states that have listed their
Denotified Tribes in the Other Backward Classes (OBC) category, thus allowing
them to get education and jobs in public institutions under a special quota, the
Gujarat government has chosen not to provide this facility to the Chharas. On
the contrary, the Chharas complain that they are constantly denied admission to
schools and colleges because of their community's status. Even when they are able
to educate themselves, however, getting a job entails facing the same prejudice
and discrimination:

> I have been applying for reporter jobs for the last five years. When
> interviewing for one job, I was asked to stay in Chharanagar and
> report crimes from there. I had not trained as a journalist to continue
> the practice of focussing on Chhara crimes. When I refused, the
> editor asked whether I would not have interviewed Kasab if I was
> a Muslim, because he was from my community. How could he
> compare us to terrorists (Ankur)?
>
> Even today when we interact with people outside of our community
> for jobs, we are sometimes asked why we don't continue the
> profitable business of making liquor. They don't understand that
> our fathers made alcohol because they had no other option (Atish).

This economic disempowerment can be seen as arising from an interaction
between the dispositional and facilitative circuits of power and will be explored
in depth in the discussion section.

It is not just in the labour market that the Chharas face discrimination. It hits right
at home. Even wealthy Chharas who can afford homes outside Chharanagar are
denied tenancy if their identities become known.

I wanted to book an apartment outside Chharanagar. Wherever I filled Chhara in the form, I was refused housing. Now I live in a posh society where the Deputy Commissioner of Police (DCP) also lives. On separate occasions, the watchman has spoken derogatorily about Chharas to me and my wife, not knowing we are Chharas. I never hide my identity, so I am going to let the society members know that I am a Chhara. They can't throw us out, but they can harass us (Dakxin).

Nor can Chharas ever think of buying or building their own home, as they believe they have been blacklisted by the banks. Every time a bank sees Chharanagar or even the encompassing area of Kubernagar on their address, the application is automatically rejected:

All of Chharanagar, even Kubernagar, seem to be blacklisted at banks. Our community people are automatically denied banking services and can never seem to take a loan. Buying or building a home is thus impossible for us (Atish).

Unfortunately, this social stigma and helplessness of the Chharas is only exacerbated and perpetuated by law. 'By the end of the 1950s most states had replaced the CTA with Habitual Offenders Acts (HOAs), and often using the exact same wording as in the repealed CTA' (Friedman, 2011, 369). In fact, Friedman documents from his own observations that '...the practice of cataloguing and identifying criminals is still very much alive in Chharanagar... Chhara identified as thieves by the police were being documented whether or not they had ever been caught in an act of theft' (Friedmann, 2011, 368).

The political oppression and discrimination faced by the Chharas are quite diverse in their manifestations, as revealed by several anecdotes they described to us. These include randomly being halted and questioned by police if they are returning to Chharanagar at night, arbitrary raids and questioning at their homes and harassment regarding any documentation that may require police verification, for example passports:

They keep harassing us with new made-up cases every time we talk about police verification for passports, etc. I have lodged a PIL regarding my father's passport, which has not been issued even six years after applying (Dakxin).

The Chharas complain that to the police, just as to society at large, there is no difference between one Chhara and another, that they are all just 'Chharas'. In fact, the police make it a point to label them in official documents:

> Even though it's illegal, Chhara gets added after our names in police documents, for example 'Dakxin Bajrange (Chhara)' (Atish).

The attitude of the local authorities towards the Chharas can be inferred by the fact that the building which earlier acted as a school for the Chharas was converted into a police station, clearly indicating that the goal is to control rather than help them develop. Also, the grounds near the building, used for community activities such as panchayats, have been denied to the community:

> There was a school for Chharanagar kids...which was turned into a police station and the school closed. The school playground was also off-limits for Chhara kids till, after much controversy, they were given a small part of the ground to play on. Our parents, the two of us had all studied at this school. We have asked that the space be given to us for community development, but for several years nothing has happened (Atish, Ankur).

> The land around the police station and the settlement is lying idle, with only a tiny part given to Chharas to play on...we used to have a panchayat of 150–200 people in those grounds but are not allowed to enter anymore and we have no other place that seats so many people (Ankur).

It is not as if the motives of the police are all about social order and discipline, either. Clearly, a community with limited power and resources makes for an easy target for harassment bribes. The Chharas' loss becomes someone else's benefit. As Atish explained, 'Policemen pay bribes to get transferred here since there is easy money to be made.'

❀   ❀   ❀

At the political level, the Chharas suffer immensely because of a rivalry with the neighbouring Sindhi community, whose attitude towards the Chharas allegedly ranges from dislike to hatred. The Sindhis seem to be better organised politically, and hence dominate political offices:

> There is rivalry with the Sindhi population, who live close by. They have political power and have oppressed us even further. The

Chharanagar MLA never visits except every five years for votes. Lighting and drainage problems are rampant (Atish).

The infrequent visits by politicians once elected is a common story in electoral politics, but what really brings the political rivalry and the power asymmetries rampant within it to light, is a particular incident regarding a bus stop that was to be established at Chharanagar:

> A Chharanagar bus stand was created but the Sindhis opposed it and got the name of the bus stop changed. We protested that the bus stop in Chharanagar must be called Chharanagar bus stop. So the Sindhis using their political network stopped the buses from entering Chharanagar. We have forty college students who have no direct bus: they have to change multiple buses to get to college (Ankur).

This incident of the bus stop, while only one, and likely not the most important example of Chhara oppression, calls for a detailed analysis because it distinctively highlights some of the important facets in Clegg's framework, and will be taken up again in the discussion section.

Act II: Budhan Theatre

The birth of Budhan Theater began with the death of a man called Budhan, a member of a Denotified Tribe (DNT) in Bengal, who was killed in what was considered a police atrocity. His story was sent to the Chharas by Mahasweta Devi, founder of the DNT Rights Action Group, who had earlier visited the Chharas. The story was enacted as a play by some members of the Chhara community, directed by Dakxin Bajrange and the play became so popular that they went around the country performing it.

Apart from the positive feedback they received from their audiences, the Chharas for the first time received widespread positive attention from the media. It was then that they realised the power of theatre to act as a bridge between themselves and the society that had shunned them for so long. Over time, the members of Budhan Theatre found increasing avenues to act on behalf of their community, and evolved into as much a movement as a theatre group:

> How the Budhan play became a Budhan movement we didn't realise...We are no more just actors. We do all sorts of activities like social work for our community and educating children in our locality (Atish).

These activities correspond to the powerful realisation among the Chharas that change might only be possible from the inside.

> We need a bottom-up approach. The community needs to rise, as they understand their own problems best. Outsiders at best can empathise and try to showcase the community's problems, bring them to only partial light...How many people will make plays on other people's sufferings? Sanjay Leela Bhansali (famous film-maker from Gujarat) won't make a film on Chharas, but Ankur Chhara can (Dakxin).

And so, the Budhan Theatre group has expanded from theatre to legal and social activism, working with other DNTs in the city and, recently, around the nation to fight along the dispositional and facilitative circuits of power. Their activities can, for ease of communication only, be broadly divided into three categories: (1) changing perceptions of outsiders about their community; (2) changing the community itself; and (3) mobilising the DNT community in India. All three activities are inextricably linked to each other, but for analytical purposes it is convenient to make this division.

Changing perceptions

> It takes time to change mentality. Unfortunate that it exists.
>
> Dakxin Bajrange 'Chhara'

Budhan Theatre retains a strong emphasis on the need to change perceptions about their community. This can be attributed to a realisation of how strong a role the dispositional circuit of power plays in their continued oppression, turning their label of 'born criminals' into a nodal point in the discourses around them and hence into an obligatory passage point in their struggle for change. Their plays are often about showing the history of their oppression and hence providing an alternate discourse of oppression and victimisation to counter the dominant one of criminality.

To accomplish this, Budhan Theatre keeps its plays brutally real, watering down none of the physical, verbal and mental violence in the past or present that they depict. Neither are their plays pre-scripted – instead, their plays 'write themselves' as they rehearse:

> Dakxin bhai just comes to us and says we'll do a new play: we'll have no idea regarding this. We will meet at 10 pm at his terrace

above the library, sit in a circle and brainstorm as to what kind of a play we should do. We either adapt a play or do a new one, but we never write a script, unless it has to be submitted somewhere (for permissions, and so on)

We enact on improvisation: we are given a character, which we think about and do some research on if necessary. We think about and imagine what to say and then say it. Dakxin bhai takes notes while we rehearse and improvise, and gives feedback on what we did or said right and what can be left out. This way we create one to one-and-a-half scenes in a day...We don't write lines: we just remember from improvised rehearsals (Atish).

The reason this works so well for Budhan Theatre is because for them these are indeed closer to re-enactments of reality than scripted performances.

We are able to do it this way, without script or dialogues, because we know what to represent. This is our life: we experience these things...we have a long experience of how each character behaves. Basically 100 per cent impact has to be there in our plays. We can't compromise on that. We focus on actual atrocities and cruelty. Tell the truth as it happened to us and our fathers. Once there was a police raid during a play rehearsal. We put that entire scene straight into the play (Atish).

Budhan Theatre's frank and unflattering depiction of the police often landed it into trouble with the local authorities, including the denial of permission to perform at several places as well as demands that it only perform pre-approved scripts. However, the group remains uncompromising on this aspect. On one occasion, they blatantly violated the police's censorship only to receive praise from the Additional Commissioner of Police (ACP), also present in the audience, for their realism. Atish described:

We can't get permissions to perform at any place since we're usually showing the bitter reality of our police. Once when doing a satire on police interrogation, we submitted a script to the cops since we needed permission to perform at Kanodia farmhouse. The cops read a few pages and said there were too many abuses. So we asked them '*aap gaaliyan nahin dete hain kya?* (Don't you abuse?)' Anyway, we removed the abuses from the script, but the opening show went ahead as planned. The farmhouse owners requested us to tone down the abuses but Dakxin bhai told them it can't be done mid-play. The ACP, who was present, praised how we had enacted this particular encounter specialist, DG Vardhan, in perfect detail. After that, we were even asked to come and perform for the police.

Despite the poverty of many of its members, Budhan Theatre believes in penniless productions: it neither spends, nor charges its audience, any money for its plays. If they are invited to perform outside the city, all they ask for is that their travel and stay be taken care of. Even donations are refused, except for books for their library which they welcome (we will return to this interesting exception in the next section). While the refusal to charge for access to their plays could have been interpreted as an attempt to maximise the reach of their message, the refusal for donations signals a different force at play, a force that comes out time and again when one interacts with the members of Budhan Theatre: pride in themselves and their identities and a severe aversion to becoming objects of others' pity.

The balance between sensitising their audiences to the history of their oppression while avoiding pity, brings out a very interesting dynamic from the members of Budhan Theatre. They understand and value the gains in social approval, acceptance and recognition the way only members of a stigmatised community can. Yet, they are clear that this process cannot be at the cost of their self-respect, perhaps realising that an emotion like pity will only be an obstacle in their struggle to be treated as equal members of society. The following anecdote is just one example of how strongly their fierce pride and expectations of respect affect their interactions with those outside their community:

> We have had a bad experience with the National Institute of Design (NID) (An elite Indian institute in Ahmedabad). A student from there won an award for making a film on Chharas, but didn't even give them a copy of the film. Other people have come and worked with the Chharas and Budhan Theatre and then lost contact – they don't even reply to calls, Facebook messages. We work with and help various people without any remuneration. We want respect, not money. We need people to stay in touch with us after an acquaintance has been made. Now NID people come and want to work with us but we refuse. They say they'll give us a stage, a platform, etc. but we don't need all that. We are already recognised internationally (mixed dialogue).

Indeed, scholars, institutions and even celebrities from both around the country and abroad have visited and interacted with the Chharas. The members of Budhan Theatre encourage this, realising that only by interacting with the 'decision-makers of tomorrow' will they gain the visibility and reach that is needed for social change. They have participated in courses and conducted workshops at several institutes of higher education in the city, including the Indian Institute of Management Ahmedabad and Indian Institute of Technology, Gandhinagar – two elite institutes located in Gujarat. A part of the reason they do this, they say, is to 'inculcate some humanity in scientists'.

But, as the quote at the beginning of this section suggests, changing perceptions is a difficult task. Discourses are powerful precisely because of the sway they hold on our patterns of thought and action, and the discourse against the Chharas seems deeply entrenched in the society around them. More problematically, there are those who gain from their disempowerment, strengthening the nodal point around this particular discourse. The local authorities especially do not seem to have let up on their attitude ranging from neglect to harassment. However, the Budhan Theatre members hope that with a gradual change in the social perspective, along with their work on other fronts, things will improve: if not for them, then for the future generations in their community. For this to happen, though, they realise that change is also necessary within the community.

Change within the community

Budhan Theatre realises that change cannot come only from outside, especially since the Chharas' involvement in liquor-making does lend some truth to the perceptions of their community's criminal activities. At the same time, they realise that change within can be as slow and difficult, as the change they are attempting outside. And so they rest their hopes with the next generation.

> The community still needs some cleaning, but you can't ask them to give up their source of livelihood, like making liquor, overnight (Ankur).

> Some people from the community oppose or do not support us. Most are with us but still a few are against our work and thought process (Indu).

> They still consider the old ways better: they ask how they will earn if we take away their livelihood, since they don't have an alternative skill (Jayendra).

> We therefore aimed at the new generation, gave them different

aspirations. Now some are studying abroad in USA, UK, while here 300 have become advocates while many others have become professors, journalists, etc. Our community has raced ahead in that sense (Ankur).

Hopefully because of Budhan Theatre, the next generation won't have to face the same stigma (mixed dialogue).

One of the primary channels for change within the community, the members of Budhan Theatre realised very early on, was education, both formal and non-formal. The establishment of their library as a community centre for non-formal education has hence been an important priority for them. This trend began when Mahasweta Devi first visited them and offered help, and they asked her to assist them with books for a library. It continues today in their acceptance of books as the only form of donation after their plays. The library acts both as a physical and symbolic centre for change and has been passionately preserved and constantly improved by the Chharas since its creation. Atish elaborated:

The old Chharanagar library ran out of space and would also flood in the rains, so that my friends and I would have to take the books home. So we moved to this new location donated by Dakxin bhai's father. It was earlier a gambling den and policemen who come to check for gambling are often surprised to find a library instead. Some policemen are even members. The library holds a multitude of books in various languages, including a few written by the members of Budhan Theatre themselves. It is also used as a centre for various activities for young children, such as art workshops. In addition to the library, however, the members of Budhan Theatre also educate the community through street plays performed within Chharanagar for the Chharas themselves. We did a play against underage marriage and women issues on every possible street and corner of Chharanagar. Women die here while pumping air in the liquor making process. The *bhatti* (furnace) sometimes bursts and everyone in the room dies, including children who might be sleeping close by. We enacted plays on these issues. We also performed plays on Right To Information Act (RTI) and Right to Education Act (RTE).

However, even as they attempt to change certain practices within their community, and other DNTs in the city as well, the members of Budhan Theatre also feel the need to preserve their cultural roots and identities. They realise that one threat of trying to integrate into the mainstream could be cultural assimilation, which they want to avoid.

> We want to keep Chhara culture alive. Western culture is spreading fast, but our culture and language are beautiful and rich (Ankur).

> We have started the 'Nomad Band' that uses as instruments utensils, tools that characterise the various communities, such as liquor-making equipment from the Chhara community (mixed dialogue).

So we come to yet another balancing act that Budhan Theatre must carefully perform: change the practices within their community that hold it back and supply fuel to the label of 'born criminals', but at the same time preserve those aspects of their culture that define them. This is comparable to the multicultural movement in the US, where the melting pot metaphor made many immigrant communities feel that they would lose their cultural identities as they melted into one. A more pluralist metaphor that has replaced the melting pot is the salad bowl, which allows several identities to live in close proximity and harmony.

Helping other DNTs

Budhan Theatre seems to have realised that as a lone community, the Chharas have limited political resources and are organisationally outflanked as per the definition of the term provided earlier. According to Clegg (1989), ignorance of potential allies is a common reason for getting organisationally outflanked. Budhan Theatre seems to be overcoming this constraint, realising that as part of a DNT as well as a broader tribal community around the country, they could be a potent political force.

> The day 8 crore people (the total tribal population in India) stand up, Modi (the current Prime Minister of India) won't be able to stand. Budhan Theater is a process, a movement to that end (Ankur).

The association among tribal communities is not just a political one. There are certain issues common to tribal communities around the country, and hence scope for a common identity. Prime among these are the displacement and disturbance to their lifestyles caused by the inexorable march of technological and economic development. Budhan Theatre has explored this issue in some of their plays.

> There is this song where a girl asks her father who these mountains,

rivers and jungles belong to. The father responds that once they belonged to the people. But, now they can neither use wood from the jungle, nor food from the river, nor climb the mountain. Now these are only for tourists, or to make expensive furniture for rich people's homes (mixed dialogue).

Hence, Budhan Theatre is reaching out to other DNTs as well, both within the city and outside the country. Part of the process is helping these communities with their issues, for example by performing plays on those issues, but also through social and legal activism if required.

> DNT communities have lived in slums in Maninagar and outside Indian Institute of Management (IIM) for years, but they obviously have no papers. Now that Maninagar is a high-profile area, the authorities want to kick them out. The Municipal Corporation demolished the slums and took away all possessions including utensils, clothes and blankets. Without food or shelter, infants and foetuses died and then they had to pay fines to get their possessions back. Budhan Theater enacted a play Bulldozer on the streets depicting this incident. Budhan Theater people also went and won cases against the Corporation in High Court and Supreme Court. Supreme Court instructed that some suitable land should be given to the displaced, so they were given land in Sarkhej with mountains of garbage, sewage and chemical waste running through it. The place is unfit for humans and they were basically being sent to a systematic death. So they have not vacated Maninagar. When an RTI was filed for the number of factories and mills in Sarkhej, the authorities replied saying they had no idea that so many factories had come up. Since the land was allotted, there has been no communication from the authorities. The Chhara community representatives have given one month's ultimatum to the Corporation, after which they have threatened to stage protests and plays outside their office (Atish).

Of course, this takes Budhan Theatre's struggle for power beyond the dispositional circuit and into the facilitative one, locking onto the power of the state and the techniques of discipline that exist with it. Here, however, the messiness of each circuit becomes apparent, with each one having its own flows and counter-flows. So while the Supreme Court can issue a directive, as with any policy such national-level directives can always be appropriated by local bureaucrats and authorities who are responsible for implementing it on the ground. Hence, again the dispositional circuit interacts with the facilitative, making the local authorities an obligatory passage point in the circuits of power.

However, Budhan Theatre's focus now is on trying to empower other communities to fight for their own rights. Their approach includes not only training them in theatre, but also looking for strategic leadership that can guide the various DNT communities.

> As happened with us, we want to arouse the other communities to fight for their rights (Atish).

> They want to adopt the Budhan Theatre model. So, our artists are going to conduct workshops in seven states. They will start in Rajasthan and the notion is to strengthen these communities to fight like we did (mixed dialogue).

> We need to focus on a political leadership for the DNTs. There also needs to be an art and culture focus, rather than conventional education. Budhan Theatre is looking at small centres in other states and are contemplating a tie-up with Swaraj University, so the university's *khojis* [student researchers] can volunteer at these centres. This will fill the human resource gap that is limiting Budhan Theatre (Dakxin).

Discussion

Our explications of the narratives above have intertwined theory with data. However, a few instances require deeper theoretical analysis and are explored in greater detail here.

Economic disempowerment: Interaction of dispositional and facilitative circuits

We mentioned earlier that the discrimination faced by the Chharas in the job market can be seen as arising from an interaction of the dispositional and facilitative circuits. The facilitative circuit, which is based among other things on the techniques of production, kicks in because of the nature of modern-day labour markets. Granovetter and Tilly (2008) posit two primary processes, ranking and sorting, which create labour inequalities in a labour market. Ranking is the way in which job positions are ranked, while sorting is the process by which people are placed in those positions. Discrimination can take place in both these processes.

The Chharas lose out everywhere in this scenario. They are denied access to legitimate skills and education, which of course disadvantages them in the sorting process. The discrimination against them is rampant. Most importantly, Granovetter and Tilly (2008) argue that social networks have a crucial role to play in the sorting process. Because of the flood of information from the open market, most firms prefer to use intermediaries that can provide better matching at lower cost. This can create ethnic dominance of certain firms and industries and communities that are unable to establish dominance lose out. Granovetter and Tilly (2008) also record how moral arguments are used to exclude competition from certain groups. All of these are ways in which the Chharas are systematically disadvantaged in the facilitative circuit.

Hence, the labour market and/or the formal education system become what Clegg terms obligatory passage points on the path to economic and financial wealth. Denied access to the organised labour market, the Chharas have no choice to engage in the unorganised labour force, with all its attendant problems, and primarily for them comprising the illegitimate manufacturing of liquor which is a skill they know, and more importantly an industry that they have access to. The denial of access to other economic pursuits arises from discrimination legitimised by the dispositional circuit of power. This is in line with Clegg's observation that the facilitative circuit 'cannot, of course, escape relations of meaning and membership' (Clegg, 1989, 224), the reason why the dispositional circuit is so central to his framework of power.

The bus stop incident: Resistance and 'organisational outflanking'

The particular incident of the Chharas protesting against the renaming of their bus stop and losing it altogether as a consequence brings out some keys aspects of Clegg's framework that are worth highlighting. For example, in contrast to earlier, multidimensional models of power, which considered visible episodes of power to be just a manifestation of the deeper, hidden dimensions, Clegg argues rather that the episodic circuit is the most economical place for the powerful to exercise power, since as long as the other circuits remain unchanged, they will remain powerful, no matter who 'wins' (Clegg, 1989):

> To the extent that power stays within the episodic circuit, it
> automatically reproduces the existing configurations of rules
> and domination because it challenges neither social, not system

integration and thus cannot innovate. This will be the case
irrespective of whether it is the putative A or the putative B which
'wins' (Clegg, 1989, 220).

Indeed, according to Clegg (1989), this is the 'greatest achievement of power'
(207) – not that it faces no resistance, but that all resistance is restricted to the
episodic circuit. Resistance of this form 'leaves unquestioned the fixity of terms
in which that power is exercised. It merely resists the exercise not the premises
that make that exercise possible. In this respect resistance is compatible with
reification and the exercise of power' (207).

This seems to be true regardless of the fact that the Chharas' protest can
be seen as arising out of their need for legitimacy, as a demand that they
be recognised as legitimate citizens. It does not seem, however, that simply
because resistance arises out of a desire to change the rules of meaning and
membership, it must act or have consequences along the dispositional circuit.
We shall explore this more clearly when we contrast at a later point the current
activities of Budhan Theatre against this resistance at the bus stop stand. This
incident also illustrates another important concept in Clegg's framework: that
of 'organisational outflanking'. Outflanking is Clegg's answer to why agencies
fail to question the circuits of social and system integration, and resist only
along the episodic circuit.

In the 'normal' course of affairs, we see once more the economy of a power
which raises questions neither of rules nor of domination. Additionally, we may
note the susceptibility of such power to resistance which is able to raise such
questions. If 'susceptibility' is merely a matter of raising questions concerning
social and system integration, why do agencies not routinely do so? Rather
than answer this question by recourse to notions of a captive consciousness,
one should look elsewhere. The notion of 'organisational outflanking', to use
the term coined by Mann (1986, 7), provides a serviceable answer to why the
dominated frequently consent to their subordination and subordinators. It is
'because they lack collective organisation to do otherwise, because they are
embedded within collective and distributive power organisations controlled
by others'. It is because they are so frequently 'organisationally outflanked'
(Mann 1986, 220–21).

The organisational outflanking of the Chharas, the way they are 'embedded
within collective and distributive power organisations controlled by others', is
easily inferred: the police, local government bodies, educational and financial
institutions, potential workplaces – indeed, all the institutions that modern-day

urban living requires us to interact with, are out of their control, and in most cases, incontrovertibly set against them. In addition, their isolation from other communities in a similar situation has made acts of resistance such as the one at the bus stop isolated incidents that fail to bring about radical change:

> Ignorance often extends to a simple lack of other similar, powerless agencies with whom, one might construct an alliance. Here resistance cannot be part of a concerted action but remains an isolated occurrence, easily surmounted and overcome, even when its irruption is not infrequent across the whole canvas of power's scope. As long as the outbreaks remain uncoordinated, they can easily be dealt with by defeat, exile or incorporation. An absence of knowledge may be premised on isolation. One would resist or could do so more effectively if one were not so isolated. An agency may simply be unaware of the other agencies that might enter its calculations as potential allies, yet may be only too aware of who its opponents might be. Even though the allies might easily outweigh the opponents if they could only connect, they cannot because they do not know of each other's location, although they might surmise their existence (Clegg, 1989, 221).

In this regard, Budhan Theatre's attempt to connect with other DNT communities takes on greater significance and relevance, as a means of countering the organisational outflanking that they face.

Conclusion

Hence, we see two broad narratives emerge from our conversations with the members of Budhan Theatre: one of disempowerment, oppression and discrimination, and the other of change and hope for a different future for the next generation of Chharas. Budhan Theatre wants the Chhara community to find its place in the economic and social mainstream without losing touch with its cultural roots and identities. They are fighting an image of criminality and trying to displace it with one of oppression and injustice, but also claim pride in their identities and dislike any form of pity or disrespect. In the process, they are reaching out to potential allies in other parts of the country who suffer a similar fate.

Through these narratives, we have also tried to reconstruct how the circuits of power might be arranged so as to produce the disempowerment that the

Chharas perceive themselves as victims of. We see how Budhan Theatre's empirical discovery of relatively effective processes of change coincide with Clegg's general model of power and resistance, and how resistance must go beyond the episodic circuit if it seeks not to reify the existing state of affairs (Fleming and Spicer, 2005).

Despite the occasional anger and frustration that members of Budhan Theatre expressed at their situation, their narratives had little hint if any of a desire for any form of retributive justice. Whether this stems from idealism or pragmatism is unclear, but whatever the reason, Budhan Theatre members seem to realise that reintegration into mainstream society is the only hope for their future generations to have better opportunities than they did. They focus on education, both within and outside the community, as a tool for achieving this goal.

Our conversations with members of Budhan also made us feel that as much as reality permeated their performances, their reality itself had started seeming like a performance to them – 'a performative reality' (Schieffelin, 1985). This was a theme that kept recurring in our conversations with them, wherein they would refer to the world as a stage in which they had been assigned certain roles. Of course, neither the concept of the world as a stage, nor that of people having role-identities is new. Yet one wonders, whether to the members of Budhan, so aware of the injustice history and society have done them, the power of their ascribed identities does not make their reality seem unusually scripted: an unnatural, unjust, forced state of existence where they must perform for the world, just to get their humanity acknowledged.

This is not in any way to say that they are bitter or disconnected from reality – quite the contrary. Their cheerfulness and sense of purpose in facing their grim reality might derive from the acceptance that life has given them a role, and an important one at that, to play on the world stage, which they choose to perform with skill and dignity.

References

Allan, Kenneth. 2011. *A Primer in Social and Sociological Theory.* Thousand Oaks: Sage.

Clegg, Stewart. 1989. *Frameworks of Power.* Thousand Oaks: Sage.

Fleming, Peter and André Spicer. 2005. 'Stewart Clegg: Towards a Machiavellian Organization Theory?' *The Sociological Review* 53(1): 95–105.

Friedman, Kerim P. 2011. 'From Thugs to Victims: Dakxin Bajrange Chhara's Cinema of Justice.' *Visual Anthropology* 24(4): 364–83.

Foucault, Michel (1979) 'Truth and Power.' In *Power, Truth, Strategy*, edited by Meghan Morris and Paul Patton. Sydney: Feral Publications.

Granovetter, Mark and Charles Tilly. 2008. 'Inequality and Labor Processes'. In *Handbook of Sociology*, edited by Neil J. Smesler, 175–21. Newbury Park: Sage.

Kamat, Manjiri N. 1998. 'The War Years and the Sholapur Cotton Textile Industry.' *Social Scientist* 26(11–12): 67–82.

Mann, M. 1986. *The Sources of Social Power*, 2 volumes, 1–38. Cambridge: Cambridge University Press.

Radhakrishna, Meena. 2001. *Dishonoured by History: 'Criminal Tribes' and British Colonial Policy*. Hyderabad: Orient Longman.

Silverman, David. 2000. *Doing Qualitative Research: A Practical Handbook*. New Delhi: Sage Publications.

Schieffelin, Edward L. 1985. 'Performance and the Cultural Construction of Reality.' *American Ethnologist* 12(4): 707–24.

8

Swaraj

An Alternative University

Nivedita Kothiyal

This chapter provides a case study of an alternative organisation – the Swaraj University, which not only critiques the neoliberal turn in modern Higher Education (HE) but also interrogates its colonial legacies, as part of the wider call towards decolonisation of education.

Understanding alternative organisations requires alternative ways of thinking of and about organisations. If the alternative organisation challenges modernity (modern industrial production system, standardisation, 'scientific' knowledge etc.) and colonialism, are the standard, always available, modern (and also its late or post- epochs and conditions, which are indexed in particular conceptions of modernity but not necessarily its rejection), 'Western', and colonising forms of organisational theorisation adequate? Can modern and colonising Organisation Theory (see Ibarra-Colado, 2006 for more) provide us with an adequate analytic of organisations that are premised in the rejection of modernity? In many ways, this chapter is not only an outline of an alternative organisation that is premised in the rejection of modernity and its assemblages (mainly modern capitalism, now neoliberal capitalism and colonialism), but also an outline of the limitations of Organisation Studies, which Burrell (1996) had correctly called NATO. The chapter helps in the mobilisation of alternate theoretical resources that are non-Western, decolonial and locally embedded.

The chapter is laid out as follows. In the following section, I trace the rise of global neoliberal university. In the next section, I outline key features of organisational practices and rehearse the existing critiques of such a set-up. The subsequent section provides an introduction to the Swaraj University. It discusses the philosophical ideas of anti-colonial thinkers such as Gandhi that undergirds the foundation and functioning of Swaraj University as an alternative organisation and describes its organising practices in contrast to that of modern neoliberal university. The final section provides a brief discussion on the ways in which Swaraj

University presents an alternative to HE institutions, as well as a call for alternate non-Western theorisation of organisations, drawing on Ibarra-Colado's (2006) naming of 'epistemic coloniality' in and of organisations and Organisation Studies.

The global rise of the neoliberal university

Across the globe, there has been exorbitant rise in fees and increasing student debt in HE. These are just two manifestations of many more profound shifts in the HE sector worldwide, i.e., the rise of the neoliberal university. This, Slaughter and Rhoades (2000, 73–74) argue, is the 'rise of neoliberal regime in public education', as a part of 'academic capitalism'. Reeling under the drastic cuts in resource/financial support by the neoliberal state, the public universities have responded by embracing 'market or market like behaviours' (Slaughter and Leslie, 2001, 154), which refer to:

> institutional and faculty competition for monies, whether these are from external grants and contracts, endowment funds, university-industry partnerships, institutional investment in professors' spin-off companies, student tuition and fees, or some other revenue-generating activity.

'Academic Capitalism' has resulted in redefinition of the purpose and role of HE and public universities, informed now by the market logic over the social purpose and economic rationality over social justice concerns. This has led to further commodification, commercialisation and marketisation of education (Saunders, 2010).

Another key feature of the neoliberal university is the rise in the rhetoric of 'need to increase global competitiveness' (Zajda, 2013, 234) of nations and markets through HE, leading to 'the global battle for world-class excellence' among HE institutions (Hazelkorn, 2009, 1). This competition is exemplified in the ubiquitously revered and ever-growing university ranking lists and league tables, both globally and locally. It has, in turn, inaugurated a blind rush to be ahead in the reputation race amongst the willing and participating institutions/universities in the 'First World' countries and has created 'relentless pressures of comparison and imitation' (Marginson, 2006, 2) for HE institutions and universities in the 'Third World' countries. On the one hand, this race creates a 'winner-take-all-markets' (Frank, 1999, 1) advantage for the existing elite institutions/universities in the West. On the other hand, it perpetuates colonialism and reinforces the 'core-periphery' relationship. As Gilmartin (2013) points out:

the local or national context is not taken into account when developing international rankings of universities. Space is flattened out, difference is elided, and the measures of university performance ... are seen as neutrally global. This hierarchical way of thinking has its roots in the colonial project, which sought to create new global, regional and local geographies of privilege and power. It is reproduced in international rankings of universities, which consistently show U.K. or U.S. universities—situated in former or current centres of colonial or imperial power—at or towards the top...[h]ierarchies that are already established are thus maintained and strengthened. Internationalisation on these terms ...relies on the problematic 'myth of progress' that underpinned the colonial project.

These neoliberal developments in HE worldwide have 'undermined, if not dislodged, the pre-existing humanistic vision and liberal view of education' (Maharatna, 2014, 61) and dismantled the university as a 'site of critical thinking, democratic leadership and public engagement' (Giroux, 2002, 427). They have also reinscribed and reinforced the Anglo-American hegemony in neocolonial ways that forces the universities/HE sector in developing countries to import the neocolonial thinking and imitate the educational models of the West, particularly from the USA and the UK (Kaba, 2012). At the same time, it stifles the spaces for re/searching non-Eurocentric paradigms (Alvares and Faruqi, 2012) of knowledge production and its dissemination at the sites of decolonised universities.

Since the 1990s, and coinciding with the economic reforms, India has witnessed growing momentum towards education reforms, especially in the HE sector. Couched in the language of deep crisis within the sector (Kamat, 2011; Kapur and Mehta, 2007), such calls demand an overhaul and restructuring of the sector. This agenda, in turn, has paved the way for more private and voluntary educational initiatives while limiting the state's responsibility for their provision (Kamat, 2004). Overall, it has accelerated the transition from a 'system embedded in welfare statism to a system partially based on quasi-market principles and finally to a system based on a neo-liberal market philosophy' (Tilak, 2012, 36). These shifts have not only led to subversion of public education by private interests, but have diluted the earlier questions of focus on access, equity and inclusion of the marginalised and disadvantaged sections of the Indian society (Nayak, 2014). This 'ethical crises within education' (Natale and Doran, 2012, 187) has made it necessary to search for meaningful ways to intervene. Central to any such intervention, is not only the need for a radical reconceptualisation of the economics of the HE sector and its institutions, but also the discovery of alternatives rooted within critical paradigms of education and learning. With neoliberalism in education becoming a doxa, Canaan (2006, 89) argues:

> It is important, in an era when there seems to be no alternative to the neoliberal agenda and we have less time to think creatively with students, to remind students that this feeling is socially manufactured.

Organising the neoliberal university

With the changing political-economic context of higher education at global, regional, national, or local levels – the organising practices of universities as learning sites/spaces are being restructured, reconfigured and reshaped (Rhoades and Slaughter, 1997). Discussing the historical role of HE institutions, Zemsky and Massey (2005, 3–4) argue:

> [i]n the 1960s and to a lesser extent the 1950s, campuses were public arenas – platforms for political theater, recruiting grounds for social activists... [w]hile certainly not every idea discussed in collegiate settings really mattered, rare was the social, political, or economic movement that did not consider the college campus as a critical venue for the airing of viewpoints and perspectives.

And further, that contemporary HE institutions:

> are seen principally as providing tickets to financial security and economic status... the lament is that they have, in their pursuit of market advantage, become dispensers of degrees and certificates rather than vibrant communities of educators who originate, debate, and promulgate important ideas. (Zemsky and Massey, 2005, 3–4).

In the following section, I outline some of the key changes, particularly the emphasis on revenue generation, the altered labour processes and associated subjectivities, and relatedly the conception of students into consumers.

Revenue generation for profit

The growing influence of 'academic capitalism', and resulting shifts in the conception of HE from being a public good to a private good, has in turn changed the 'regimes of policies and practices' (Rhoades et al., 2004, 317) in the contemporary modern university. A discernible shift has occurred in the ways in which HE is conceived, funded and financed by developing newer revenue streams. Such a shift is not just to offset the increasing withdrawal of state's support and provisions but also to forge the new identity of HE institutions as economic actors and active players in the market and be business-like. Such a neoliberal conception of HE institutions, Rhoades *et al.* (2004, 317) argue, manifests itself as follows:

> In the USA, colleges and universities are not simply partnering with business, they are developing, marketing and selling products commercially in the private-sector marketplace. Essentially, they are looking to generate profits, whether that is through patents and technology transfer, through the technologically mediated delivery of education and educational materials, or through various non-academic consumption items.

The quest to develop newer revenue streams and emphasis on profits has significantly altered the existing practices in the domain of research and education, paving the way for more commercialisation, marketisation and commodification of the university (Saunders, 2010). In a context dominated by discourses of global knowledge economy, it is narrower conceptions and imaginings of knowledge, work, and workers that flourish in the modern neoliberal university. On the one hand, knowledge is constituted discursively as only information, and is 'codified and embedded in technologies' (Levidow, 2002, 4). On the other hand, knowledge production through research has become excessively commercially orientated, favouring knowledge that has a commercial potential and is able to realise 'better value for money', thus undermining critical liberal education. While citing reasons of 'lack of funds or lack of work', academic programmes in liberal arts and humanities, for example, which impart knowledge with lesser commercial potential are being merged, reduced and reorganised (Rhoades and Slaughter, 1997, 10).

Changing academic labour processes and subjectivities

The World Bank pushed 'New Public Management' agenda in academia has profoundly influenced, altered the professional identities and subjectivities of the academics, the ways in which academics understand their positions within the university and the nature of the academic work they do:

> Radical change, or restructuring, of an institution of higher education

means either fewer and/or different faculty, professional staff, and support workers. This means lay-offs, forced early retirements, or major retraining and reassignment, as in: the closure of inefficient or ineffective institutions; the merger of quality institutions that merely lack a critical mass of operations to make them cost-effective; and the radical alteration of the mission and production function of an institution – which means radically altering who the faculty are, how they behave, the way they are organized, and the way they work and are compensated (Johnstone *et al.*, 1998, 22).

On the one hand, there has been a rise of 'core-periphery' employment relationship in the neoliberal university, with adjunct faculty increasingly being hired on restrictive and temporary employment contracts, forced to deliver packaged commodified knowledge in a 'Fordist style' teaching to large sized classes (Gaffikin and Perry, 2009, 120). The 'McDonaldisation' of the university further commodifies academic labour by creating a 'reserve army' of alienated and proletarised academics. On the other hand, the privileged 'research only' tenured faculty members, who are supported by differential incentive system to internalise the academic subjectivity of 'entrepreneurial professoriate' (ibid), are increasingly being subject to 'audit technologies (that) standardize and regularize expert knowledges' (Davies and Bansel, 2010, 7). The hegemonic discourses of efficiency and quality in the neoliberal university indexes academic craft into narrowly defined but measurable indices; it also dismantles the space for generation of new and pluralistic knowledge while diluting the will to critique and resist.

Students as consumers

The student-as-consumers discourse has begun to significantly shape the pedagogical practices within the neoliberal university, thus raising concerns over the concept of university and if it has 'really hollowed out…and has become an empty signifier' (Barnett, 2014, 13). The pervasive consumerism has changed the 'terms on which education takes place in universities' by forcing the 'pedagogic relationships to comply with market frameworks' (Naidoo, Shankar and Veer, 2011, 1145). This has fostered 'market subjectivity' amongst students (Varman, Saha and Skålén, 2011, 1163) refashioning them as Homo-economicous who then make use of 'economic rationality to make education decisions' (Saunders, 2010, 54). The consumerist turn in education has effected another transformation. The students in a neoliberal university are not only consumers but have themselves become *products* synonymous to being a 'bundle of skills' with self-identification of 'skills as aspects of personhood with exchange value on the labor market' (Urciuoli, 2008, 211). On another extreme, it has led the students to embody 'corporate personhood' and imagine 'oneself to be an entity that requires a brand' (Gershon, 2014, 281).

Contemporaneous with the student-as-consumer discourse is the equivalence of learning with training and educational outcomes with employment outcomes epitomised by credentialism. It has led to demands for extreme vocationalisation and modularisation of the curriculum (Saunders, 2010) in synchronisation with the neoliberal employability discourse. Thus, the liberal-humanist values guiding higher education, with its emphasis on critical literacy, are displaced and replaced by market-centric subjectivities.

Swaraj University and Nayee Taleem: Alternate organising in and for education

Mahatma Gandhi, as part of his anti-colonial struggle, propounded an alternative vision to the-then prevailing colonial education system. In his critique of modernity and modern Western civilisation, Gandhi articulated his strong reservations against the colonial model of education:

> The present system of education is useless. Those boys who get their education in schools and colleges, they get only literacy, but over and above literacy something more is needed. If that literacy renders our other parts of the body inactive, I would say I don't need such literacy (Gandhi, 1998).

Instead, he advocated 'Nayee Taleem':

> [m]y definition of Nayee Taleem is that if the person who has received Nayee Taleem, is enthroned, he would not feel vanity of power, on the other hand, if he is given a broom, he will not feel ashamed. For him both the jobs will be of equal importance. There would be no place to vain rejoicing in his life. None of his actions will be unproductive or useless. No student of Nayee Taleem shall be dull, because each part of his body would be active and he would have nice neuro-muscular co-ordination. When the people would do manual labour, there would be no unemployment or starvation. My Nayee Taleem and the village industries are mutually complementary. When they both will be a success, we will attain true Swaraj (Ibid).

For Gandhi, Nayee Taleem: a self-supporting education in provincial/mother language with an emphasis on productive craft learning, enabled 'well-balanced all-rounded education' by strengthening intellectual development, independent thinking and character building.

Inspired by the Gandhian ideals of Swaraj and Nayee Taleem, the Swaraj University was co-founded in 2010 by Nitin Paranjape, a community media practitioner, Reva Dandage, a development practitioner and promoter of self-directed learning, Manish Jain, who promotes the unschooling movement in the South Asian region, and Deborah Frieze of The Berkana Institute, a US-based non-profit that promotes 'leadership development' projects based on community conversations on issues of interest. Located on the outskirts of Udaipur, Rajasthan, the campus is set in 15 acres of land, with an organic farm, herb gardens, and an ayurvedic medical centre.

The Swaraj University was designed as a two-year long self-directed learning programme. Built on the principles of self-designed learning and green entrepreneurship, the university does not provide any degrees or diplomas to its students, or *khojis* (explorers) as they are called. Instead, it encourages them to learn through apprenticeship under their mentors or *ustaad*, promotes sustainable life-styles and teaches its graduates to adopt democratic decision making within their organisations through practice-based learning. In the absence of any pre-determined learning areas or objectives and curricula, the *khojis* design their own programmes depending on their individual interests and desires. Such a self-designed programme is expected to help *khojis* to:

> [e]xplore their learning styles, questions and passions without the institutional constraints that smother interest and joy, and breed mediocrity; Engage consciously with unlearning, *jugaad* (playful improvisation), deep dialogue and gift culture; Design individualised learning webs that are based on authentic real world trans-disciplinary projects and inter-generational relationships; Build feedback frameworks and mechanisms to reflect on their learning; Use the close, supportive learner community as a base from which to engage with local, regional and global communities (Swaraj University n.d. a).

In this, they are supported by *ustaads*, as well as *mitras*, facilitators, founders and committed advisors. The programme uses a mix of workshops, learning journeys and apprenticeship; of which the first is organised at the beginning of each term or 'gathering'. The functioning of the Swaraj University is supported in the form of gifts and grants from individuals and aid organisations. Its management is non-hierarchical and embodies the philosophical foundations of the Swaraj: a commitment to social justice and democracy, co-creation, organic agriculture, gifting, alternate leadership, collective decision-making and sustainable living.

The gift culture

While, the neoliberal modern university operates on the dogmas of modern economics, Homo-economicus and now TINA (There Is No Alternative), organising practices in the Swaraj University attempts to recover and reclaim the gift culture based on philosophies and traditions of gift giving that are deeply embedded in the diverse knowledge and cultural systems:

> The entire [Swaraj] university is designed to function in the spirit of the gift culture. There is a strong commitment to de-commodifying knowledge and learning...Several experiments and practices such as copyleft have been initiated to understand the gift culture (Jain, 2012).

The cultural values of 'generosity, care and mutuality' are projected as an alternative to the commodification present in the 'realm of monoculture and artificial scarcity, monopolized packaging and distribution, and institutionalized hierarchy and exploitation... [thus enabling de-institutionalisation and] moving beyond Experts, Money, Technology and Nation States' (Jain and Jain, 2008, 5–6). Instead of universities becoming like markets under academic capitalism, Swaraj University nurtures the idea of 'limiting the space/control of markets' (ibid) in all the domains of human endeavours and activities. By invoking the spirit of ancient and local traditions of *pyaoo* (a kiosk to offer free and clean drinking water during summers to one and all), *sewa* (selfless service), *gupt daan* (undisclosed giving) and *aparigarha* (non-acquisitiveness), there is an attempt to develop an alternative understanding of generating the resources. Instead of burdening the students with tuition fees and pushing them into debt traps, the spirit of 'gift economy' and 'gift culture' is deployed to make education at Swaraj University affordable and accessible:

> Swaraj University is not accepting any grants from big donor agencies. We operate on the idea of *Gift Culture*, accepting gifts of various kinds from friends, supporters and well-wishers. You can also contribute in our journey by gifting books or films for the

library, or old laptops for the media resource centre, games and sport
activities for the *khojis,* or gift us your time and share your skills
and/or wisdom. Financial contributions to support scholarships
for *khojis* are also welcome (Swaraj University n.d. b).

At the same time, the concept of fees are reframed into willing contribution
towards meeting the lodging, boarding, and travelling costs of the programme,
while charging no tuition fees. It suggests:

> For those whom it is possible, we ask a contribution against
> the above mentioned expenses. And if you can, your additional
> contributions will help to support other peoples' participation.
> However, if you cannot afford this for any reason, then please
> let us know and we will arrange for a scholarship for you (Swaraj
> University n.d. b).

These practices, in turn, make education possible for all irrespective of their
ability and willingness to pay, in a sharp contrast to academic capitalism which
focuses more on the highest bidder for the education (Slaughter and Rhoades,
2004).

Ustaads as mentors

Guru shishya or *ustaad shagird parampara* (the master-disciple tradition) has
been a part of the traditional discourses on *taleem* or education, and is still a
living tradition in the 'world of music, dance and indigenous medicine, religious
seminaries or *math*' (Chanana, 2007, 6) and artisanal communities (Jaitly, 2007).
In such living oral traditions, learning that encompasses values, knowledge,
worldviews and wisdom embedded within local culture, is handed down from
one generation to another. The *guru* or *ustaad* 'embodies the tradition which is
slowly and beautifully assimilated through a long, close relationship' (Schippers,
2007, 124) in a stark contrast to the hegemonic (neo)colonial modern education,
which happens through 'decontextualised bookish learning, largely transmitted
as information to be memorized' (Rampal, 2008, 320). Although such existing
indigenous intellectual and spiritual traditions have been assaulted, dismantled
and then replaced by the imperialist conquests and subsequent colonial rule
(Alvares, 2011), it still continues in the neoliberal globalised modern university
and academia (Simpson, 2004); as they remain sites of 'hegemonic construction
and imposition of western knowledge and the concomitant delegitimation of
indigenous knowledges' (May and Aikman, 2003, 139).

At the same time, new possibilities and spaces for resistance to such intellectual colonisation have been crafted by the 'marginalised' indigenous populations (Alvares, 2011) and made possible through progressive activism beyond the university (Amsler and Canaan, 2008). As a part of its commitment to decolonisation of education, the Swaraj University has organised its pedagogical practices with the aim to reclaim and revalue the 'diverse living knowledge systems' and 'wisdom traditions' (Jain, 2012). The faculty or *ustaads* in Swaraj University include 'non-PhD teachers, traditional artisans and village healers and farmers, jail inmates, children, mentally challenged adults, and others' (Jain, 2013). This helps in 'validat[ing] a wide range of *teachers* in local communities' (Jain, 2012).

Rajaram Sharma, a nationally recognised Picchwai artist from Udaipur is an exemplar of an *ustaad* keen to teach his art to 'anyone who is interested in learning, irrespective of the caste or religion'. While, he has no formal processes for selection, he looks for a serious commitment to learning in the prospective *shishya*:

> There is no selection process as such. There is no examination paper. It is totally dependent on the interest of the person who wants to learn. The first thing we ask them is why do they wish to pursue this art? If it is only for hobby, then we don't want to waste our time...[w]e have to keep our craft alive and earn our livelihood. (Shikshantar Andolan, 2010).

Sharma stayed with his *Guru* for fifteen years and learned the art. According to him, '[t]he *Guru*, the learner, even the new people starting out, all work together' (Shikshantar Andolan, 2010). One of his *shishya* describes the pedagogic practice as '[t]he *guru* creates such a close relationship with us...[e]ven when he is in the middle of his work, we can still go to him with our questions...[w]e ask our *guru* the same thing many times, he will answer us patiently'. While another *shishya* describes the experience as 'we can sit [to learn] until we feel satisfied... [*Guru*] is available to guide us. Until now, he has not taken any fees' (Shikshantar Andolan, 2010).

Such an approach leads to 'shap[ing] the envisioned *creative common collective* of sharing and caring' (Rampal, 2012, emphasis in original). Thus, a shift of emphasis from the *Ivory Tower* mode of education to a more democratised pedagogy helps breaking the 'conventionality of a strict hierarchy of knowledge conceived in terms of dichotomies' (Rampal, 1992, 61).

Student as *khoji*

What also makes neoliberal HE a dehumanising experience are the ways in which knowledge has been reified as information and learning reduced to mere receiving of this information by the learner:

> The modern university has, in various ways, become a highly irrational place. Many students and faculty members are put off by its factory like atmosphere. They may feel like an automation processed by the bureaucracy and computers or feel like cattle run through a meat processing plant. In other words, education in such settings can be a dehumanizing experience. (Ritzer, 1993, 143).

Thus, making her passive and in a receptive role (Rampal, 1989) and limiting her scope to make a contribution to her own learning (Alvares, 2011).

In a sharp contrast, students at the Swaraj University are considered as *khoji* or seekers:

> We encourage and support each of the *khojis* to enter the process of exploring their own 'experiments with truth' (which is the title of Gandhi's biography). From Day one, students are asked what they want to learn, what is important to them, what is their deeper search, and are introduced to several key processes of self-design learning such as unlearning and deep listening (Jain, 2013, 90).

The unlearning experience also encompasses going beyond print literacy and loosening the shackles of the disciplinary effects of modern education geared towards the production of the smooth running of industrial corporations. Sakhi, a *khoji* from Nasik, describes her experience as

> [h]ere [at the Swaraj University] I am not just rushing to get a degree. I am also trying to figure out how I want to live my life and what kind of a person I want to be in the future (Shikshantar, n.d.).

One such unlearning experience in Swaraj University is a 'learning journey on cycles, without money, technology or first aid, with the aim of going to the heart of India – its villages – and learning from nature and those living in harmony with it' (Swaraj University, n.d. c). Unlearning, then becomes:

> an intentional experiment in breaking out of our fear of money and re-connecting ourselves with the gift culture. It is based on

surrendering to the goodness and generosity of people, nature and the universe to provide both food and shelter, as well as love and care. It is about revaluing and recovering many of our gifts which have been made invisible. For all of us who have participated in the *yatras*, the act of leaving home without money is the first mental hurdle to overcome. We as urban people, are not used to being so vulnerable. This vulnerability, we have learned, is key to accessing the gift culture (Jain and Jain, 2008, 77).

And so, learning is redirected towards 're-build[ing] positive relationships with people that are not mediated by money or institutional status' (ibid).

Another distinguishing feature of Swaraj University is its commitment to fight against the dehumanising 'hidden curriculum' of modern education, which includes compulsion, competition/comparison, commodification, compartmentalisation of knowledge, decontextualisation, and monoculture (Jain, 2013). This deep conviction to resist the hegemonic model of 'McEducation' has emerged from unsettling personal experiences of the co-founders of Swaraj University. As Reva Dandage (Swapathgami, n.d.) admits:

> My own experience with education was not great. I failed in 12th grade in almost every subject. Two of my peers who also failed, committed suicide shortly afterwards. This moved me tremendously...I began looking for alternatives that acknowledged who people are and their various learning styles and gifts. So I spent the next seven years visiting, learning about, and working with free schools in the U.S., England, and Israel, as both a student and a staff member. The purpose was to learn and to find out what I could start back in India...I felt inspired to create something here.

The unfairness and injustice of ranking and labelling millions of young people, especially the disadvantaged and marginalised as 'failures' or 'rejects' by an education system that relied more on fear and carrot and stick approach to enforce conformity than to ignite passion and explore deeper purpose, also unsettled Manish Jain of Shikshantar (personal communication). For him, 'it is personally very painful every time I meet a young person in India who describes himself as 'I am tenth class fail'. Failure has become a part of their identity' (Jain, 2013, 86). As a result, one of the organising practices of Swaraj University is to keep the admission open to anyone in the age bracket of 18–25 years with no requirement of prior degree or certificate to join the programme.

Unlike the competitive selection processes undertaken in traditional universities, the selection process in Swaraj University has been designed to enhance mutual understanding and assess if the future *khoji* is a potentially good match with the learning processes practiced in the Swaraj University. The different steps in the selection process call for an honest engagement, intense reflections and wider discussions by the aspirant *khoji* within and with her significant others including family members. An intensive orientation programme helps the future *khoji* decide if Swaraj University is the right place for her future leaning journey. Once a *khoji* joins the Swaraj University, she is set on a path of self-directed learning, far away from the popular voices of media, society and educational institutions, in an environment that is amenable to exploration, is safe and nourishes creativity (Swaraj University n.d. c). This learning path is supported by ensuring:

> Each student designs their own personalized learning programs based on their dreams for their lives and their community. They learn/work on authentic projects which affect the lives of others; students are initiated in peer co-learning and community living and the mundane but important day-to-day life questions of shit, waste, food, water, energy, entertainment, power and conflict; students have the power to choose their own mentors (Jain, 2013, 90).

These self-learning processes help the *khoji* visualise the interconnection between their choices, thus action, and the impact it may have on the communities and the nature. It further inculcates and strengthens '*social intelligence* which include[s] wisdom, leadership and social responsibility as attributes of an intelligent person' (Rampal, 2008, 315). Though, there are challenges when the cohort of *khojis* come from different backgrounds such as metro, urban/semi-urban and rural, value systems and experiences (Jain, 2012), the constructivist stance of the pedagogy followed not only facilitates personal constructions of knowledge through negotiated experiences but also establishes meaningful communication by developing a deeper empathy for each other's constructs (Rampal, 1992).

The resistance against 'credentialism' is taken forward in Swaraj University by another organising practice that further questions the legitimacy of degrees by the practice of 'No to degrees and certificates':

> [W]e do not give any degrees after the course. We are proud of being totally unrecognized and un-deemed, since we believe in creating portfolios based on one's own experiences rather than degrees and

certificates as a proof of one's education. We are also part of the campaign, *Healing Ourselves from the Diploma Disease*, a national campaign to say NO to degrees and certificate and promote a better evaluation framework such as that which is based on experience and portfolios (Swaraj University n.d. d).

These practices in Swaraj University recognise how valuing of the credentials reinforces the existing elitism in the mainstream education institutions and promote the myths of 'meritocracy'. Such valuation further disadvantages young people who come from diverse settings and generally lack the cultural capital to sustain themselves within such a system, which strips them of their identities, local relationships and knowledge systems (Janssens-Sannon, Jain and Jain, 2005). The alternative practice of devaluing the credentials here aims to rupture the stronghold of 'monopoly of institutionalised experts and professionals' and make a dent on the injustices and unfairness of the 'violent global political economy' of the neoliberal modern education (Janssens-Sannon, Jain and Jain, 2005). It is also an effort made to reclaim a self, unshackled by the imperatives of becoming another clog in the massive machinery of capitalist-consumerist economic system. As Manish reflects:

> I have seen the self-image and body language of many young people who were branded as failures change when we talk to them about their gifts and about their being 'walkouts' instead of dropouts or failures. I also believe that we have re-ignited many young people's imaginations to break out of the clutch of TINA thinking, and lots of exciting self-organizing experiments and networks are growing out of these efforts (personal communication).

The Swaraj University is a small experimental endeavour for educational transformation (Jain, 2012). It offers an alternative logic-based on Gandhian critique of modernity, scope and direction for conventional universities, which have embarked on a neoliberal trajectory, to 're-imagine and re-invent' themselves in a radical and progressive way. At the same time, this experiment also needs to engage with the counter-critique of 'tradition' offered by Ambedkar, and ensure that a call to return to traditions does not sidestep and gloss over the questions of inequality and exploitation associated with caste system in India.

Contribution for organisations and organisation studies

This chapter makes three contributions. The first two of these are for organisations in the area of education, particularly in HE sector and located in the so-called 'Third

World'. It discusses the organising practices of the neoliberal, global university such as emphasis on revenue generation (not only as an objective but a political rationality), altering the form and content of academic labour and subjectivity and configuring students into consumers. By juxtaposing these practices with organising practices of the Swaraj University, the chapter outlines the urgent need for alternative forms of education and knowledge production to emerge (Amsler and Canaan, 2008) and demonstrates a possible way to move from the 'discourse on how to move from the university to practicing pluriversity' (Tamdgidi, 2012, xiii).

Outlining an agenda for alternative imaginaries to neoliberal hegemonic order, Leitner *et al.* (2007, 319) wrote that it ought to promote:

> collective rather than individual welfare; collaboration rather than competition; consensual rather than hierarchical decision making; recognition and respect for diversity rather than the promotion and commodification of individual identity; equity, justice, and social welfare rather than efficiency and competitiveness; and care for the environment rather than productivity, growth, and exploitation.

While such an agenda is a call to counter the neoliberal onslaught in the sector, it does not pay adequate attention to the ways in which questions of neoliberalism, quest for modernity, and colonialism are inter-linked, historically, in *our* part of the world. In another context, Lukose (2005, 915) argues:

> [w]hile attention to [neoliberal] globalization as a new cultural force is crucial to understanding the changed cultural, political, and economic conditions under which much of the postcolonial world now struggles, situating globalization within long-standing histories of the production of modernities around the world is in turn crucial to understanding claims about...homogenization.

There is, therefore, the need to see neoliberalism, and relatedly the neoliberal university, not simply as a 'new cultural force', but which is part of the historical trajectory of modernisation in the country. In light of which, we need to situate the criticism/s of neoliberal organisations, as part of the long-standing struggles for modernisation. Having recognised this as part of its organising premise, the Swaraj University rejects neoliberalism and colonialism, but also, and perhaps more importantly, modernity infused in ideas such as 'schooling society', '[formal] Education for all', 'monoculture' (Jain, 2013); and as products or commodities such as degrees and diplomas.

Finally, the field of organisation studies, as Burrell (1996) argued, remains dominated by NATO. That is, the state of the field can be characterised by the predominance of theorisation that emerges from the North Atlantic experience and history; and where like in the case of the military NATO, the US dominates. Since then, the emerging critiques of the field, which seek to challenge this North Atlanticism, remain Euro-centric, colonising and emblematic of 'epistemic coloniality' (Ibarra-Colado, 2006). The Swaraj University experiment draws on anti-colonialist thinkers such as Gandhi, and by emphasising 'situated knowledges', it draws our attention towards critical interventions that are decolonising. As organisations such as the Swaraj University decolonise our education and our minds, Organisation Studies ought to follow suit. We must, therefore, move beyond the Euro-centric conceptions of modernity and its late- and post-conditions, to recover alternate, decolonial modes of organising and studying them. We must dig beyond and further the gaze of the modern analyst (Chakrabarty, 2002) and look in our past, in the pre-modern, pre-colonial organisation of education and society. There is, however, in the present times an inherent danger in doing so, particularly in India. As the Hindu right distorts the past to produce essentialist histories that reconfigure colonialism and resurrect singular Hindu identity, we must look at and to the past – critically and cautiously.

References

Alvares, Claude and Shad Saleem Faruqi. 2012. *Decolonising the University: The Emerging Quest for Non-Eurocentric Paradigms*. Penang: Universiti Sains Malaysia Press.

Alvares, Claude. 2011. 'A Critique of Eurocentric Social Science and the Question of Alternatives'. *Economic and Political Weekly* 46(22): 72–81.

Amsler, Sarah S. and Joyce E. Canaan. 2008. 'Whither Critical Pedagogy in the Neo-liberal University Today? Two UK Practitioners' Reflections on Constraints and Possibilities'. *Enhancing Learning in the Social Sciences* 1(2):1–31.

Barnett, Ronald. 2014. *Thinking and Rethinking the University: The Selected Works of Ronald Barnett*. New York: Routledge.

Burrell, Gibson. 1996. 'Normal Science, Paradigms, Metaphors, Discourses and Genealogies of Analysis'. In *Handbook of organization studies*, edited by S. Clegg, C. Hardy and W. Nord, 642–58. London: Sage.

Canaan, Joyce E. 2006. 'Teaching Social Theory: Reflections from a Teaching Diary'. In *Learning and Teaching Social Theory*, edited by Jon Cope, Joyce Canaan and Dave Harris, 73–97. Birmingham: Higher Education Academy Subject Centre for Sociology, Anthropology and Politics (C-SAP) Monograph No. 8.

Chakrabarty, D. 2002. *Habitations of Modernity: Essays in the Wake of Subaltern Studies*. Chicago: University of Chicago Press.

Chanana, K. 2007. 'Situating the Academic Profession in Indian Tradition, Modernisation and Globalisation: Implications for Research and Knowledge'. United Nations Educational, Scientific and Cultural Organization (UNESCO). Accessed in June 2015. Available at http://portal.unesco.org/education/en/files/54063/11870007425Karuna_Chanana.pdf/Karuna_Chanana.pdf.

Davies, Bronwyn and Peter Bansel. 2010. 'Governmentality and Academic Work: Shaping the Hearts and Minds of Academic Workers.' *Journal of Curriculum Theorizing* 26(3): 5–20.

Frank, Robert H. 1999. 'Higher Education: The Ultimate Winner-take-all Market?' CHERI Working Paper #2. Accessed on 24 May 2015. Available at http://digitalcommons.ilr.cornell.edu/cheri/2.

Hazelkorn, E. 2009. 'Rankings and the Battle for World-Class Excellence.' *Higher Education Management and Policy* 21(1):1–22.

Gaffikin, Frank and David C. Perry. 2009. 'Discourses and Strategic Visions: The US Research University as an Institutional Manifestation of Neoliberalism in a Global Era.' *American Educational Research Journal* 46(1): 115–44.

Gandhi, M. K. 1998. *Gandhi on Education*. Edited by J. S. Rajput. New Delhi: National Council for Teacher Education (NCTE).

Gershon, Ilana. 2014. 'Selling your Self in the United States.' *PoLAR: Political and Legal Anthropology Review* 37(2): 281–95.

Gilmartin, Mary. 2013. 'The Colonial Tendencies of Internationalisation.' *QJB–Querelles Jahrbuch für Frauen-und Geschlechterforschung* 16. Accessed on 25 May 2015. Available at http://www.querelles.de/index.php/qjb/article/view/11/10.

Giroux, Henry A. 2002. 'Neoliberalism, Corporate Culture, and the Promise of Higher Education: The University as a Democratic Public Sphere.' *Harvard Educational Review* 72(4): 425–64.

Ibarra-Colado, E. 2006. 'Organization Studies and Epistemic Coloniality in Latin America: Thinking Otherness from the Margins.' *Organizational* 3(4): 463–88.

Jain, Manish and Shilpa Jain. 2008. *Reclaiming the Gift Culture*. Udaipur: Shikhantar.

Jain Manish. 2012. 'Decolonisation Insights from the Swaraj University Experiment'. In *Decolonising the University: The Emerging Quest for Non-Eurocentric Paradigms*, edited by Claude Alvares and Shad Saleem Faruqi, 381–94. Penerbit: USM.

———. 2013. 'McEducation for All: Whose Agenda does Global Education Really Serve?' *Critical Literacy: Theories and Practices* 7(1): 84–90.

Jaitly, Jaya. 2007. 'Crafting an Education for the Educated.' *Seminar* 570. Accessed on 25 May 2015. Available at http://www.india-seminar.com/semframe.html.

Janssens-Sannon Shreya, Manish Jain and Shipla Jain. 2005. *Healing Ourselves from the Diploma Disease*. Udaipur: Shiskhantar.

Johnstone, Donald Bruce, Alka Arora and William Experton. 1998. *The Financing and Management of Higher education: A Status Report on Worldwide Reforms*. Washington DC: World Bank.

Kaba, Amadu Jacky. 2012. 'Analyzing the Anglo-American Hegemony in the Times Higher Education Rankings.' *Education Policy Analysis Archives* 20: 21.

Kamat Sangeeta. 2011. 'Neoliberal Globalization and Higher Education Policy in India'. In

Handbook on Globalization and Higher Education, edited by Roger King, Simon Marginson and Rajani Naidoo, 273–85. Cheltenham: Edward Elgar Publishing.

Kamat, Sangeeta. 2004. 'Postcolonial Aporias, or What Does Fundamentalism Have to Do with Globalization? The Contradictory Consequences of Education Reform in India.' *Comparative Education* 40(2): 267–87.

Kapur, D. and P. B. Mehta. 2007. 'Mortgaging the Future.' *India International Centre Quarterly* 34 (3/4): 154–66.

Leitner, H., J. Peck and E. Sheppard. 2007. 'Squaring up to Neoliberalism.' In *Contesting Neoliberalism: Urban Frontiers*, edited by Helga Leitner, Jamie Peck and Eric S. Sheppard, 311–27. New York: Guilford Press.

Levidow, Les. 2002. 'Marketizing Higher Education: Neoliberal Strategies and Counter-Strategies.' In *The Virtual University? Knowledge, Markets and Management*, edited by Kevin Robins and Frank Webster, 227–48. Oxford, UK: Oxford University Press.

Lukose, Ritty. 2005. 'Consuming Globalisation: Youth and Gender in Kerala, India.' *Journal of Social History* 38(4): 915–35.

Maharatna, Arup. 2014. 'Invasion of Educational Universe by Neo-Liberal Economic Thinking: A Civilizational Casualty?' *Economic and Political Weekly* XLIX(37): 61–70.

May, Stephen and Sheila Aikman. 2003. 'Indigenous Education: Addressing Current Issues and Developments.' *Comparative Education* 39(2):139–45.

Marginson, Simon. 2006. 'Dynamics of National and Global Competition in Higher Education.' *Higher Education* 52(1): 1–39.

Naidoo, Rajani, Avi Shankar, and Ekant Veer. 2011. 'The Consumerist Turn in Higher Education: Policy Aspirations and Outcomes.' *Journal of Marketing Management* 27 (11–12): 1142–62.

Natale, S. M. and C. Doran. 2012. 'Marketization of Education: An Ethical Dilemma.' *Journal of Business Ethics* 105(2):187–96.

Nayak, D. 2014. 'The Logic of Neo-liberalism in Education.' *Economic and Political Weekly* XLIX(13): 10–13.

Rampal, Anita. 1989. 'Distant Learning and Distancing the Learner.' *Social Scientist* 17(9/10): 96–99.

———.1992. 'School Science in Search of a Democratic Order?' *Social Scientist* 20(7/8): 50–74.

———. 2008. 'Scaffolded Participation of Children: Perspectives from India.' *The International Journal of Children's Rights* 16(3): 313–25.

———. 2012. 'Educating for a Common Collective: Pedagogies of Sharing and Caring.' Paper presented at the *International Conference on Sustainability and Rural Reconstruction*, Southwest University, Chongqingng, China.

Rhoades, Gary, Alma Maldonado-Maldonado, Imanol Ordorika and Martín Velazquez. 2004. 'Imagining Alternatives to Global, Corporate, New Economy Academic Capitalism.' *Policy Futures in Education* 2(2): 316–29.

Rhoades, Gary and Sheila Slaughter. 1997. 'Academic Capitalism, Managed Professionals, and Supply-side Higher Education.' *Social Text* 15(2): 9–38.

Ritzer, George. 1993. *The Mcdonalization of Society.* Thousand Oaks, CA: Pine Forge Press.

Saunders, Daniel B. 2010. 'Neoliberal Ideology and Public Higher Education in the United States.' *Journal for Critical Education Policy Studies* 8(1): 41–77.

Schippers, Huib. 2007. 'The Guru Recontextualized? Perspectives on Learning North Indian Classical Music in Shifting Environments for Professional Training.' *Asian music* 38(1): 123–38.

Shikshantar Andolan. 2010. 'Colors of Devotion'. YouTube video, 17:48. Posted on 17 December 17. Accessed on 26 September 2016. Available at https://www.youtube.com/watch?v=JyLfEeu8EAQ.

Shikshantar. n.d. 'A Day in the Life of Swaraj University'. Video. Accessed on 26 September 2016. Available at http://shikshantar.org/videos/day-life-swaraj-university.

Shore, Cris. 2010. 'Beyond the Multiversity: Neoliberalism and the Rise of the Schizophrenic University.' *Social Anthropology* 18(1): 15–29.

Simpson, Leanne R. 2004. 'Anticolonial Strategies for the Recovery and Maintenance of Indigenous Knowledge.' *The American Indian Quarterly* 28(3): 373–84.

Slaughter, S. and L. L. Leslie. 2001. 'Expanding and Elaborating the Concept of Academic Capitalism.' *Organization* 8(2): 154–61.

Slaughter, Sheila and Gary Rhoades. 2000. 'The Neo-liberal University.' *New Labor Forum* 6 (Spring–Summer): 73–79.

Slaughter, S. and G. Rhoades. 2004. *Academic Capitalism and the New Economy: Markets, State, and Higher Education.* Baltimore: Johns Hopkins University Press.

Swapathgami. n.d. 'Swaraj University: Interview with Reva Dandage'. Accessed on 5 April 2015. Available at http://issuu.com/shikshantar/docs/121010081509-ba52791d6f0e4b6da2618c277c04b49d.

Swaraj University. n.d. a. 'The Two Year Programme'. Accessed on 20 March 2015. Available at http://www.swarajuniversity.org/program.html.

———. n.d. b. 'We Welcome Contributions of All Kinds!' Accessed on 20 March 2015. Available at http://www.swarajuniversity.org/contribute.html.

———. n.d. c. 'Year 1'. Accessed on 25 March 2015. Available at http://www.swarajuniversity.org/year-wise-flow.html.

———. n.d. d. '4 Step Process to Join'. Accessed on 30 March 2015. Available at http://www.swarajuniversity.org/join.html.

Tilak, Jandhyala B. G. 2012. 'Higher education Policy in India in Transition.' *Economic and Political Weekly* 47(13): 36–40.

Tamdgidi, Mohammad H. 2012. 'Editor's Note: To Be of But Not in the University.' *Human Architecture* 10(1): vii–ixv.

Urciuoli, Bonnie. 2008. 'Skills and Selves in the New Workplace.' *American Ethnologist* 35 (2): 211–28.

Varman, R., B. Saha and P. Skålén. 2011. 'Market Subjectivity and Neoliberal Governmentality in Higher Education.' *Journal of Marketing Management* 27(11–12): 1163–85.

Zajda, J. 2013. 'Globalization and Neo-liberalism as Education Policy in Australia'. In *Neoliberal Education Reforms: A Global Analysis: A Critical Analysis,* edited by Hüseyin Yolcu and David Turner, 234–52. New York: Routledge.

Zemsky, Robert and William F. Massy. 2005. *Remaking the American university: Market-smart and mission-centered.* New Brunswick: Rutgers University Press.

9

Alternative Organisations
Spaces for Contestation

Ankur Sarin and M. S. Sriram

Markets, today represent not just arenas of exchange but a way of life that organises activities based on values assigned (explicitly or implicitly) by the market (Sandel, 2012). In the veneer of economic objectivity and value neutrality, market-based values continue to displace other values that emphasise different sensitivities and alternate normative forms of organising society. The ecological destruction resulting from the deepening of 'market societies' is tangible and increasingly indisputable. And so are the inequalities that appear to be the natural (and perhaps celebrated) outcomes in such societies. While the glaring and pernicious effects have been alarmingly met with indifference and an inertial bias for the status quo, it has also been met with organisations that seek to challenge what is increasingly apparent as a dangerous way of life.

In this chapter, we study organisations seeking to promote social change that forces them to engage with markets, even while they resist the dominant principles characterising the markets in which they work are based. Despite subscribing to visions of development that are clearly inconsistent with those promoted by dominant discourses of market-based development, these organisations have no option but to engage with markets. In doing so, they often have to reject mainstream measures of success and constantly strive to challenge the market structures even as they continue to operate in them and perhaps even depend on them to achieve their goals. Conventional frames of understanding organisations may lead us to unfavourable views of such organisations, in comparison with others who might be operating in the same spaces, with greater alignment with dominant market logics. However, we argue this would be severely underestimating the work such organisations do. Instead, they reflect more on the measures used and the horizons privileged by these measures than the societal and ecological value created by such organisations.

While we do not think that such contestations are limited to only these, the organisations we focus on this chapter are Dastkar Andhra (DA) and its sister organisations: Selco Solar Limited (Formerly, the Solar Electric Light Company, India), Decentralised Cotton Yarn Trust (DCYT) and Pratham Books. The Oxford Dictionary defines contestation as 'the action or process of disputing or arguing'. As we elaborate, each of the organisations discussed here is not only engaged in the practice of making markets work better for specific populations but also simultaneously challenging norms that legitimise current market activity. Therefore, even as they continue to participate in them, they seek to overturn assumptions that underlie participation by actors driven primarily by commercial motives.

We elaborate on ways that each of the organisations works, to address market failures by engaging with markets and not shying away from them. We describe the motivations explaining the origin of these organisations and the manner in which these are expressed. We then probe reasons why engaging with markets becomes a necessity for them, the tensions the engagement creates and different ways that organisations have tried to address them. In analysing their contrasting trajectories vis-a-vis their stated missions, we argue that such organisations have no alternative but to continuously contest and negotiate conflicting ideologies.

Introduction to organisations

DCYT

Founded by Ms Uzramma, who had earlier founded DA, DCYT is working in developing the technology that enables setting up of small-scale units to decentralise the production of cotton yarn and bring it closer both to the cotton producer as well as the weaver. This serves as a counterpoint to the current dominant practice of transporting cotton from farms in villages, production in large, capital intensive and centralised plants and then resale of the yarn back to weavers dispersed over large areas. Further, the small-scale technology 'handle the delicate cotton fibres gently, avoiding the force and violence of conventional processing, keeping the springiness of the live fibres all the way into the cloth' ('Malkha: The Freedom Fabric, n.d).

The goal has been not only a move to a more ecologically efficient production process that creates value in the villages but also to create a product that is superior to ones produced using conventional processes. The argument is that by keeping value addition (ginning, spinning, and weaving) nearer the production in villages

– makes the process more ecologically sustainable and optimal. The activities of Malkha are now centred around villages in Telangana. There are no costs of transportation, the production is local and might also avoid urban migration. The workers (ginners, spinners, and weavers) work in a familiar workplace in workshops close to their homes, rather than a large machine-driven centralised workplace.

While the production and value addition could happen in a decentralised place, nearer to the place of production, it is imperative to engage with the markets because the local production would be in excess of the requirements and there would be areas that do not produce fabric or garments that are natural places to sell. The fabric created from this process is marketed under the name, Malkha and has been described as 'soft, it breathes, absorbs, holds colour, reflects its handmade heritage in its texture' ('Malkha: The Freedom Fabric', n.d.).

DA organisations

DA, Dastkar Andhra Marketing Association (DAMA) and Dastkar Andhra Retail Agency (DARAM) are groups of closely knit non-profit organisations that are working in the handlooms space (http://www.dastkarandhra.org). The organisations work with over 450 weavers in twenty five villages spread over eight districts in the states of Telangana and Andhra Pradesh in India. DA's primary work is on policy research and advocacy. The need to contest the discourse of handlooms being a sunset sector led DA to work on the entire value chain in handlooms and create DAMA and DARAM. DAMA's role was seen as 'innovating and providing professional services to the producer base of household textile production, and in the process catalysing the evolution of responsible producer entities that would be responsive but not subservient to market forces' (DAMA Annual Report, 2002–03). It was important for DA to contest the ever-emerging market for alternative fabric through highly mechanised centralised production systems and at the same time engage with the markets to demonstrate that the handlooms are a viable alternative and they could indeed provide a meaningful livelihood for the weavers.

While DAMA focuses its attention on weavers and the production and procurement process, DARAM was created to work with issues around retail of the final product and better understand the interface with customers. The three main functions that DA and its sister organisations perform are divided into three different silos – the policy advocacy being done at DA, the interface with the weavers – providing inputs like design, dyeing technology, better weaving techniques and other inputs that were traditionally provided by the master weaver is being done by DAMA. DAMA has over a period of time actively engaged with designers, set up dye houses – experimenting on natural dyes and encourage entrepreneurs to replicate DAMA's dye houses to ensure that the larger eco-system for the weavers is in place. While on one hand DAMA works on the inputs side, a more important aspect DAMA's function is in providing market access, by procuring fabric from the weaver cooperatives. DARAM is facing the customer, in the market. DARAM completes the feedback loop both for DAMA and DA. Unlike DCYT discussed above, DA does not advocate decentralisation. It works for preservation of handlooms as a heritage livelihood opportunity. Its direct engagement with the market is largely to provide a feedback loop for its basic functions. Engagement with the market at both the buyer and supplier end enables DA be aware of changing tastes and preferences and remain grounded in the experiences of producers and consumers.

SELCO

Established in 1995 by Dr Harish Hande, SELCO is a private limited company that describes itself as a 'social enterprise providing sustainable energy solutions and services to under-served households and businesses'. The organisation currently employs around 375 employees in over five states in India – primarily in Karnataka, Gujarat, Maharashtra, Bihar and Tamil Nadu. The organisation claims to have sold, serviced and financed over 2,00,000 solar systems through forty five energy service centres (http://www.selco-india.com/about_us.html). The organisation distinguishes itself from others working in the space of sustainable energy by the emphasis it pays to customisation of the product to users' needs and the creation of a local eco-system that provides maintenance and after-sales service to customers.

The emphasis of SELCO is not so much as solar energy as working with an alternative source of energy. They recognise the problem that the traditional grid-based energy supply does not reach the last mile and the last household. The set-up costs are too high for the grid-based energy to reach sparsely populated areas and remote villages and remote households in villages. Solar energy is an alternative source which is off-grid and provides a localised solution. While SELCO uses all the tools available with the mainstream markets – including engaging with the carbon markets as a source of revenue, its own approach to the markets is distinctly different as we shall see. The SELCO model is about providing the appropriate and adequate solutions for lighting needs for those who are not on the grid.

The second form of contestation for SELCO – though not done directly but through negotiations and collaboration – is with the credit markets for the poor. Given that solar as an alternative is extremely expensive for people who are off-grid, and that it involves a private investment in something that ought to be a public good, the normal microfinance markets with interest rates that cover the transaction costs and the profits turn out to be unviable for the customers of SELCO. Engaging with public institutions to provide affordable credit while questioning the natural emergence of sub-prime market for the poor is another way in which SELCO is contesting the status quo on how the markets emerge. This engagement and contestation is very critical to SELCO's main business of selling solar solutions to the poor. The popular notion of solar energy has been pedalling of solar lanterns to the poor on a use and throw basis. That involves mass production and traditional selling to the 'bottom of the pyramid' – the relationship with the customer terminates at that level. Unlike this popular imagination of the market, the customised solutions that SELCO creates is about continuing relationship with the customer for maintaining the systems through an elaborate after-sales service, particularly on the batteries. This activity has to be viable and sustainable in the institutional and economic context in which their customers are located. Otherwise they would be driving their customers into deep debt. Negotiating and working with these constraints not only helps the customer but also SELCO, because the experience these customers have, results in referrals of other customers to SELCO, making its own business sustainable. Unless SELCO is able to make the complete package affordable to the poor, they do not serve the purpose. Therefore, when one is contesting the market, one is not restricted to their own line of business and sales.

Pratham Books

Set up in 2004 with the objective of putting a book in every child's hand, Pratham Books wants to provide the children the joy of reading material that is outside of the curriculum. Pratham Books does not use any form of differential pricing and strives to make the books affordable so that more children have access to a greater number of books. While DCYT is engaging largely with the production process and the aspect of decentralisation, Pratham Books is basically contesting the existing market structure on a single point – the pricing of the books. Pratham Books believes that by making the books more affordable – without compromising on the content, and the quality of presentation, it is making books accessible to a larger number of children, thereby moving a step towards its goal of a book in every child's hand.

Unlike SELCO, Pratham Books, which is a not-for-profit, uses this status as a tool for contestation of the markets. Being a non-for-profit removes its need to service the investors and the element of profit could be transferred as lesser cost for the books. It also uses the moral position of being a not-for-profit to negotiate better terms from authors and illustrators, and uses extreme efficiency in production (multilingual production as against single language production) and inventory management to drive the costs down. The selling proposition of Pratham Books is that you get more books for a static budget. However, Pratham Books has not challenged the distribution chain and sells through the traditional channels through which the books reach the children and their schools.

Markets as spaces of contestation

Working with market-based models while pursuing a social objective is an increasingly growing phenomenon that has come to be housed under different terms like 'social entrepreneurship (Dees and Anderson, 2003)', 'business at the bottom of the pyramid' (Prahalad, 2009) and social business (Yunus, 2009, 320). In many dominant accounts of these frameworks, engagement with markets is seen to be essential for the 'sustainability' of the social intervention the organisation is seeking to make. Therefore, market participation is looked at favourably primarily because of the advantages it is supposed to confer in the generation of financial resources for the organisations. The challenge for these organisations is then primarily to tackle the social problem they wish to mitigate in a manner such that at the minimum, it covers all investments and costs of creating that impact. The viability of the solution within the existing market structures becomes a primary constraint (if not goal) of the enterprise, restricting the scope of the problem being addressed or even redefining it in a manner that is consistent with the solution.

We define engagement of this nature as market reinforcing rather than contesting. The market is typically seen as a non-political institution, governed simply by the laws of demand and supply. Therefore, the intervention tries to increase the scope of an existing market, make it work more efficiently and bring into its ambit perhaps previously underserved populations by product or service innovations. However, it poses no (or at best limited) challenge to the underlying structure of the market that might have been responsible for it being exclusionary or discriminatory in the first place. In many cases, such engagement might succeed only in changing the identity of actors, hopefully bringing in those with more benevolent motivations.

We do not dispute the social impact that even such interventions can potentially create. However, we believe the impact in these cases is in large part dependent on the extent of benevolence of the new set of actors. If the actors exit or the motivation changes, they are unlikely to leave behind a market structure that is very different from the one they entered to start with. In this sense, they are no different from the logic of charity that these organisations are trying to displace – a failure that we attribute to a blind-sighted worship of markets that ignores their social context.

The celebration of market as a means of organising economic activity is in large part based on the assumption of existence of choices and competition. The assumption is a questionable one, even in general. However, it is particularly questionable in the context of resource-poor environments in which the choices are often limited to choosing one exploitative condition over another. Therefore, market participation can not only fail to lead to any significant welfare gains in the short term but can also lead to reinforcement of exploitative conditions in the long term. For instance, weavers may lose their ability to innovate and be creative with their designs if they are reduced to simply taking designs from the final retailer. Similarly, consumers can get locked into product eco-system (example, a standardised solar energy solution) that is inefficient from the perspective of his or her specific needs.

Markets serve as means of exchange as well as information discovery. However, markets are also socially and politically embedded and market value is continuously being socially constructed (Zajac and Westphal, 2004; also see Biggart and Delbridge, 2004; Fourcade and Healy, 2007 for reviews). This implies that the returns to different actors from market transactions are contingent on social and political structures, values and norms. For example, environmental laws and norms affect the kind of colour dyes permissible in a market. Clearing the path for a low-cost, albeit toxic, chemical dye to enter a market would have immediate implications for producers of natural dyes and garment manufacturers that wish to sell products using the dye.

Markets: Necessity of engagement

Markets are often criticised as being indifferent to concerns about equity, while ensuring efficiency. From this perspective, social or public action is necessary only to counter the inequitable outcomes that might result from the otherwise efficient functioning of markets. However, such a reading often assumes that the notion of efficiency is a value free term. Closer attention to definition of efficiency, simply stated as the lowest cost of achieving an intended goal indicates the problems with the assumption of value neutrality. What the goals are, where they emerge from and the principles that underlie creation of a 'consensus' around them, need to be examined. It is this examination that leads not only to the need for challenging existing functioning of markets but also the need for engaging them.

※   ※   ※

Complete disengagement with markets can be unproductive and potentially mitigate the desire to innovate (with notable exceptions, like the Bhagwan Mahaveer Viklang Sahayata Samiti or BMVSS and their work with the 'Jaipur Foot'). BMVSS can afford to disengage with the market because of the specificity of the product and service it is offering. However, it is quite different for handlooms, which have to jostle for space in the customers' mind space. For example, while the decline of the handlooms industry in India can be traced to many policy choices (Tyabji, 1980), the misguided state support also increasingly distanced weavers from markets (Annapurna *et al.*, 2012), thereby converting something that should have survived in the market place into a captive silo – where governments were directed to buy handloom fabric from co-operatives and khadi outlets. Most benevolently described, the government tried to protect the weaver from the market, diverting public funds for supporting what they claimed to be an article of faith. In this misguided or apathetic benevolence, the state effectively guaranteed to pick up whatever was produced by cooperatives. This reflected the paternalistic attitude that the state adopted towards cooperatives, handlooms and handicrafts. Such support might have provided a stable means of livelihood in the short term, the effects in the long term have been rather debilitating.

For one, the approach completely ignored the choices available to weavers and their ability to exercise their agency to be strategic in their choices. Moreover, the state in its quest for legibility (Scott, 1998) ignored the fact that weavers differ in their skills and abilities. The near unconditional guarantee from the state implied that the weaver had no incentives to innovate (Sundari, 2015). While this did not imply that weavers stopped innovating completely, they did so primarily for traders (mostly in the form of 'master weavers') who continued to serve the market. Moreover, since the traders worked with a sub-set of weavers only – typically the highly skilled ones – innovation as a practice was reduced to a sub-set of weavers. As a result, the higher-quality and the more innovative weavers largely started serving niche and elite markets. On the other hand, the government system, which served the mass market and became the interface via which a bulk of the consumers interacted with handloom, failed to keep up with changing production systems' preferences. This adversely affected mainstream perceptions of quality and further exacerbated the problem of 'adverse selection' with the state procurement system.

Similarly, a challenge that SELCO has often faced is competing with organisations that bring in charitable money to subsidise their operations. A profile of the founder describes the consequences of purely non-market based motivations:

> In the short-term they may install a handful of units but after the funding depletes and issues of maintenance surface, the recipients are left with expensive, inoperable equipment and the organisation that delivered the product has moved on to another cause. What is worse is the long-term impression it has left on the market, because organisations that want to deliver sustainable services cannot compete with unreasonably low to no prices affixed to charity (http://india.ashoka.org/fellow/harish-hande).

While SELCO argues that both from the perspective of sustainability as well as from the perspective of signalling it is important to be free of charity – the argument being charity destroys the sustainability of the market – at the same time, it believes that the asymmetries in the market place have to be contested. In particular, the status quo of the marketplace is to be contested to make these markets accessible to the poor. The questioning of the status quo not only contests the way the markets are organised, but also contests the rents that the status quo seeks.

Success in competitive and valued markets is also often used to legitimise investments upstream in the production process and create new structures in production. As described earlier, DCYT has rationalised the need to restructure production in a manner that was favourable to the rural artisan and farmer not only on account of concerns of fairness, but also for the creation of a better product. Therefore, even as DCYT passionately pursues more decentralised forms of production, it celebrates the international recognition that the fabric receives. For instance, tastes and preferences in Europe are often pointed to as references validating DCYT's work (Uzramma, 2014).

Similarly, the approach of Pratham Books also has been that of being collaborative with the channels that reach the customer. It recognises that recreation of the entire distribution chain will take its focus away from the core competence of Pratham Books – that of creating content and printing it. However, the engagement with the distribution chain has to be proactive and continuous. Every time the sticker price of a book falls, the distributor's margins falls. Pratham Books uses the moral suasion to push its books. It is not the distribution chain that Pratham Books is challenging. It is contesting the pricing structure of the other players that are operating in the difficult market of children's books.

Markets: Forms of contestation

While a strong concern for equity and social justice motivates their work, the predominant reason for contesting the market by organisations like DCYT, DA, SELCO and Pratham Books is to establish that the markets are not 'efficient' from the perspective of groups they are seeking to work with. The contestation has been both cooperative (using the rules of the game) and combative (changing the rules of the game). Using the rules of the game implies recognising that there is a producer and there is a potential consumer and one needs market mechanisms to bridge these two players. However, 'combating the rules of the game' implies engaging with the functioning of the bridging mechanism. While some organisations have worked on how the bridging mechanism functions from the producer side, others have done so from the consumer side. In either case, market structure becomes just an instrumentality, but the target 'person' (producer/consumer) turns to be the focal point and the organisation has tried to intervene with that part of the market structure that it believes most adversely affects the target person.

Commitment to contestation

All four organisations have elements of what we describe as contestation, as explicit goals and reason for their existence. Further, they signal their commitment not just through claims, but decisions that have implied financial burdens.

For instance, given the increasing recognition to climate change, sustainable energy has received a lot of attention from all quarters – government, financial investors and entrepreneurs. Organisations like d.light (www.dlight.com) have grown at a rapid pace and received widespread recognition (http://www.dlight. com/about-us/recognition/) and investment (http://www.dlight.com/about-us/solar-energy-investors/). In the relatively short time of eight years, it 'has sold over eight million solar light and power products in 62 countries, improving the lives of almost 47 million people' and seeks to 'reach 100 million people by 2020' (http://www.dlight.com/about-us/).

The growth of SELCO seems unworthy of attention by these metrics.

However, SELCO sees its objectives as far beyond the provision of sustainable energy solutions to underserved populations. Instead it sees its work as:

> an effort to dispel three myths associated with sustainable technology and the rural sector as a target customer base: (1) Poor people cannot afford sustainable technologies; (2) Poor people cannot maintain sustainable technologies; (3) Social ventures cannot be run as commercial entities.

Instead of targeting aggressive growth numbers, SELCO sees itself challenging fundamental assumptions about customers it plans to impact and ways they can be served. This does not imply SELCO lacks ambition for social impact. However, instead of compromising on its theory of change that demands the kind of intensive customisation inimical to scale, it has created a SELCO incubator (http://www.selcoincubation.org) whose mission is to 'nurture & empower the next generation of sustainable energy entrepreneurs for the under-served communities' (http://www.selcoincubation.org/mission).

SELCO also sees scale as a hindrance to achieving its objective of providing customised solutions for the poor. The usual formulation of the markets based for profit organisations is to rapidly scale on a standardised template and achieve economies in the cost of delivery of services thereby delivering superior profits to the investors. SELCO counter posits this need with the recognition that there are still a large number of underserved and un-served poor who have no access to power, and they need to be served. This large residue to be served is to be served through growth of the SELCO movement, rather than scaling of SELCO. This growth of the SELCO movement is to be achieved by offering the business model of SELCO of customer centricity, moderate profits, and complete solutions including engaging with the financial institutions – to anybody interested in learning about their model in an open way and also incubating entrepreneurs who could follow this model elsewhere and grow.

In fact, to stay true to this commitment of growth of the business model, rather than scaling of the business per se, SELCO has had to resist investments by large energy behemoths and even fight out investors pushing it in the direction of aggressive growth via standardised products and working with a lean workforce (Yale School of Management, 2007).

Similarly, DCYT is explicit in its articulation of its disagreement with dominant forms of production and market organisation. It describes its work as 'an alternative to the present industrial model where ghettoisation of the worker and pollution of nature is the norm' and as an attempt 'to rid the artisanal textile chain of its dependence on large spinning mills that distort the small-scale, village-based nature of handloom cloth making' (http://malkha.in/about-malkha/).

As a source of comparison, it may be of interest to bring in another example from the handlooms sector. Desi Trust as well as Charkha Womens' Multipurpose Cooperative Society are engaged in activities that are very similar to Malkha – trying to bring in localisation, rid the chain of machinery, chemical dyes, and other elements of technology that reduce the primacy of labour. However, it does not change the way the final consumer, the wearer of garments engages with the last link in the handloom value chain – the retail shop. But for this link, Desi has changed the rules of engagement of each one of the links right from the production upwards. It has brought in non-traditional weavers into the weaving cycle, by offering them training; it has brought production of handlooms into a significantly labour-intensive agrarian cluster. By doing this in an area that has not been entrenched by the skill sets and the master weavers, by engaging in a greenfield area that is not bogged down by historical baggage, it has created an alternative value chain that could be demonstrated to the outside world. In a way, the skill sets of the weavers of Desi (considering that they are all first-generation, newly trained weavers) is similar to the low-skilled weavers from whom the government has been traditionally purchasing. We have argued above that this segment has been destructive for the weavers themselves. However, Desi has established a niche segment for these weavers by having its own chain of stores, and selling the garments at lower prices than the ethnic wear shops like Fabindia. It has been able to achieve this because Desi has been able to pick up a set of non-weavers whose alternative employment – of peeling areca nuts – is less lucrative than weaving simple fabric. This intervention of Desi could fundamentally change the way handlooms are looked at – as a heritage to be preserved – a significant departure from the worldview of Dastkar. However, what Desi is contesting is not only the traditional value chain – it is also contesting the way other non-market interventions are engaged with the handlooms' sector.

The impact of Pratham Books has been on two counts – the other players in the market have moderated their prices and the prices of children's books have fallen in real terms and also in some cases in nominal terms. The players are also conscious of the quality of books they produce – both in terms of content and look and feel. What Pratham Books is proving through its disruptive model of producing high-quality books across a variety of languages is that the market-based players tend to seek rents clearly exceeding the value added. Further, it has drawn attention to the demand for 'non-academic' books for children.

In addition to the contestation at the market place, there are two other areas in which Pratham Books engages in contesting the market system for childrens' books. The first is in having content that moves beyond mythological, moral, inspirational, message-based stories to normal, social and largely contemporary stories. The second is about engaging with markets that do not appear lucrative and markets that need to be developed. One example is their publication in Urdu. They cannot use the economies of scale provided by the multilingual production because Urdu script moves from right to left and the market is somewhat limited. However, this is a language where reading is dominated by the moral texts and needs a creative break of interesting stories. Publishing in Urdu is going against the wisdom of the market, but selling the books in Urdu has to be done in the same market place.

By removing the profit constraint, the case of Pratham Books illustrates that a not-for-profit player intervening in the market can potentially reduce the rents available to market actors and compel them to improve the quality and kind of products produced.

Sites of contestation

Dividing the market into a demand and a supply side, organisations have contested different sides of the market. Seeing the fulfillment of certain needs as socially necessary, organisations working on the demand side have recognised the failures in the functioning of traditional markets to meet these needs. These organisations have tried to contest markets by paying attention to underserved customers in ways that pure market reinforcing organisations would perhaps never be motivated to. Making the specific needs of these consumers as their non-negotiable, and tried to design and pursue interventions to meet these needs. This explains why SELCO has stayed away from standardised products. However, SELCO has not done this necessarily in violation of market principles. SELCO has several design features that ties it to markets. As we have discussed earlier, close attention is paid to ensure that the solar lighting solution being provided is financially viable for the customer. SELCO does not itself provide the financing but instead works with regional rural banks. This poses an additional constraint but also poses a check for due diligence. This also ensures that SELCO is not pumping an artificial demand in its pursuit to do good.

On the other hand, interventions like DCYT and DA (as well as Desi and the more famous, Amul) are primarily in the value chain without necessarily changing the way that consumers access the market. This choice is often a result of where the organisation sees the market failure. For DCYT and DA, their target population – weavers, cotton growers and others engaged in the production of fabric in rural areas – have been adversely affected by changes in the production process that distanced them from markets and transferred value outside of the village.

As Syama Sundari of DA points out, traditionally the weaver was always a part of the market and perhaps that is why they did not collectivise. Over time as the market changed and the buyer and producers became increasingly distant, the weaver was reduced to depending on traders (the 'master weaver'), the handloom cooperative, or the government. While the 'master weaver' engaged the weaver with the markets, it passed all costs associated with 'market failure' on to the weaver, exploiting the monopolistic position and asymmetries of information. The handloom cooperatives turned out to be ineffective because of their ineffective engagement with the markets and constantly seeking patronage from the state. While in form the handloom cooperatives were structured as Weavers' cooperatives, in spirit, they worked more as a labour cooperative, procuring whatever the weaver produced, and trying to maximise the work days for the weaver. The engagement with the consumer end of the value chain depended heavily on state patronage. Working within this space, DA has made 'the need for transparency in transactions at all levels and control of different aspects of the production process by the producers themselves' as guiding principles in its engagement with weavers to reach its long term aims of 'Facilitating participation and equity within and demonstrating the viability of the handloom industry' (http://www.dastkarandhra.org/dastkar-andhra.htm). However, DAMA's choice of the institutional form for intervention are handloom cooperatives, even if it implies that the growth in terms of business slows down to match those of cooperatives. Similarly, despite the relative success of a retail outlet clearly targeted to elite, it has refrained from opening up additional ones. While an actor driven purely by short-term market considerations would have gone further down the retail route, as we have seen in the case of Fabindia, expanding on that front diverts the attention to economic value add in the form of profits than the eco-system value addition the DAMA believes in providing the handloom weavers. DAMA believes that it would rather draw on their experience to support cooperatives develop retail expertise than get into the retail frenzy.

To understand DA's contestation of mainstream markets, it is useful to counter pose it to Fabindia, the largest actor in the handloom space. Like DA, Fabindia began its work in support of and to showcase the skills of the handloom weaver.

Much of Fabindia's reputation and image was established because of its strong association with handlooms. The commitment to handlooms was strong enough for it to display signs in its retail stores stating: 'Let's not think of an irregular weave or print or a stitch as a defect. Handloom by definition means a glorious uncertainty when it comes to uniformity (Khaire and Kothandaraman, 2007)'. The message essentially sought to persuade the customer to accept the woven fabric for what it was and explicitly stated where Fabindia's allegiance laid between pleasing the customer and working with the constraints of the handloom process.

The message still remains in the company's website, albeit in the 'Returns and Exchanges' section: 'Let's not think of an irregular weave or print *or a stitch* as a defect. Handloom by definition means a glorious uncertainty when it comes to uniformity (emphasis added, http://www.fabindia.com/intl/returns-and-exchanges/). The phrase might seem innocuous but has important meaning for the trajectory followed by the organisation from working exclusively with handlooms to working with 'handcrafted,' even if that working on fabric made in power looms or mills. Although this shift was protested within the organisation by old timers (Singh, 2010), the imperative for the shift was the desire for aggressive growth. The 'glorious uncertainty' was incompatible with the imperatives of scaling at the desired pace. Therefore, from selling the customer whatever the handloom could make, it shifted to 'handcrafting' whatever the customer wanted to buy.

This attention to the production or value chain does not imply that DA and DCYT have not tried to intervene at the customer end. As mentioned earlier, DCYT has paid a lot of attention to branding and marketing what it believes to be a superior fabric. However, it imagines a more important role for itself in addressing a larger problem. Rather than being content with the creation of one new fabric, it believes it can bring around a sectoral change by filling a vital gap. As Uzramma (2014) explains:

> Yarn-making specifically suited to Indian diversity of cotton varieties is the missing link in our otherwise potential, green, low-energy cotton-to-cloth production chain. If we had that we could regenerate our diversity of cotton varieties. We still have the handloom. Link the flexible technology of the handloom with diversity of cottons through adaptable spinning and what will you get? A unique, hard-to-beat cotton textile industry. It's only the middle stage that's missing.

Bringing change at the producer end (DCYT, Desi, DA) is more difficult and usually not apparent. The question these organisations also face is when and where do they integrate it with the mainstream systems. For instance, in Amul, the producer collectively took charge of not only the milk supply system (procurement), but also processing into its control and integrated (without contesting) the distribution and marketing and was able to do so at a large scale. Indeed, during the initial days of Amul, it was constantly fighting the established players all the way from the dairy farmer to the processing plant, but had totally outsourced its sales and distribution to Voltas, a large private sector player. It was only much later that Amul took charge of that part of the engagement.

In the case of Pratham Books it may appear that it is difficult to understand the sites of contestation. They after all work with the same set of writers and illustrators, print the books in commercial printing establishments, and distribute the books through the same value chain that the mainstream markets are choosing to do. However, their dual point of contestation is in providing quality material and pushing the prices down. Unlike SELCO where the contestation is in customisation of the product and providing an opportunity to buy by engaging with a financial institution that is willing to lend to the poor at a benevolent rate, Pratham Books pushes the price down and pushes volumes up, thereby being a significant enough player in the market to influence the pricing of other players who are providing books for the poor.

In each of these cases, we find that the first point of engagement and contestation is on the vulnerable side of the value chain. In case of SELCO, the poor consumers are vulnerable and the terms of engagement needs to be changed for them, but not in engaging with the procurement of solar panels nor with the technology. Similarly, in the case of Pratham Books, the contestation is on the pricing of the books – in order to make it more accessible to the poorer child, a vulnerable side of the value chain. In case of DA, DCYT, Desi and Amul, it is assumed that the consumers are able to engage on even terms with the market, and therefore what needs to be contested is the engagement with the market value chain that affects the vulnerable producer.

Challenging the non-material

> I want to suggest to you that we should look at the handloom not
> as an outmoded relic of the past but as a low-carbon production
> technology for the energy-stressed future (Uzramma, 2014).

The quote above emphasises a strategy that all four organisations adopt in their contestations by challenging conventional ways of looking at the products and markets they serve. The framing of handlooms as a 'low-carbon production technology' is a clear repositioning of the handloom from something that belongs to the past to something that has an important role to play in the future. In doing so, Uzramma seeks to garner new legitimacy for handlooms to be able to get the necessary support for it to compete against processes of production that appear to be more modern. In doing so she reiterates Suchman's (1995, 585) observation that any institution is 'valuable and worthy of support because its structural characteristics locate it within a morally favoured taxonomic category'.

Recognising that the ability to succeed using the instrument of markets is contingent on the legitimacy accorded to their work by different participants in the market, organisations that contest existing markets have to challenge the discourse in which their work is located. For DA, the challenge takes many forms, including frequent research articles in academic journals that also receive policy attention. This may not seem to be consistent with conventional views of field-based organisations, but an essential goal of DA's work is to change the discourse around handlooms, to challenge the notion that it is a technologically obsolete and dying craft. Similarly, SELCO's efforts can also be understood as positioning alternate energy as a financially viable manner of meeting energy needs in locations that would be unviable through centralised grids. In doing so, it repositions alternate energy as not only 'clean' energy but also the 'right' energy depending on the circumstance. Finally, by holding on to its non-profit status in a market dominated by for-profit actors, Pratham Books also wants to challenge the notion that philanthropy is unsustainable.

Conclusion

As economic activity comes to be increasingly governed by the profit logic, it raises questions of whether organisations pursuing non-market objectives but needing to be embedded in the larger economy can negotiate the tensions. The label of 'social enterprise' (Dees and Anderson, 2003) is often used for these organisations. However, questions of mission drift (Sarin and Sriram, 2012) and examples of organisations using the non-market objectives as primarily rhetoric abound (Sriram, 2010). We believe that, among other things, what the organisations we have highlighted have in common is a vigorous engagement with markets that is informed by a very acute sense of the context and social forces in which the social problem they are tackling is placed. As a result, they do not see the market in simple neo-classical economic terms. Instead, they are conscious and often driven by the idea that values, beliefs, and culture is central to understanding markets (Zelizer, 1988). Therefore, they are driven to engage with the market in a way that is potentially disruptive and perhaps leave more enduring possibilities of mitigating the social problems being tackled. They are able to do so by not only working on the ground but also paying close attention to how their work contests dominant ideas and meanings. Therefore, they simultaneously recognise and work on both the material and non-material, spanning conventional models of organisation.

Nicholls (2010) distinguishes between three models of social entrepreneurship: *functional, critical* and *transformational*. Functional refers to 'actions that addresses existing institutional voids and market failures through new products and services', critical 'action that reconfigures markets to create new and greater social value' and transformational 'action that challenges institutional arrangements at a field level through advocacy and political action'. Organisations described here have to adopt facets of all three models to succeed in the kind of contestation they are engaged in. In doing so, we don't believe these are typical of the organisations favoured by the dominant discourse around social entrepreneurship. The 'industrialised' view has taken a very narrow view on sustainability to refer primarily to financial sustainability of an organisation even at the expense of other broader understandings (Hobbes, 2014).

Undoubtedly, there are several challenges that these organisations face. The most significant being that of growth and scale as they negotiate dominant mainstream institutions. For instance, the rapid growth of an organisation like Fabindia whose success has been instrumental in reviving handloom in mainstream markets also serves a cautionary tale in terms of the compromises that had to be made. Similarly, they have to negotiate a paternalistic state that has tried to intervene in markets in ham-handed ways. A failure that continues to persist, as exemplified by the Gujarat state finance minister while inaugurating 'the first ever international buyer-seller meet for handloom and handicraft products':

> This (handloom and handicrafts) is an important sector for us because it touches the life of many rural artisans and our focus is now to expand their market and through this event we want to explore new markets for these products. While we have sales through our emporiums in state and in India, we now prefer sales internationally. And for that to happen, the incomes of the artisans must increase. There are so many events that take place every day - so many gifts are given…Corporate houses, if they can sell the stuff or buy the

stuff of artisans, under the CSR activity, they would be doing a great favour to them (Express News Service, 2015).

To conclude, the work of organisations such as DCYT, SELCO, DA and Pratham Books argues for a need to go beyond binary positions that are pro or anti markets. Instead, markets are better seen as contested spaces in which value is continually defined because of material and non-material factors. The act of trading itself reflects moral judgments about the boundary or markets (Anteby, 2010), but that is not where moral values and ideologies end. Ideologies and moral values impinge on all aspects of the structure and functioning of markets, significantly impacting both the distribution of the value created in the markets, as well as the nature and quantity of value created.

References

Annapurna M., B. Syamasundari and Wiebe Bijker. 2012. 'Mobilising Discourses Handloom as Sustainable Socio-Technology.' *Economic and Political Weekly* xlvii(25): 41–51.

Anteby, Michel. 2010. 'Markets, Morals, and Practices of Trade: Jurisdictional Disputes in the U.S. Commerce in Cadavers.' *Administrative Science Quarterly* 55(4): 606–38.

Ashoka. 'Fellow: Harish Hande.' Ashoka India. Accessed 1 December 2015. Available at http://india.ashoka.org/fellow/harish-hande.

Biggart, Nicole Woolsey and Rick Delbridge. 2004. 'Systems of Exchange.' *The Academy of Management Review* 29(1): 28–49.

DAMA. March 2002. *Dastkar Andhra Marketing Association Annual Report*, 11. Secundrabad.

Dastkar Andhra. Accessed 15 December 2015. Available at http://www.dastkarandhra.org/dastkar-andhra.htm.

Dees, J. G. and B. B Anderson. 2003. 'Sector-Bending: Blurring Lines between Nonprofit and For-Profit.' *Society* 40(4): 16–27.

Express News Service. 2015. 'Promote Handicrafts: Minister to Corporates.' *The Indian Express*, 28 February, Ahmedabad edition, sec. Gujarat. Accessed on 15 April 2017. Available at http://indianexpress.com/article/cities/ahmedabad/promote-handicrafts-minister-to-corporates/.

Fabindia. 'Return & Exchanges.' Accessed on 15 April 2017. Available at http://www.fabindia.com/pages/return-and-exchanges/pgid-1124142.aspx.

Fourcade, Marion and Kieran Healy. 2007. 'Moral Views of Market Society.' *Annual Review of Sociology* 33(1): 285–311. DOI:10.1146/annurev.soc.33.040406.131642.

Hobbes, Michael. 2014. 'Stop Trying to Save the World Big Ideas Are Destroying International Development.' *New Republic*, 17 November. Accessed on 15 April 2017. Available at http://www.newrepublic.com/article/120178/problem-international-development-and-plan-fix-it.

Khaire, Mukti and Prabakar Kothandaraman. 2007. 'Fabindia Overseas Pvt. Ltd.' Harvard

Business School Case, 807–113.

'Malkha: The Freedom Fabric'. n.d. *Making Cotton Sustainable*. Accessed on 12 December 2015. Available at http://www.sustainablecottons.com/638/.

Nicholls, Alex. 2010. 'Fair Trade: Towards an Economics of Virtue.' *Journal of Business Ethics* 92(S2): 241–55. DOI:10.1007/s10551-010-0581-3.

Prahalad, C. K. 2009. *The Fortune at the Bottom of the Pyramid: Eradicating Poverty Through Profits*. Revised and updated 5th Anniversary edition. Upper Saddle River, New Jersey: Wharton School Publishing.

Sandel, Michael J. 2012. *What Money Can't Buy: The Moral Limits of Markets*. New York: Farrar, Straus and Giroux.

Sarin, Ankur and M. S. Sriram. 2012. *Social Enterprises and the Pursuit of Mission: Form Matters*. Fourth International Social Innovation Research Conference, University of Birmingham.

Scott, James C. 1998. *Seeing like a State: How Certain Schemes to Improve the Human Condition Have Failed*. New Haven: Yale University Press.

Singh, Radhika. 2010. *The Fabric of Our Lives: The Story of Fabindia*. Viking, Penguin Books India.

Sriram, M. S. 2010. 'Commercialisation of Microfinance in India: A Discussion of the Emperor's Apparel.' *Economic and Political Weekly* 45(24) (June): 65–73. Accessed on 15 April 2017. Available at http://www.epw.in/journal/2010/24/special-articles/commercialisation-microfinance-india-discussion-emperors-apparel.

Suchman, Mark C. 1995. 'Managing Legitimacy: Strategic and Institutional Approaches.' *The Academy of Management Review* 20(3): 571–610. DOI:10.2307/258788.

Sundari, Dr Syama. 2015. Personal Communication.

Tyabji, Nasir. 1980. 'Capitalism in India and the Small Industries Policy.' *Economic and Political Weekly* 15(41/43): 1721–32.

Uzramma. 2014. 'Cotton Cloth as Continuity.' India Habitat Centre, New Delhi, October 21. Accessed on 15 April 2017. Available at http://malkhaindia.blogspot.in.

Yale School of Management. 2007. 'SELCO 2009: Determining a Path Forward'. Design and Social Enterprise Case Series. Accessed on 15 April 2017. Available at http://som.yale.edu/our-approach/teaching-method/case-research-and-development/cases-directory/selco-determining-path.

Yunus, Muhammad. 2009. *Creating a World without Poverty: Social Business and the Future of Capitalism*. Reprint edition. New York and London: Perseus Books Group.

Zajac, E. J. and J. D. Westphal. 2004. 'The Social Construction of Market Value: Institutionalization and Learning Perspectives on Stock Market Reactions.' *American Sociological Review* 69(5): 748–49. DOI:10.1177/000312240406900507.

Zelizer, Viviana A. 1988. 'Beyond the Polemics on the Market: Establishing a Theoretical and Empirical Agenda.' *Sociological Forum* 3(4): 614–34.

Contributors

Bhaskar Chakrabarti is a Professor in the Public Policy and Management Group at the Indian Institute of Management Calcutta. He is a PhD from the University of British Columbia, Canada and holds an MPhil in Social Anthropology from the University of Cambridge, UK. His research interests are broadly in the areas of decentralisation and local governance, public service delivery and public-private partnerships. His work has been published in various journals including *Journal of South Asian Development*, *The Eastern Anthropologist*, *Government Information Quarterly* and the *Commonwealth Journal of Local Governance*.

Joydeep Guha is at the Indian P&T Finance and Accounts Service. He is a graduate of the Fellow Programme from the Indian Institute of Management, Calcutta. His research interests centre on the areas of information technology and politics, political networks and public administration. His research has been published in *Man in India* and *Government Information Quarterly*. He has been involved in major e-Government projects, including design and implementation of ERP in the Department of Post.

Srinath Jagannathan is an Assistant Professor at Indian Institute of Management, Indore. He was formerly a faculty member at the School of Management and Labour Studies at Tata Institute of Social Sciences, Mumbai. He completed his Fellow Program in Management from the Personnel and Industrial Relations Area of Indian Institute of Management, Ahmedabad. His areas of interest include critical appraisals of worker's experiences of insecurity and injustice, resistance, and the organisational apparatus that provides the infrastructure for police encounters in India. His work has been published in journals such as *Organization*, *Journal of Business Ethics*, *Culture and Organization and Critical Perspectives on International Business*.

George Kandathil is an Assistant Professor in Organisational Behaviour area at Indian Institute of Management, Ahmedabad. He completed his PhD from Cornell University and MTech from Indian Institute of Technology Kanpur. He has worked in the spacecraft and automotive industries for a few years. His broad research interests lie at the interface of information systems implementation, organisational sociology and critical management studies. George has published his research in some of the international management journals.

Anvika Kapoor was a post-graduate student at the National Institute of Design, Gandhinagar, before which she studied Industrial Design at the Symbiosis Institute of Design, Pune and Coventry University in England. She has done several design research projects for companies like Google, Nokia and the Bill & Melinda Gates Foundation, and now works as a freelance graphics designer and researcher.

Apoorv Khare is an Assistant Professor in Marketing at Indian Institute of Management Tiruchirappalli. He graduated from the doctoral program at Indian Institute of Management Calcutta. He is an MBA from Devi Ahilya University Indore. He has worked in pharmaceutical and banking industries. His research interests are broadly in the fields of subaltern consumption, consumption behaviour in postcolonial societies and consumer culture theory. He has published his research in *Journal of Marketing Management* and *Journal of Public Policy and Marketing*.

Nivedita Kothiyal is an independent researcher and teaches part-time at The York Management School, University of York. Until recently, she was an Associate Professor at Institute of Rural Management Anand (IRMA) in India. She holds a PhD in Human Resource Management and has over 15 years of experience in research, teaching, consultancy, and training. Her research is interested in decent work, gender and diversity management, workforce development and skill building, and CSR. In her research, she draws on postcolonial theory and critical management studies. Her research has been published in field-leading journals, including the *British Journal of Management* and *Indian Journal of Industrial Relations*, and edited volumes including Sage's *Handbook of Qualitative Business* and *Management Research Methods*.

Rajnish Rai is a visiting faculty in Indian Institute of Management, Indore. His areas of expertise include value creation and appropriation in inter-firm alliances of simultaneous cooperation and competition and a critical examination of the socio-political situatedness of organisational wrongdoing. In his other life, Rajnish Rai is a member of the Indian Police Service (1992 Batch) and is currently posted as Inspector General of Police, North Eastern Sector in the Central Reserve Police Force. He completed his Fellow Program in Management from the Indian Institute of Management, Ahmedabad. He also holds a Master's degree in Patents Law from the National Academy of Legal Studies and Research, Hyderabad, apart from another Master's degree from Indian Institute of Management, Bangalore in Public Policy and Management. His work has been published in leading journals such as the *Journal of Management, Organization, Journal of Business Ethics* and *Economic and Industrial Democracy*.

Ankur Sarin is a member of the faculty in the Public Systems Group at the Indian Institute of Management Ahmedabad. His areas of teaching and research include social policy and social entrepreneurship. More recently, as part of an action research project (www.rterc.

in), he has been working on making the Right to Education an instrument not only for increased access to education, but also one that promotes student engagement with social policy. He has been a Researcher at Mathematica Policy Research and has a PhD in Public Policy from the University of Chicago.

Prateek Shah is a doctoral fellow in the Innovation and Management in Education Area at the Indian Institute of Management, Ahmedabad, where he also received his Post-Graduate Diploma in Management. His prior education includes a BS and MS in Computer Engineering from the Georgia Institute of Technology, Atlanta.

M. S. Sriram is currently Visiting Faculty at the Indian Institute of Management, Bangalore. Prior to this he was the ICICI Bank Lalita D. Gupte Chair Professor in Microfinance and the Chairperson of Finance and Accounting Area at the Indian Institute of Management, Ahmedabad. He is a graduate from Institute of Rural Management, Anand and completed his doctoral studies at IIM Bangalore. His research work is largely in the area of agricultural and rural finance, cooperatives and microfinance. He has published five books *Beyond Microcredit: Putting Development Back into Microfinance* (one of the earliest books on Indian Microfinance) and two volumes on *Flow of Credit to Small and Marginal Farmers in India*. He has written the annual Inclusive Finance India Report for 2015 and 2016. Sriram has served on several expert committees appointed by the Indian Government, Reserve Bank and NABARD, and recently served as the Chairman of the Expert Committee on Kerala Cooperative Bank. He is currently on the board of NDDB Dairy Services, Micro Credit Ratings International, a Trustee of Pratham Books and Dastkar Andhra. In addition to the above, Sriram has been a writer in Kannada. He has five books of fiction and four books of essays to his credit.

Rohit Varman is a Professor of Marketing at Indian Institute of Management, Calcutta. He is a PhD from University of Utah and MBA from McGill University. His research interests are broadly in the fields of Critical Marketing and Consumer Culture Theory. He has also taught at Deakin University, Indian Institute of Technology, Kanpur, University of Reading and at University of Utah. He was a Visiting Research Professor at Karlstad University, Sweden. Rohit has published his research in several international management journals that include *Journal of Consumer Research, Human Relations, Journal of Retailing* and *Organization Science*. He serves on the editorial boards of *Journal of Macromarketing, Journal of Marketing Management* and *Journal of Historical Research in Marketing*. He is an Associate Editor of *Consumption, Markets, and Culture*.

Devi Vijay is an Assistant Professor at the Indian Institute of Management, Calcutta. Currently, she is also a Fulbright-Nehru Postdoctoral Research Fellow at the Mailman School of Public Health, Columbia University. She graduated from the doctoral program at the Indian Institute of Management, Bangalore. Her doctoral dissertation examined the evolution of collective action frames and a new organisational field in the context of community-based organising for the provision of palliative care in Kerala, India. Her subsequent research builds on this work and, in various contexts, examines facets of institutions, inequality and collective action.

Ram Manohar Vikas is an Assistant Professor of Marketing at Institute of Rural Management, Anand. He is a PhD and MBA from Indian Institute of Technology, Kanpur. He has worked in construction and consultancy industries for several years. His research interests are broadly in the fields of consumer culture theory with emphasis on subaltern consumers. He has also taught at Indian Institute of Management, Lucknow. Vikas has published his research in international management journals that include *Journal of Consumer Research, Journal of Macromarketing* and *Consumption, Markets, and Culture.*

Index

capitalism
  criticisms against, 8–9
  gains vs costs of, 9
  managerialist impulse of, 9–10
  necrocapitalistic practices of, 9
  trajectories and configurations in
    postcolonial settings, 16–17
  trajectories of exploitation within, 10
CETSCALE, 16
Chakrabarty, Dipesh, 3, 14, 16, 22, 221,
Charkha Womens' Multipurpose
  Cooperative Society, 236
Chatterjee, Partha, 3, 17, 22
Chhara community, 183–184
  bus stop incident, 191, 200–202
  economic disempowerment of, 182,
    184, 188, 199–200
  labeled as born criminals, 19, 183, 185,
    187–188
  political oppression and discrimination
    faced by, 188–191
  registration as a criminal tribe,
    185–186, 188
  resistance and organisational
    outflanking of, 200–202
Chharanagar, 187–189
Chharas, 19
Chhattisgarh Mines Shramik Sangathan
  (CMSS), 159–160, 162–165, 179–180
Chia, Robert, 27
Chiapello, Eve, 6, 8
Chipko Movement, 154
Clegg, Stewart, 184–185, 187, 200–201
Communist Party of India (CPI), 160
consenting to alternative state, 43–51
Conway, Dennis, 8
Cotton Yarn Trust, 20
Criminal Tribes Act (CTA), 184
Critical Management Studies (CMS),
  12–13

critical theory of organisations in India,
  12–14

Dandage, Reva, 212, 217
Dastakar Andhra, 20
Dastkar Andhra (DA), 226–228, 237–241,
  243
Dastkar Andhra Marketing Association
  (DAMA), 227–228
Dastkar Andhra Retail Agency (DARAM),
  227–228
Decentralised Cotton Yarn Trust (DCYT),
  226–227, 229, 233, 235, 237–240, 243
Deem, Rosemary, 10
'degree/certification' culture, 20
Denotified Nomadic Tribe (DNT), 19
Denotified Tribe (DNT) Rights Action
  Group, 191–192
deology
  Marxist-Leninist, 160–161, 167, 177
Desi Trust, 236, 240
Dhattiwala and Biggs (2012), 26
Durbar, 26, 27, 39, 43, 45, 48, 51, 53
Durga Puja festival, 59
Durkheim, Emile, 12

Eagleton, Terry, 178
economic structures, 60–61
  craft sectors, 61
  institutional maintenance, 86–88
  institutional practices and scripts,
    62–63
  types of coordination practices, 61
  Weber's switchman metaphor, 60
Eder, Klaus, 155, 178
Escobar, Arturo, 9

Fabindia, 236, 238–239
feminist theory, 12

Jha, Shivanand, 40–42
Johri, Anil, 36
Johri, Geetha, 35–36, 42, 53

Kaviraj, Sudipto, 17
Klein, Naomi, 10
Koopmans, Rudd, 178
Kumhar caste, 63, 68–69
Kumortuli Mritshilpa Karigar Samity, 63
Kumortuli Mritshilpi Samity, 63
Kumortuli Mritshilpi Sanskriti Samity, 63

labour process theory, 12
Lash, Scott, 4
Latour, Bruno, 96
Leitner, H., 220
Lenin, Vladimir, 161
liberal capitalism, 4
life process of capital, 3
local knowledge system(s), 20
Lukacs, Georg, 153
Lukose, Ritty, 220
Lury, Celia, 4

Mahatma Gandhi National Rural
  Employment Guarantee Act
  (MGNREGA), 125–126, 129–131. see
  also panchayats, functioning of
bureaucracy-politician relationship in
  implementation of, 143–146
guidelines, 129, 134, 145–146, 148,
  149n13–14, 149n16
implementation of, 131, 134, 136, 141,
  147–148
people perception of, 142
role of Panchayat Samiti, 134
social construction of, 142–147
software, 134, 141–142
violation of norms at panchayat level,
  136

mainstream organisational and
  management thought
  contemporary capitalism and phase of
    capitalist accumulation, 8–9
  creation of extra-ideological violence, 6
  employees as entreploys, 11
  limitations of, 6–12
  managerialist ideology, 7
  new spirit of capitalism, 6
Maintenance and Welfare of Parents and
  Senior Citizens Act 2007, 103
Managed Annihilation (Bavington), 9
management discourse, contemporary,
  11–12
management scholarship in India, 14
managerial reasoning, 13
managementality, 2,
Mander, Harsh, 100
Mann, M., 201
March, Artemis, 96
Marcuse (1968), 154
marginalised lives of homeless, 18–19. see
  also absence of homeless from shelters,
  reasons for
  deaths, 100
  invisibility of, 97–101
  shelter plans for, 98–99
marketing theory, 152
markets
  criticism of, 231
  efficient functioning of, 231–232
  forms of contestation, 233–241
  as sites of contestation, 237–240
  as spaces of contestation, 230–231
  as 'sustainability' of social intervention,
    230–231
Marx, Karl, 5, 12, 153
Marxism, 12
Marxist-Leninist ideology, 160–161, 167,
  177

Printed in the United States
by Baker & Taylor Publisher Services